INTERNATIONAL LAW FRAMEWORKS

By

DAVID J. BEDERMAN
Professor of Law
Emory University

CONCEPTS AND INSIGHTS SERIES

New York, New York
FOUNDATION PRESS
2001

COPYRIGHT © 2001 By FOUNDATION PRESS
              11 Penn Plaza, Tenth Floor
              New York, NY 10001
              Phone Toll Free 1–877–888–1330
              Fax (212) 760–8705
              fdpress.com

All rights reserved
Printed in the United States of America

ISBN 1–58778–025–9

 TEXT IS PRINTED ON 10% POST CONSUMER RECYCLED PAPER

FOR ANNELISE GABRIELLE
AND HER BETTER WORLD TO COME

*

PREFACE

International law is the law of nations. But public international law can also be the law applied to individuals, relationships, and transactions across national boundaries. International law is also the basis of international business and trade. It dictates the uses of international common resources and the management of common transnational problems. In short, international law can mean many different things. This volume develops a framework for understanding international law: what it means today, not only for practicing lawyers, but also for statesmen, policy-makers, human rights advocates, environmentalists—anyone who has an interest in our world and international relations.

Public international law is its own legal system, with unique ways of making rules and enforcing them. Because of its sense of separation from municipal or domestic legal systems, international law has been criticized as not being "law" at all. I will carefully examine this criticism throughout this volume. At the same time, I will also show that international law and domestic law interact in a number of ways, and at a number of different levels.

As a consequence of all this, this book is organized around four parts. The first unit considers what I call the "sources and methods" of international law. These are quite different from the cases and statutes that most law students have confronted in their studies, or most attorneys use in their practices, or most decision-makers are likely to have experienced in their offices. This unit will examine, among other things, treaties and the role of custom in making international law. It will also consider the nature and history of international law as a legal system.

The second unit will focus on the subjects and objects of international law. It used to be that the law of nations considered only States to be worthy of legal attention. Today, individuals, juristic persons (including business associations), and organizations are also properly "subjects" of international law. I will briefly examine the continued role of States and State sovereignty in international law, as well as the place for international organizations. Moreover, I will look at new "objects" of international control, including ocean areas and the international environment, as well as the international economy. Most importantly, I will discuss how the rights and duties of individuals are vindicated and enforced in international law.

This leads us to the third part of the volume, on the relationship between domestic law and international law. This is the portion of the book most closely-geared to the demands of an American law practice. At the same time, I hope to introduce readers to other countries' views on such issues as jurisdiction, diplomatic immunity, sovereign immunity, the Act of State doctrine, making and breaking treaties, and other concerns in the conduct of a nation's foreign policy.

The fourth, and final, unit of the book deals with issues of war and peace. After all, international law's success as a legal system is largely dependent on its ability to manage and resolve disputes. I will consider, therefore, different approaches to the peaceful settlement of disputes, including the role of international adjudicatory and arbitration bodies, such as the International Court of Justice. I will also look at the limits placed by international law on the use of force and on the conduct of hostilities.

As already suggested, this volume is intended to be a broad conspectus or *tour d'horizon* of international law. Not all topics can be considered, much less in substantial depth. (All material in this book is current as of July 2000.) Rather, the purpose of this book is to describe the frameworks—the essential architecture—of international law rules and how they are made. The foundations of international law run deep. So does its importance for the role of law—and lawyers—in a peaceful, prosperous, and just world.

DAVID J. BEDERMAN

Atlanta

TABLE OF CONTENTS

PART THREE. INTERNATIONAL LAW AND U.S. LAW

PART FOUR. WAR AND PEACE

TABLE OF CONTENTS

*

INTERNATIONAL LAW
FRAMEWORKS

*

PART ONE

SOURCES AND METHODS OF INTERNATIONAL LAW

Chapter 1

Nature And History Of International Law

International law are those rules of conduct that are binding on international actors in relations, transactions and problems that transcend national frontiers. A hundred years ago, a student coming to this subject—or a lawyer practicing in this area—would have called it the "law of nations." And, indeed it was: States were regarded as the only legitimate international actors, the only entities capable of exercising international rights and duties. But in the twentieth century, States ceased to be the sole subjects of international legal rules. This is certainly one of the most significant developments in this area of law, for it makes possible the application of norms of conduct to a wide range of individuals, institutions, and businesses. In short, it has "democratized" law for international relations and opened vast vistas of practice opportunities for legal advisors around the world.

A. A Thematic History

How have we come to this juncture, a true globalization of law and legal practice? To answer that question in a way that would be relevant to the needs of a practicing international lawyer today can be accomplished with a few broad strokes. The history of international law is long and richly-textured, and a knowledge of how international law rules have evolved over time can be positively crucial for practicing international lawyers. If what Justice Oliver Wendell Holmes, Jr. said of the common law is true—that it is premised on experience, not logic—it is doubly so for international law. The reason for this is that law in international affairs serves an intensely pragmatic purpose: the changing needs of the international community. The test by which that need is served is the experience that only time can bring.

Whether a rule of law for international relations can trace its origins to ancient times and classical antiquity is (fortunately enough) of little concern today. Suffice it to say, norms of international conduct have only developed when there is an authentic system of States and international actors in place. International law has never flourished in times of anarchy (think of the "Dark Ages" in Europe from 500—1100 AD), nor, for that matter, in times of hegemony (consider the Roman Empire from 50 BC—300 AD). The ideal environment for the development of international law have been times of "multi-polar" international relations, where a number of States have competed and cooperated in a particular part of the world. Such conditions existed in various regions of Asia (China and the Indian sub-continent), as well as Africa, over the last three millennia.

But whether because of historical serendipity, or (more likely) Western ethnocentrism, the date that is commonly given as the birth of international law is one of peculiarly European significance. The year is 1648, the end of what has come to be known as the Thirty Years War (1618–48). This was a period of ferocious and bloody religious conflict in Europe, a war that resulted in the decimation of close to twenty percent of Europe's population. These events—culminating in the Peace of Westphalia, a comprehensive peace treaty signed by virtually all European nations—led to two significant observations about the development of international law.

The first, as already suggested, is that international law needs States in order to grow and develop. But more than that, it needs States with strong internal institutions and a profound self-awareness that we would today call nationalism. And it just so happens that the Thirty Years War saw the rise of modern nation-States like Great Britain, France, Spain, Portugal, Sweden, and Russia. The Thirty Years War also provided the ultimate intellectual and political justification for nation-States: States needed to be *sovereign* in order to confront the challenges that war and domestic upheaval brought.

So was born the notion of sovereignty in the writings of such political theorists as Jean Bodin, Thomas Hobbes, and (later) John Locke and Jean–Jacques Rousseau. Sovereignty became the linchpin of the notion that States are independent and autonomous, and accountable only to the whim of their rulers, or (in what was then the exceptional case) to the popular will of the people. States thus owed no allegiance to a higher authority—not to God, nor a moral order or ideological ideal. States answered to nothing but themselves, and to the extent that a rule of law was possible between States, it was only because States had specifically consented to be bound by such rules.

There was a second phenomenon heralded by the 1648 Peace of Westphalia. It is that the defining moments for international law of the last three and a half centuries have come only after periods of intense global conflict. One can almost linearly chart the progress of new international organizations, new substantive rules of international conduct, and new procedures of dispute settlement between international actors by the dates that mark the end of cataclysmic wars: the 1763 Definitive Peace (concluding the Seven Years War or Great War for Empire), the 1815 Final Act at Vienna (ending the Wars of the French Revolution and Napoleon, 1791–1815), the 1919 Treaty of Versailles and Covenant of the League of Nations (completing the First World War, 1914–18), and the 1945 Charter of the United Nations (marking the end of World War Two, 1939–45). It thus appeared that international law was the step-child of war and destruction, offering a utopian hope of order and moral renewal.

So far, this historical narrative is pretty grim: international law has only prospered by extolling State power and sovereignty, and as an antidote to national conflict. Before one gets too discouraged by this doubtful pedigree of international law rules, it would be useful to chart other influences on norms of international conduct. One such consideration is that the notion of sovereignty—and its handmaiden of *positivism* (that States are subject to no moral authority above them)—has not always been ascendant, and is not so today. Indeed, international law was seen in the Middle Ages as an outgrowth of universal values and norms, largely derived from Roman law (the *ius gentium* (which applied to all peoples), and the *ius civile*, or civil law), religious institutions (the law of the Roman Catholic Church, or canon law), and common European customs involving such transnational issues as trade and control of conflict (the *ius commune*).

The earliest "classical" scholars (or publicists) of international law were writing before and during the Thirty Years War and were often reacting to the excesses of sovereignty and positivism. Writers such as Francisco de Vitoria (1486–1546), Alberico Gentili (1552–1608), Hugo de Groot ("Grotius") (1583–1645), and Samuel Pufendorf (1632–94) tended to emphasize the moral imperatives of law between nations and were part of a larger *natural law* tradition—a "common law" of States backed-up by religious and philosophical principles of good faith and good will between men and nations. But by the late 1600's, publicists were starting to consider that the actual experience of State relations was the real basis of obligation in international affairs. This is the positivist tradition, reflected in the works of Richard Zouche (1590–1660), Cornelius van Bynkershoek (1673–1743), and Emmerich de Vattel (1714–69).

Of these great writers (who are still consulted on some points), Grotius and Vattel represented the best attempts at a naturalist and positivist synthesis of rules for international actors. Grotius has earned the title "father of international law," largely on the reputation of his volume *De jure belli ac pacis* ("On the Laws of War and Peace"), first published in 1625. But Vattel probably had greater practical influence. His treatise, *Le droits des gens* ("The Law of Nations"), published in 1758, was widely-read in European capitals and was admired both by the Founders of the United States (in 1776 and 1787) and the Jacobin leaders of France (in 1789). Vattel's positivism was the favored instrument of international relations in the age of revolutions and was followed by the leading 19th century American writers on the subject: Chancellor James Kent, Professor Henry Wheaton and Justice Joseph Story.

There was bound to be a collision between positivist and natural approaches to international law. It came in the early 1800's and was waged over the most compelling social issue of the day: the institution of slavery and the slave-trade. The practical problem for international lawyers of that day was whether a small group of States (Great Britain and the United States) could unilaterally seek to suppress the international traffic in slaves. That question turned on whether the slave-trade violated international law. For those who believed in natural law principles—that State conduct was subordinated to moral values—then the answer was easy: slavery was an abomination. But for positivists, who embraced State sovereignty and the necessity of ascertaining State consent for new rules of international conduct, the issue was more difficult. And, ultimately, in a series of cases decided by English and U.S. courts, the positivist view won and the decision was made that slavery and the slave trade could only be suppressed if States explicitly agreed that their nationals could not legally engage in it. Happily, this result was achieved by the late 1800's, although it came only after the bloody Civil War in the United States.

Positivism reigned supreme in international relations from 1848 to 1919. Gone were the days of nation-State building and the popular revolutions in Europe and the Americas. In their place was a period of colonialism and imperialism, in which explicitly (and exclusionary) European political and value systems were forcibly transmitted to Africa and Asia. Among these was a peculiarly European notion of a law of nations for "civilized" nations. Despite the fact that China, Japan and India each had their own historic conceptions of international rules of behavior, in the face of overweening European military and economic power, their price of admission into the global order was acceptance of Western international law.

Ultimately, the European domination of international law collapsed in the charnel house of World War One. Four empires (the Austrian Hapsburg, German Hohenzollern, Russian Romanov and Ottoman Turkish) disintegrated into new ethnic States. Only the

British Empire remained, and three new powers entered the international scene: Japan, the United States, and the communist Soviet Union. The 1919 Treaty of Versailles and the Covenant of the League of Nations (history's first attempt at an organization for global peace and security) was probably doomed to failure. What with the United States remaining outside the League, the Soviet Union disengaged, Britain and France morally and physically exhausted, the world was powerless to respond to the aggressions of new totalitarian powers (Germany, Italy and Japan).

But, to some degree, the League did break the pattern set in early centuries that substantive innovations made in international law came only after periods of warfare. The League set-upon a relatively ambitious program for *codifying* international law, systematizing the rules of international conduct. A permanent international judicial tribunal was established. Conference diplomacy became more regular. International institutions began to operate in a more predictable fashion. And, just as important, the League became concerned with issues of significance to people, and not just governments: economic development, protection of the rights of minorities, and prevention of disease. But, ultimately, the League was unable to do the one task it had set for itself—keep the peace.

The cataclysm of the Second World War re-made the globe. First, it accelerated the process of decolonization. The British and French colonial empires collapsed by the early 1960's, and by the 1980's there remained no part of the world that was under unwilling colonial domination by Europeans. This meant that the international community—the family of nations—grew into a large, rowdy clan. Before 1945, the group of "civilized" nations had never numbered more than fifty. By 1960, it had increased to a hundred, and (in the year 2000) has topped-out at about 195 States. The sheer increase in State entities (quite apart from other international actors) has changed the face of international law in fundamental and irreversible ways.

World War II and the Cold War rivalry that followed (particularly between the U.S. and Soviet Union) also set in motion a host of technological, social, environmental, and economic phenomena that we now identify as "globalism." Whether it is the integrated international economy and trade disciplines, nuclear power and proliferation, space exploration and computer applications, environmental pollution and habitat degradation, or intellectual properties and entertainment, we are gradually living in a shrinking, interdependent world. International law has been compelled to respond to the functional demands of the international community.

Lastly, the end of World War Two brought a vision of world order that had only been incompletely realized by the League of

Nations. Enshrined in the United Nations Charter, this dream created an organizational architecture for the international community. With the U.N.'s political organs at its center, this system has reached out into every aspect and spectrum of human cooperation. It has created progressively more complicated and supple legal and regulatory regimes for virtually all functional areas of international concern.

At the same time, this world order has managed to place State concerns (including sovereignty and maintaining international peace and security) side-by-side with the principle of protecting and extending the dignity of individual human beings. This vision is not exclusively one of State power and a positive grant of rights by nations to people. Instead, it is at least partly premised on a natural law notion of the inherent worth of human beings, and is manifested in the creation of rules by which a State must treat its own citizens. So the pendulum of natural and positive approaches to international legal obligation has swung back to a more neutral position in which the international community recognizes values separate and apart from State sovereignty.

B.   Dispelling Some Myths

Why, then—if international law is so historically legitimate and ethically relevant, so doctrinally robust and functionally necessary—do so many people (including lawyers and policy-makers) believe it does not exist? Why does it seem to be the step-child of legal studies, a discipline in search of its own reality? Why do international lawyers (including this one) seem to have a perpetual chip on their shoulder?

No other area of law is compelled to justify its very existence, and yet, international law seems condemned to perpetually do so. The answer lies, I think, in confronting—and exploding—several myths about international law and international legal practice.

Myth #1: International law is its own, separate and distinct legal system. This is actually a half-truth. As already indicated, international law began as a "law of nations," where States were the only relevant actors in international affairs and only countries had rights and duties in that legal system. This notion has radically changed in the last century, to the point that institutions, individuals, business associations, and other entities are also capable of being actors under international law.

One consequence of this development is that international law has come to exhibit many features of "mature" domestic legal systems, even as it remains a fairly primitive or youthful regime. There is a rough (very rough) correlation between doctrinal areas in international law and those in most domestic (or "municipal") legal systems. For example, the law of treaties (considered in Chapter 3) shows many common structural characteristics as contract law. Likewise, there is a strong flavor of property law in the international law of territory (discussed in Chapter 10), tort law in the international law of State Responsibility (Chapter 8), constitutional law in the operation of international organizations (Chapter 6), and civil rights law in the international law of Human Rights (Chapter 9). This is no coincidence. International law has consistently borrowed from domestic legal systems as it has sought to fill-in doctrinal gaps, a process of using "general principles" (described in Chapter 2).

It would be a profound mistake to think that domestic law has not been affected by the development of international rules of conduct. And that is the myth in thinking that international law is "separate and apart" from domestic legal systems. By various means, international law has been incorporated and applied into domestic law. These methods of incorporation will be considered generally in Part Three of this volume (and particularly Chapter 14).

It is fair to say, though, that this process has been long and slow. Although at one point in the Middle Ages all European legal systems were substantially influenced by an international *ius commune*, as modern nation-States developed they tended to be more and more exclusionist of "foreign" law, and (to some degree) international law was regarded as not being quite domestic. Some areas of domestic law (including maritime commerce and international trade) have always been influenced by international norms and expectations. However, it was only in the late 1800's and early 1900's that technological developments (like communications and transport) started to make the world smaller and allowed for the acceleration of economic integration, a phenomenon that has continued apace to this very day. Domestic legal systems have been obliged to transform themselves in the face of this process of globalization.

So the best way of thinking about international law in this respect is that it may well be "separate" from domestic legal systems, but it is not "apart." Or, in the simple and stirring words of U.S. Supreme Court Justice Gray in *The PAQUETE HABANA* case (discussed in the next Chapter): "international law is part of our law."[1]

Myth #2: International law is all theory and no practice. Like Myth #1, this statement contains a kernel of truth, but is otherwise a profound distortion. International law has historically been

---

1.   175 U.S. 677, 700 (1900).

enriched by religious values, moral philosophy, political attitudes, and international relations theory. But much of domestic law has been similarly influenced by such "non-legal" or "outside" notions, and no one suggests that it is theory-bound and, thereby, lacks practical application.

To talk about the "theory" of international law is nothing more than asking how someone (whether it be a policy-maker or attorney) actually uses that law. Understanding the historic nature and uses of legal rules in international relations helps one to identify appropriate and useful *sources* of international legal obligation (considered in the remainder of this Part). Having engaged in the lawyerly task of collecting the sources and materials that describe international law, one can then offer an intelligent opinion of the *doctrines* or *rules* of international conduct and behavior. Only then can a lawyer or policy-maker offer helpful advice, whether it is suggesting a course of diplomatic action, structuring a business transaction, framing arguments in a legal proceeding, or deciding an international dispute.

To thus criticize international law as being "too theoretical" is really no criticism at all. Theory is just one of the tools in the international lawyers tool-chest. And certainly there is plenty of "practice" for international law—and international lawyers.

Myth #3: International law is not "real" law. This statement is the heart of darkness for detractors of this subject. And, I must admit, that it is a pernicious myth and exceedingly difficult to debunk. It takes elements of the two previous propositions (international law is not like domestic law, and it is too theoretical) and conflates them into an awesomely broad condemnation of this area of legal pursuit. Repeated enough times, it becomes the proverbial "big lie."

If all this myth were articulating is that international law does not have the characteristic features of mature domestic legal systems, I would have no quarrel with it. Although hardly an original sentiment (the legal philosopher John Austin observed this in the early–1800's), it is still true that the international legal system does not have a supreme "law-maker" or legislature (like Congress or Parliament), a commanding "law-enforcer" or executive, or an authoritative "law-interpreter" or judiciary (like the Supreme Court or a Constitutional Court). Indeed, if we had a World Parliament (capable of making binding law on the whole globe) and a world police force, the face of international relations would be utterly different. In fact, it would not be international relations at all; it would be World Government. And World Government (like anarchy or hegemony) is the antithesis of international law for a world of many separate and independent political entities.

International law remains a primitive legal system. It makes its law through a combination of consensual and coercive means. Enforcement is often through unilateral "self-help," rather than by multilateral action. As will be considered in the next Chapter, the practices of the international community (known as customary international law) is an actual source of law—and an exceedingly effective one. Likewise, the network of bilateral and multilateral treaties that not only adjust potential disputes between nations, but also prescribe rules for the future, is also terribly significant. At the same time, international law is certainly evolving towards an administrative and regulatory model for prescribing rules of conduct for such areas of functional cooperation as the international economy and finance, protection of the global environment, and management of common resources.

To say that international law is "unreal" because it does not exhibit the characteristic features of what we take to be "real" legal systems (such as our own) is both false and misleading. It is false in the sense that international doctrines and institutions are evolving to replicate the successful forms of law-making in domestic legal systems. But, much more than that, because international law serves the interests of a special constituency (the global community) and a special value (the rule of law in international relations), it is unreasonable and unfair to expect that it should precisely mimic domestic legal systems in order to earn the label as a "real" kind of law.

Myth #4: No one obeys international law. This is the ultimate, *realist* critique of international law and relations. It depends on a utilitarian and rationalist attitude that States and other international actors conduct themselves only out of self-interest. When that self-interest coincides with community norms of behavior, the realist might say, then international law will be obeyed. But when the law conflicts with national self-interest, the law will be ignored or flouted. And, the realist concludes, any law that can be followed or not at the whim of the legal actor, is no law at all.

This myth raises the most fundamental question in international law: what is the basis of obligation in international affairs, or, put even more simply, Why do States obey international law? My answer would be that States and other international actors do, indeed, follow international law norms out of self-interest. But that self-interest is expressed as more than a situational observance of a particular rule at a particular time. Instead, nations have a self-interest in promoting a systemic rule of law in international relations, a "culture" of law observance. As one international law scholar has noted: "almost all nations observe almost all principles of international law and almost all of their obligations almost all of the time.''[2] And while the handful of examples of violations of international law norms are extraordinarily well-publicized, the literally thousands of instances of law compliance go unnoticed and unheralded. Countries have a self-interest in the predictability and stability that law and legal relations bring to the international community.

Does that mean that States never disobey international law? Of course not. But that cannot be the operating standard for any "real" legal system. Even in the most highly-advanced domestic legal systems, lawlessness may well be rife. Whether it is traffic infractions, tax evasion, or violent crime, all legal systems recognize that unlawful behavior does occur. The question for international law and the international legal system is whether unlawful conduct is flagrant by the wrong-doer and tolerated by everyone else. If it were, that might raise the specter that the law is but a fiction, to be observed or ignored at whim.

But that is not the case for international relations today. Protests to actions that are regarded as violating international law are quick and vociferous. Even when States engage in legally dubious conduct, they will still attempt to justify or rationalize their behavior on legal grounds. These defenses might be spurious, and the avenues for effective relief from unlawful behavior limited, but still the attitude and culture of international law is that actors may not justify bad behavior by expediency or strength.

Myth #5: International law is what the United States says it is. The United States as currently the world's only superpower does occupy a significant position in international relations. And there has always been a concern in international law that the "Great Powers" exercise disproportionate influence on the development of international law and the content of international legal doctrines. It is patently false to believe that one State—even a superpower—can unilaterally captain the course of international law.

For American students and attorneys of international law there is a special need for caution. There is an alluring tendency to be selective with one's sources of international law rules, to believe that unless a United States statute, or judicial decision, or authoritative treatise suggests a particular legal rule, then that norm is not followed by other countries around the world. The United States' practice of international law and its incorporation into the domestic constitutional culture in this country—what is sometimes called "Foreign Relations Law"—is distinctive. That is why it will be specially treated in Part Three of this book. But otherwise, U.S. international lawyers must scrupulously avoid a dangerous and

2. Louis Henkin, How Nations Be-
have 47 (1979).

parochial trend toward assuming that what is good as an international legal rule for the U.S. is good for the rest of the world.

Myth #6: International lawyers are not real lawyers. This is profoundly misguided because it trivializes and ignores the international legal practice that is growing by leaps-and-bounds in the new, global economy. It simply follows as a matter of logic that as the United States continues to prosper from international contacts—whether financial, economic, cultural or intellectual—money will be made from lawyering those transactions and relationships.

Almost without notice, international law issues have come to pervade domestic legal practice. When an attorney seeks to enforce a U.S. court judgment in a foreign country, that involves international law (implicating treaties and jurisdiction, discussed in Chapter 16). When a company owned or operated by a foreign sovereign is sued, that also raises international law (foreign sovereign immunities, considered in Chapter 17(A)). Or if a personnel dispute arises for an employee of an international organization headquartered in the U.S., that too involves the immunities of international institutions (Chapters 6 & 17(C)). Many criminal enterprises have international aspects (narcotics trafficking is just one example), and that includes the international law of criminal jurisdiction (Chapter 16). U.S. investments overseas may be expropriated or otherwise interfered with, and that raises the international law of State Responsibility (Chapter 8). Lastly, human rights concerns are litigated in U.S. courts, whether as immigration, asylum and refugee issues, or as civil enforcement of human rights norms (Chapters 9 & 17).

International law practice is here to stay in the United States, as in Europe, East Asia and elsewhere. But, more than that, practicing international law is not just about a secure professional future. It is also about doing well by doing good: being involved in a practice area that promotes the rule of law, peace and justice everywhere. And those who study international law may not even practice it. Instead, they may serve as heads-of-State or as heads-of-government, diplomats, policy-advisers, business executives, and cultural leaders.

Not surprisingly, this myth is regarded as personally offensive to international lawyers. It suggests that the unique set of skills and talents that attorneys bring to international problems are somehow undeserving of recognition and respect. If anything, international lawyers number among the most supple and sophisticated of practitioners today, capable of adjusting their practices to meet emerging technological developments, new forms of international regulation and activity, and fresh client demands.

Chapter 2

General Principles and Customary
International Law

Essential to understanding the nature of international law as a legal system is comprehending the sources of international legal rules. It would be hard to practice within any legal system without knowing, quite literally, where one *finds* the law, and international law is no exception. This is true whether one believes in the positivist nature of international law, or that the sources of international law are a neutral and objective means of providing rules of conduct in international relations, or that these sources are readily accepted by all international actors.

Happily, there is a definitive statement of the sources of international law. It can be found in Article 38 of the Statute of the International Court of Justice (ICJ), or World Court, which indicates that, in disputes submitted to it, the Court shall apply:

a. international conventions, whether general or particular, establishing rules expressly recognized by contesting states;

b. international custom, as evidence of a general practice accepted as law;

c. the general principles of law recognized by civilized nations;

d. ... judicial decisions and the teachings of the most highly qualified publicists of the various nations, as a subsidiary means for the determination of rules of law.

Despite this handy summary of the sources of international law, substantial confusion remains as how actually to find these sources, and, much more importantly, how to effectively use them as an international lawyer.

One thing to realize at the outset is that of the five sources of international law mentioned in Article 38, three are given clear prominence. These are general principles, custom, and treaties. They will be discussed in turn in this Part. The remaining sources are of a secondary, or "subsidiary," nature and meant to be used really as evidence of what is (or is not) a rule of international behavior. This is a significant distinction. Just as an advocate would not cite a law review article as conclusive "precedent" in a case, neither would an international lawyer use a subsidiary piece of evidence in favor of more authoritative sources.

But, more than that, general principles, customary international law, and international agreements—the core sources of international law—operate with a peculiar and powerful synergy in making international legal rules binding and enforceable. To understand how this dynamic works, I will examine general principles first, and then turn, in this Chapter, to customary international law.

A.   General Principles

Article 38, paragraph 1(c) of the ICJ Statute refers to "general principles of law recognized by civilized nations." Notice, though, that it does not say "general principles of *international* law." Rather, the emphasis is on general principles of domestic law (sometimes called "municipal law"), as recognized in the legal systems of "civilized nations." The point here is that the very sources of international law recognize that the international legal system remains primitive and unformed, and that often recourse must be had to "borrowing" legal rules from domestic law. General principles of law are the ultimate seed-bed and gap-filler of international law rules.

How does a legal rule become a general principle? The process by which a principle is "elevated" from domestic law to the realm of international law is subtle and complex. The very language of Article 38 is suggestive that a principle would have to be "recognized" not just in one legal system, but, rather, in most of the world's legal cultures. So when Article 38 speaks of "civilized nations," it is referring to jurisdictions embracing the common law tradition (the United Kingdom and its former colonies, as well as the U.S.), the civil law derived from ancient Roman law (prevalent in all of continental Europe, Latin America, and most of Africa and Asia), significant religious legal cultures (including Islamic law), and ideological legal systems (including socialist law as practiced in China and elsewhere).

In order for an international lawyer to argue that a general principle of law is a binding rule of international law, it would be necessary to canvass all of the world's great legal systems for evidence of that principle, and also to reference manifestations of that principle in the actual domestic law of as many nations as possible. This is no easy task. Simply citing a few U.S. Supreme Court decisions, or to quote a Latin legal maxim, will not do the trick.

There is a bit of a paradox in the incorporation of general principles as international legal rules. The more abstract the principle, the greater consensus of legal systems, but also the less useful the rule. Some general principles of this sort include a rule of good faith in international obligations (known as *pacta sunt servanda*) and the doctrines of necessity and self-defense. These are useful doctrines, but they are short on specifics. But the less abstract (and more concrete) the principle, the more useful it is, but also the more difficult it is to find a consensus among domestic legal systems.

A good example of this paradox at work is the rather prosaic principle that there should be a period of repose for international claims. Every domestic legal system has this principle. In common law we would call this a statute of limitations or laches; in civil law it is known as extinctive prescription. But is it a general principle applicable in international law? In 1903, an international arbitral tribunal ruled that there was sufficient consensus to make it a rule of international claims practice (and thus to bar a nearly 30–year old claim). But the tribunal could not say definitively whether the international statute of limitations was 10 years, 30 years, or 50 years.[1] The abstract principle of prescription was thus recognized, but no specific rule or time-limit. Such are the pitfalls of general principles.

Nevertheless, general principles continue to exert a strong influence on the sources of international law, even as the international legal system has grown and matured. General principles have been developed on such issues as good faith in the exercise of international rights (the abuse of right doctrine), due process issues before international tribunals (especially on evidentiary questions and burdens of proof), and the modalities of State Responsibility (like rules of contributory or comparative fault). As will be noted later, general principles played a key role in the development of international environmental law (see Chapter 12), and in substantive rules of international economic law (Chapter 13).

It would be a mistake to think that international tribunals will invariably resort to general principles to fill a gap, or *lacunae*, in international law. The ICJ declined, for example, to apply domestic law rules of easements or servitudes in the *Right of Passage* Case (discussed below), and refused also to elevate municipal law trust principles in cases involving areas under international trusteeship or custodianship. Despite these caveats, an international lawyer would be well-advised not to forget general principles as a source for binding rules of international conduct.

B. Customary International Law

Custom is a source unique for public international law. It also presents special problems of interpretation and methodology. Most

---

1. *Gentini* (Italy) Claim (Venezuelan Mixed Claims Comm'n 1903), Jackson Ralston, Venezuelan Arbitrations of 1903, at 720 (1904).

of these problems stem from the fact that in most mature legal systems, lawyers typically assume that the only binding rules are those made by legislatures (or, by delegation, to administrative agencies or bureaucrats) or by courts. We tend to forget that law can also be made by the consent of communities of people, without any formal enactment by governmental entities. Indeed, such customs or practices are sometimes not even written down. Think of a group of businesspeople who formulate their own rules for conducting certain types of transactions. (We call these "usages of trade.") Or imagine that the standard of care exercised within a certain community for a particular activity becomes the relevant basis for determining negligence. Although we do not tend to think of custom as a legitimate source of law, we do know that industry customs are enforced in commercial disputes, just as an industry benchmark can be held up as the standard of negligence.

So custom remains a powerful, if subliminal, source of law, even in "mature" legal systems. But public international law is not a mature legal system at all—it remains strikingly primitive. And customary international law is a source of signal strength and flexibility for international law. It allows international legal actors to informally develop rules of behavior, without the necessity of resorting to more formal and difficult means of law-making (like treaties). Custom "tracks" or follows the conduct of such actors as States, international institutions, transnational business organizations, religious and civic groups, and individuals involved in international matters.

There are two key elements in the formation of a customary international law rule. They are elegantly and succinctly expressed in Article 38 of the ICJ Statute. Custom is "evidence of a general practice accepted as law." To show a rule of customary international law, one must prove to the satisfaction of the relevant decision-maker (whether it be an international tribunal, domestic court, or government or inter-governmental actor) that the rule has (1) been followed as a "general practice," *and* (2) has been "accepted as law."

The first part of the equation (the general practice element) is an objective inquiry: have international actors really followed the rule? has the practice been consistent? has the practice been followed for a sufficient period of time? The second part of the equation (the "accepted as law" element) has often been called a subjective, or even psychological, inquiry. It asks *why* an international actor has observed a particular practice. This is specifically known as *opinio juris sive necessitatus* (or just "*opinio juris*"), and it attempts to ascertain whether a practice is observed out of a sense of legal obligation or necessity, or, rather, merely out of courtesy, neighborliness, or expediency.

There is an inherent tension between these two elements, and practicing international lawyers (as distinct from legal academics) suspect that they are deliberately redundant. The tendency has been, in proving whether something is a rule of customary international law, to simply satisfy oneself that a particular practice is really followed by States and other international actors and to forget about *why* the rule is observed. But there really is a need to have an extra element, an additional "ingredient" for the recipe that makes customary international law. Otherwise, international actors will be bound to follow practices that may not really reflect their own expectations of lawful international conduct, or, worse yet, may be unreasonable or anachronistic. Whether one thinks of an *opinio juris* requirement, or instead focuses on the reasonableness or utility of a rule of custom, something in addition to the fact that States and other actors follow the practice is necessary.

How, then, does an international lawyer prove that a norm of international conduct is really a "general practice" that qualifies it as a binding rule of customary international law? States rarely oblige by disclosing and handily collecting all of their relevant international practices in one location. (The exceptions include such legally sophisticated nations as the United States, United Kingdom, Japan, and others which periodically publish compendiums of their practices of, and positions on, international law.) Remember, customary practices are often not formally recorded at all. More than that, what States *do* should matter a lot more than what they *say*. But, necessarily, international lawyers rely on written evidence of State practice (even if it is diplomatic correspondence, military manuals, or newspaper accounts of contemporary events). And while customary international law is very much a "struggle" between competing positions, no international lawyer would desire that in their exuberance to *show* what their positions are, States would more readily resort to muscular and violent means of asserting their rights.

An excellent illustration of the hard work of lawyering evidence of State practice is shown in *The PAQUETE HABANA*, a case decided by the U.S. Supreme Court in 1900.[2] The facts and issues presented in the case were deceptively simple. Two Cuban fishing boats had been captured by U.S. naval forces in the Spanish–American War and condemned as "prizes" of war. The question was whether small coastal fishing boats were immune from capture under customary international law. The U.S. government confi-

---

2.   175 U.S. 677 (1900).

dently asserted they were not so protected. The attorney for the Cuban boat owners, J. Parker Kirlin, was obliged to show the content of customary international law. Drawing from sources as varied as medieval English royal ordinances, agreements between European nations, orders issued to the U.S. Navy in earlier conflicts, and the opinions of treatise writers, Kirlin staged one of the most stunning upsets in U.S. Supreme Court history. He persuaded the Court that his clients, and not the U.S. government, knew better what customary international law was. The Court held that custom barred the capture of small fishing boats.

Kirlin's victory was not only a demonstration of an eclectic and scholarly collection of evidence of State practice. It was a *tour de force* of powerful argument insofar as Kirlin persuaded a majority of the Justices that the immunity granted to coastal fishing boats was grounded in humanitarian concerns, as well as supported by legal obligation. The United States had particularly relied on one earlier case, *The YOUNG JACOB*, decided by the English High Court of Admiralty in 1798.[3] That case had held that the practice of immunizing fishing craft was not a rule at all, but instead was only "comity" or courtesy. The English court had ruled that the practice was not supported by *opinio juris*, and the United States (some 100 years later) seized on this as a basis for arguing that protecting enemy fishing boats was a matter of "grace" only. Kirlin persuaded the Court, however, that within the intervening century the practice *had* become obligatory; it was no longer optional and was, indeed, binding on the United States.

Kirlin had the advantage, of course, of proving a customary usage that was supported by an impeccable evidentiary pedigree: nearly two centuries of consistent and well-documented State practice. But must all evidence of a general practice be confirmed by this high threshold of uniformity, consistency and longevity of the usage? The International Court of Justice has indicated that uniformity need not be perfect, and that minor inconsistencies in the observance of the practice are acceptable. Likewise, the ICJ has held that for a rule to be established as customary, the corresponding practice need not be in absolutely rigorous conformity with the rule. Instead, the conduct of States in such situations should be consistent with such rules, and to the extent they are not, such inconsistencies should be treated as breaches of the rule, and not as an indication of the emergence of a new rule.[4]

There also is no requirement that a practice necessarily be observed for a long period of time before it will be confirmed as a

---

3. 1 C. Rob. 20, 165 Eng. Rep. 81 (Adm. 1798) (U.K.).

4. See *Military and Paramilitary Activities* (Nicar. v. U.S.) (Merits), 1986 I.C.J. 98.

binding custom. The history of international law is replete with examples of State practice that enjoyed such immediate popularity, and around which formed such a complete consensus of the international community, that they were recognized almost as "instant custom." One well-known example was the development of State claims to offshore oil and gas deposits, under a theory of continental shelves (discussed more in Chapter 11) that took barely 15 years to form into binding law. It is not the age of a practice that makes a custom. Rather, it is the high degree of consistency and uniformity of observance by most (if not all) of the international community, that satisfies the objective element of confirming it as a "general practice."

If one thinks it is easy to prove a rule as a general practice, one might do well to consult the French counsel in *The S.S. LOTUS* case decided by the Permanent Court of International Justice (PCIJ) (the ICJ's predecessor) in 1927.[5] Another nautical case, the facts are again wonderfully simple. A French vessel, the LOTUS, negligently collided with a Turkish vessel on the high seas (beyond any nation's control) killing 8 Turkish nationals. The LOTUS foolishly sailed into Istanbul, whereupon Turkish authorities arrested the French officer on whose watch the accident occurred and charged him with negligent homicide. France protested Turkey's assertion of criminal jurisdiction over a French national for an act which occurred on a French vessel outside of Turkey's territory.

The law of the sea and criminal jurisdiction aspects of this case will be considered in Chapters 11 and 16 respectively, but the question here is how the PCIJ determined the relevant customary international law principle. To France's dismay, the Court ruled at the outset that since France was challenging Turkey's exercise of jurisdiction, it was incumbent on France to show that Turkey violated customary international law. The Court thus assigned France the burden of proving that Turkey breached international law. That pretty much sunk France's chances of winning the case, because it meant that the French counsel was obliged to collect sufficient evidence of State practice indicating that Turkey's prosecution was improper. Unfortunately for France, its advocates were given the task of showing evidence of State practice indicating that exercise of criminal jurisdiction over a foreign national on a foreign-flagged vessel on the high seas was improper.

That proved impossible. The PCIJ was able to distinguish every earlier case or incident relied upon France for the proposition that the State of nationality or the "flag-State" had exclusive jurisdiction in circumstances such as this. Not only was there a lack of objective evidence supporting France's supposed general practice,

5. 1927 P.C.I.J. (Ser. A) No. 10 (Fr. v. Tur.).

but even if there had been (the Court intimated) it would merely show that States had often abstained from instituting criminal proceedings, but had not necessarily felt obligated to do so. Even if the French lawyers had shown (which they could not) a "smoking gun" of an earlier incident where Turkey had declined to prosecute a foreign national, that would not have been conclusive. The only possible way that France could have carried its burden was to have documented a case where a *Turkish* vessel had collided with a foreign ship, that foreign country had prosecuted a Turkish mariner, and then Turkey had protested and prevailed. Only in this classic "shoe-on-the-other-foot" scenario could France have proven a contrary general practice accepted as law by Turkey.

The LOTUS has proven to be a most problematic case for international lawyers. Its core holding is that international law is a permissive system: everything is allowed, except that which is expressly prohibited. The burden was thus placed on the country challenging another's conduct. Aside from this presumption (which has certainly been questioned and attacked in the context of exercises of jurisdiction), *The LOTUS* remains a powerful cautionary tale for international lawyers attempting to prove the existence of a general practice accepted as binding customary international law.

All of this begs, however, the larger question of how exactly customary international law gets made. This problem is particularly acute when one realizes that for most evolving rules of international behavior or conduct there is *no* consensus. Instead, as I have suggested already, there is a dynamic "struggle for law," in which countries are actively competing in a marketplace of rules. A country might, by both its words and deeds, attempt to build support for a new custom. Other nations might join this bid. Another group of countries might actively resist the creation of a new norm. They might lodge diplomatic protests, and—in extreme circumstances—actually undertake affirmative steps to block the formation of a new practice or, at a minimum to deny that new usage the legitimacy of *opinio juris*.

The International Court of Justice has developed some definitive methods for identifying an emerging custom under these conditions of conflict and competition. It is important to appreciate these approaches because they illustrate not only the practical reality of custom as a source of international law, but also show how the ICJ and international advocates can use custom to achieve different sorts of client objectives and decisional outcomes. The best way to understand these approaches to custom is by comparing two cases decided by the World Court.

The first of these, The *Asylum* Case,[6] implicated a most peculiar custom. The case arose when a Peruvian military leader, Victor Raul Haya de la Torre, took refuge in the Colombian embassy in Lima after leading an unsuccessful coup attempt. Elsewhere in the world, this would have resulted in a very long stay for Haya de la Torre, for while all nations respect the inviolability of foreign embassy premises (for more on this see Chapter 17(C)), there is certainly no rule requiring a host State to allow a political refugee safe passage out of the embassy, out of the country, and to the asylum State. Nowhere, that is, except Latin America, where evolved a regional custom of diplomatic asylum.

Imagine, then, the surprise of the Colombian authorities, who, after waiting a decent interval, made what they assumed was a *pro forma* request to Peru to grant Haya de la Torre safe passage to Colombia. The Peruvians turned them down flat, asserting that they were not bound by the regional custom of diplomatic asylum. And the Court ultimately took Peru's side in the dispute, ruling that the regional custom was not binding. As in *The LOTUS* Case, once it became clear that Colombia bore the burden of showing that Peru's conduct violated international law (as opposed to Peru being required to explain its actions), the result was inevitable.

The most significant aspects of this case was the ICJ's treatment of a State's reaction as proof of its opposition to the formation of a custom and its discounting of regional custom as a source of international law. What the Court ruled was that where a regional (as distinct from a global) custom was concerned, silence on the part of the State in the face of an emerging practice meant that that State objected or protested to the rule. In short, a silent or ambiguous response meant rejection. This was contrary to the general presumption that States were obliged to protest loud and often if they wished to avoid being bound by a rule of emerging global custom.

This general presumption for global custom seems unfair. After all, it somehow expects that all countries in the world have minions of international lawyers in their employ who have nothing better to do that closely monitor what other nations are "bidding" and "claiming" as new rules of custom, and then effectively protest them. The reality of legal staffing for Foreign Ministries around the world is quite different. Nevertheless, it has always been understood that customary international law could never really develop if it required the affirmative and express consent of nations to produce a binding State practice. Hence the general presumption is that, for global custom, silence means acceptance of a new rule.

6.   1950 I.C.J. 266 (Colom. v. Peru).

Why, then, did the World Court, change the calculus of consent for regional custom in the *Asylum* Case? One can only conclude that the Court wished to suppress regional custom, and there is no more effective way to do so than to declare a presumption that fundamentally disrupts the formation of such regional practices. While the ICJ has no qualms about applying rules derived from regional (or at least non-global) treaties, it was concerned that development of distinctive bodies of regional rules—not just for Latin America, but perhaps also for Europe, Africa and Asia— might unduly interfere with the universal aspirations of international law. More pertinently, the allowance of easy-to-make regional customs might also challenge the institutional role of the World Court as a place for authoritative pronouncements on international legal rules. I speculate this because in an analytically similar case, *Right of Passage Over Indian Territory*, decided by the Court in 1960,[7] the ICJ reached a very different conclusion.

The problem raised in that dispute was Portugal's asserted right to be able to transit both civil administrators as well as troops and munitions from the Portuguese colony of Goa (on the coast of India) to little Portuguese-controlled enclaves in the interior of India. It was the late 1950's—a critical time for the process of decolonization around the world—and India made no pretense of its desire to drive the last vestiges of colonialism from the Indian subcontinent. So the Indian authorities denied Portugal's right of passage, assuming (correctly) that if the enclaves could not be re-supplied they would be ripe for the picking.

The ICJ could have decided the dispute as a matter of global custom: whether there was some inherent right of passage by one nation over the territory of another, especially in situations where part of one nation's territory was completely surrounded by another. The judges on the Court declined to undertake this analysis, and one can hardly blame them. It would have been a daunting and difficult task of collecting many centuries of State practice over many continents, in order to derive a set of global customary rules for these situations.

Instead, the World Court chose to limit the scope of the analysis to an exceedingly narrow shutter. The question became whether Portugal and India (and its predecessors, the British and Maratha rulers) had developed a special, or local, custom allowing Portuguese right of passage. The Court sifted through evidence of the course of dealing between the two sides over the course of many centuries. The ICJ ultimately concluded that Portugal's right of passage for civil administrators was binding custom on India, although India retained the right to exceptionally suspend such

---

7.   1960 I.C.J. 6 (Port. v. India).

passage. But as for a right to move troops and weapons over Indian territory, previous permissions to do so had been "mere" comity or courtesy, and in so lacking *opinio juris* it failed as a custom.

The Court essentially decided that it was futile to declare a global custom in a case where it was easier to simply describe and characterize a "course of dealing" between the two parties to the dispute. And in using a local or special custom, the Court resorted to the typical presumption that silence in the face of an emerging practice means acquiescence or acceptance. In these bilateral situations, it appears especially incumbent on States to protest if they are unhappy with the legal positions taken by their neighbors.

For example, in the 1951 *Anglo-Norwegian Fisheries* Case,[8] the United Kingdom and Norway contested access to fisheries off the Norwegian coast. Norway had attempted to claim ocean areas through some creative cartography: by drawing "straight baselines" from points along its rugged coastline and asserting that the enclosed areas were exclusive Norwegian fisheries. Norway's zealous "bidding" of a straight-baseline rule, combined with Britain's lack of effective (and well-documented) protests in the early–1900's, meant that Britain had waived its subsequent objection. The Court indicated that Norway's straight-baseline were thus not "opposable" by the U.K.

In the Court's divergent treatment of regional custom and local (or special) custom, one also has two very different models of the role of international dispute settlement machinery. In the *Asylum* Case, the ICJ was emphatic in asserting that it was its prerogative to declare the content of customary international law, not only for the benefit of the parties to the case, but, more importantly, to the global community at large. And whenever the ICJ takes on the difficult task of defining principles of global custom, it is as much to declare what the law is as to settle a dispute. But in *Right of Passage*, one observes a far more modest (and typical) role for the Court: simply settling the dispute, without making great pronouncements. That is why, in such situations, recourse to special custom and to the very particular course of dealing between two nations is so very attractive for the ICJ. Essential to either approach is the Court's understanding of the role of consent in making customary rules.

If one regards this pattern of assumptions and presumptions about the formation of customary international law as troublesome, one would be correct to be concerned. It would seem that, with the exception of regional custom, fortune favors those States that aggressively stake-out new rules and hope that other nations simply do not notice or fail to act in a timely or compelling manner.

8.   1951 I.C.J. 116 (U.K. v. Nor.).

Aside from the basic question of what constitutes an effective protest of an emerging custom, how can one know whether a new practice is successfully supplanting an old usage? One could, I suppose, look at the extent, frequency and consistency of departures from old customs, and tally the numbers of States that adhere to one rule or the other, or try to trace a linear progression as States shift from one practice to another.

Another question that needs to be considered is what role do new States have in the process of customary international law formation. Are newly-independent countries bound to the existing rules of custom, almost as the price of admission to the "community of nations," even though they have had no role in making those rules? This seems to be the preferred approach (although in contrast to rules of State succession for treaties, considered in Chapter 5). The international community does not give new States the alternative of "opting-out" of rules of custom they do not like. Instead, if a new State dislikes a rule of custom, it can compete in the global marketplace and struggle to change it.

If this dynamic and consensual model of customary international law appeals, bear in mind that some rules of international conduct have become so important that we will not let any State opt-out of them, even if they have loudly and conscientiously protested. For example, the minority white government of South Africa persistently objected to the development of customary international law condemning that government's practice of *apartheid*, or racial separation. But to no avail; the international legal consequences of South Africa's failure to observe that custom were notable. Similarly, rules against genocide (systematic destruction of groups of people based on ethnic, cultural or linguistic identity), committing war crimes, or engaging in aggressive war have come to acquire special status.

For example, there are some rules of custom that are so significant—some of them have just been mentioned—that the international community will not suffer States to "contract" out of them by treaty. For example, two States may not conclude a treaty reciprocally granting themselves the right to commit genocide against a selected group. These peremptory rules are called *jus cogens* norms. Likewise, some customary international law obligations are so significant that the international community will permit *any* State to claim for their violation, not just the countries immediately affected. These are *erga omnes* norms.

Accordingly, we have some principles of customary international law that seem to transcend State consent and are seemingly immune from the "bidding" process of objection. How these particular rules of "super-custom" are designated and achieve the exceptionally high level of international consensus they require is a bit of a mystery. But do not let this enigma detract from what would otherwise be the conclusion that custom is a unique source of strength for international law, precisely because it ensures that rules of international conduct are current with the needs and expectations of the international community. Likewise, the methods for finding the evidences of State practice are very supple and require substantial imagination and skill in researching. The last element of the customary international law equation—whether it be *opinio juris* or the reasonableness or utility of a rule—brings into sharp focus the essential question of why States (and other international actors) choose to obey international law.

Chapter 3

Treaties

Along with general principles and custom, treaties are an essential source of international law. Indeed, it is easy to think of written agreements between countries as being *the* source of international legal rules. Although customary international law and general principles remain an important part of the dynamic of international law formation, treaties and treaty-making are gradually becoming the dominant source of rules for international conduct.

This Chapter considers the law of treaties and proceeds by analyzing (A) some important nomenclature about types of international agreements, (B) the relationship between treaties and custom, (C) the process by which treaties are concluded, (D) the methods by which treaties are applied and interpreted, and (E) the ways in which treaty obligations are suspended or terminated. This Chapter, therefore, looks at how international agreements are born, how they live, how they have meaning, and how they die.

A. Treaty Nomenclature

Popular understanding notwithstanding, there is no legal difference between various kinds of international instruments because of the name they are given. In other words, "treaties," "pacts," "protocols," "conventions," "covenants," and "declarations" are all terms to convey international agreements. Some of these terms may connote more or less solemnity or formality, but it does not matter for purposes of characterizing an accord as an international agreement, binding under international law. (You should know, however, that the term "treaty" *does* have a particular meaning in U.S. constitutional law, and this will be considered in Chapter 15.)

Much ink has been spilt by international law academics in trying to distinguish various kinds of treaties, depending on some essential characteristics or subject-matters. This has largely been futile. Most international agreements defy easy categorization. For example, some scholars have attempted to identify treaties that are more like *contracts* between nations, and those that have more the flavor of *legislation*, definitively establishing rules of conduct between countries. Many international agreements have aspects of both properties: they try to settle relations between nations, while also ordaining rules. The contracts-legislation duality is a significant one, and it does explain the peculiar problems that international lawyers face in interpreting and applying treaties. But it does not serve as a reliable guidepost for categorizing international agreements.

Likewise, some writers have tried to differentiate treaties that purport to write-down existing rules of customary international law ("codification"), as opposed to freshly legislating rules of international conduct ("progressive development"). This distinction is supposed to explain whether a new treaty is likely to garner sufficient international support. It rarely does. Treaty projects that "merely" codify existing law are among the most contentious in modern diplomatic history. (Just ask the International Law Commission (ILC), the U.N. body that has been deliberating rules of State Responsibility for over 50 years!) On the other hand, the international community can often mobilize substantial support for entirely novel forms of law-making—if the circumstances are compelling enough.

The only sensible typology of international agreements is the simple distinction between *bilateral* treaties (made between two nations) and *multilateral* treaties (concluded between three or more countries). This distinction will need to be kept in mind when conducting treaty research, whether in historical collections of treaties made before 1919 (like Parry's and Marten's), international collections (like the League of Nations Treaty Series (LNTS) or the U.N. Treaty Series (now available on-line)), or national treaty sources (for the United States, "U.S. Treaties and Other International Agreements" (U.S.T.) or "Treaties and Other International Acts Series" (T.I.A.S.)).

That leaves the question of what actually defines an international agreement. Fortunately, international law provides an answer in the 1969 Vienna Convention on the Law of Treaties (VCLT). The VCLT is, quite literally, a treaty on treaties. Almost every question of treaty law is settled in that document, and it is an essential bit of reading for every international lawyer. (Just as the Uniform Commercial Code (UCC) and the Convention on International Sale of Goods (CISG) are the "bibles" for commercial litigators in the U.S.) In any event, VCLT article 2 thoughtfully provides that an international agreement is one "concluded between States in written form and governed by international law."

Let us consider the elements of this definition in turn. For starters, the VCLT only governs treaties between States. That might compel one to conclude that only States can enter into binding agreements, but that would be wrong. International organizations can enter into agreements with other institutions or with countries. Such instruments, though, are not covered by VCLT— they are governed by a separate Convention and by customary international law. Likewise, individuals and companies can enter into agreements with nations (whether for procurement contracts, resource concessions, or loans), but, again, they will not be covered by VCLT, but rather by yet other sets of written rules and by custom.

Must all international agreements be written? To be covered by the "default" rules of the VCLT, yes. That does not mean that oral agreements concluded between nations, or even unilateral declarations made by countries, are invalid. In a number of cases, the World Court has enforced such verbal agreements or unilateral declarations. For example, the PCIJ in the *Eastern Greenland* Case enforced an oral promise by the Norwegian Foreign Minister to renounce Norwegian claims to Greenland, especially when the promise was motivated by the *quid pro quo* of Denmark foregoing claims to Norwegian territory elsewhere.[1] The same goes for unilateral declarations made by States, even without consideration. The French President's 1973 announcement of his nation's termination of atmospheric nuclear testing in the South Pacific was held to be legally binding on France.[2]

The key factor in deciding the binding character and enforceability of unilateral declarations is whether the declaring State intended to create a legal obligation or induce reliance on the part of other States. If this sounds circular, it probably is. But it is increasingly important for international lawyers to distinguish between binding and non-binding agreements. The latter, called sometimes "gentlemen's agreements" or "aspirational texts" or "soft law," are intended by their parties not to be legally obligatory. That does not mean they are purely political or hortatory. A non-binding accord might start the process of forming a State practice which, when accompanied by *opinio juris*, would make a custom. An aspirational text might later mature into a fully enforceable and binding treaty.

That leaves the last element of a treaty covered by the VCLT— the agreement has to be "governed by international law." This, again, is controlled by the intent of the parties. One can imagine that States might enter into agreements of such a purely technical or desultory nature that there is no intention to have them enforceable by international law standards. Generally, this element of the VCLT's definition of a treaty is self-proving. Absent a specific provision that the agreement would be governed by other than

---

1. *Legal Status of Eastern Greenland* Case (Den. v. Nor.), 1933 P.C.I.J. Ser. A/B, No. 53.

2. *Nuclear Test* Cases (Austl. & N.Z. v. Fr.), 1974 I.C.J. 253.

international law (perhaps the domestic laws of one of the parties), then it will be assumed to be.

B. The Relationship Between Treaties and Custom

As has already been intimated, profound tensions can arise between rules based on treaties and those based on custom. Before proceeding to consider treaty formation, interpretation and breach, it is important to clarify the relationship between treaties and custom in certain circumstances.

The first is presented by the question of whether treaties can bind non-parties. The straightforward answer to this—the one you might expect from even a superficial understanding of contract law—is "No." Agreements can never bind non-parties. There are situations where an international agreement might confer *benefits* on a non-party. And, once conferred, such benefits cannot be withdrawn, without the consent of the beneficiary. Treaties, therefore, should not be binding or legally enforceable against States that decline to participate. This is known as the principle of *ius tertii*.

This seems standard Contracts "black-letter," and (for the most part) it is a correct statement of international law. Nonetheless, there are some notable exceptions where duties in international agreements can be applied to non-parties. There are a handful of "objective regimes," treaties which have been understood to be binding even on non-parties. The United Nations Charter—the "Constitution" of the post-World War Two international order—has been found by the ICJ to create rights and duties for non-members (see Chapter 6). Some newer environmental regimes, including the 1959 Antarctic Treaty, have also been found to have this objective character, as have some aspects of regional economic integration (including the European Union).

A more complicated problem is presented where a State deliberately does not become party to a treaty, but it is nevertheless asserted that it has become bound to a custom codified or progressively developed in the agreement. This was the situation in the *North Sea Continental Shelf* Cases,[3] where Denmark and The Netherlands asserted that the Federal Republic of Germany was bound to a rule of equidistance in delimiting their respective continental shelves, even though Germany had purposefully not signed the 1958 Convention on the Continental Shelf. Needless to say, Germany had declined to sign that instrument precisely because adoption of the equidistance rule would have had disastrous

3. 1969 I.C.J. 3 (F.R.G. v. Den./ Neth.).

consequences for its legal claim to offshore oil and gas in the North Sea.

The ICJ ruled that the equidistance rule—unlike the basic concept of a nation's claim to a continental shelf—was a progressive development, and not a codification of existing custom. Holland and Denmark could not, thereby, assert that the equidistance rule contained in the 1958 Convention had quickly matured into a custom (the dispute arose in the mid–1960's, and was decided in 1969). This saved Germany from proving that it had persistently objected to the new custom, as distinct from merely rejecting the treaty.

The important thing to remember here is that a rule can develop through a parallel evolution in both treaties and custom. Even though a country rejects a treaty provision containing a rule, if it fails to object as that same norm is renewed in State practice, it will later become bound to it. If treaty rules and custom can converge, they can also clash. Despite the fact that more and more areas of international law are being governed by rules contained in international agreements, it would be profoundly mistaken to believe that, in case of conflict, custom will be trumped by treaty. It is vital to keep in mind that custom and treaties are co-equal sources of international law; there is no inherent hierarchy between them.

Indeed, a number of diplomatic incidents and tribunal decisions have given customary international law norms precedence over treaty rules. In diplomatic correspondence between the U.S. and United Kingdom, just before America's entry into World War One,[4] the U.S. successfully protested the British practice of stopping U.S. vessels and arresting German nationals. Britain justified this practice based on an extensive network of treaties, but the U.S. relied on a customary rule granting immunity to neutral vessels. Absent an explicit agreement between Britain and the U.S. sanctioning such arrests, the U.S. was correct to rely on custom. In the *S.S. WIMBLEDON* Case, the World Court (in its first case),[5] was faced with a collision between customary principles of neutrality and treaty-based rules of access to an international canal. The PCIJ opted for the treaty and compelled Germany to grant passage through the Kiel Canal to a vessel carrying munitions to Poland (then engaged in a war with the Soviet Union). Germany was thus caught in a classic "whip-saw." By satisfying its obligations under the Treaty of Versailles, it was violating its customary international law obligation of neutrality to the Soviets (which was *not* a party to Versailles).

4. The S.S. China Incident, [1916] For. Relations of the U.S. Supp. 667.　　**5.** 1921 P.C.I.J. Ser. A, No. 1 (Fr./U.K./It./Jap. v. Ger.).

The last ground for potential conflict between treaties and custom is presented with *jus cogens* obligations. These are definitionally "peremptory norms"—rules of custom that may not be abrogated by treaty. Like provisions of domestic contracts that are "void for public policy," treaties which violate *jus cogens* (such as an agreement sanctioning genocide) are void when made, or, if a peremptory norm later develops in conflict, such an agreement is subsequently voidable.

So the interaction between treaties and custom can be subtle, and is by no means clearly understood. International lawyers realize that they must assess both treaty-based and customary sources for a particular rule. It is not enough to assume that if a duty is contained in an international agreement, it will necessarily trump a contrary custom. Nor can it always be supposed that a treaty rule will never bind a non-party.

C.   The Process of Treaty–Making

Most aspects of the process by which States enter into international agreements are technical, of interest only to the staffs of foreign ministries around the world. Happily, the VCLT prescribes most of the rules on this subject, and they are rather uncontroversial. Once it is accepted that the entity entering into a treaty has the *capacity* to do so (and that turns on whether it is a legitimate subject of international law, considered in Chapter 5), the treaty process unfolds in a fairly predictable way.

The first step is the negotiation, in which diplomats or representatives are given instructions and authority (called "full powers") to draft, and then sign, an agreement. The question of authority can sometimes be tricky, but largely turns on elemental notions of agency. High government officials (heads of state, heads of government, and Foreign Ministers) are always assumed to have the power to enter into treaties. Lesser officials need to have this authority expressly stated.

The reason why this is important is that for some treaties, a State will be assumed to be legally bound at the moment of signature. It thus may be significant to know the authority of the individual making that signature. But for the vast majority of international agreements there is a subsequent step in the treaty-making process. Known generically as "ratification," it is the act by which a State makes clear its intent to be legally bound by the treaty. In the United States, for example, the class of international agreements known as "treaties" must be signed under the authority of the President and then submitted to a two-thirds vote in the Senate for "advice and consent." Once that is secured, the President can then "proclaim" the treaty, and at the moment of proclamation it is deemed ratified and binding internationally.

But there are often substantial delays (often lasting years or decades) between the time that a treaty is signed by an authorized official and the time it is ratified according to the constitutional processes of the individual States parties. (For example, it took the U.S. nearly 40 years to ratify the 1948 Genocide Convention.) During this interim period, Article 18 of the VCLT controversially required that States, at a minimum, do not act in a way to defeat the object of the treaty, *unless* they make clear their intent not to ratify the instrument.

The real moment of danger in any treaty-making process is when a State regrets the deal it has struck and attempts unilaterally to change the legal effect of the treaty by making "reservations" to the agreement. Some treaty regimes have spectacularly unraveled when one country sought such changes. Perhaps the most historically-significant example of this was the U.S. Senate's refusal in 1920 to advise and consent to the Treaty of Versailles and League of Nations Covenant (ending World War One and creating a new international organization) without substantial reservations. President Woodrow Wilson refused to make those changes, and the U.S. never became a party to a significant institution designed to protect international peace and security. Whether this led to later aggressions by Nazi Germany, Fascist Italy, Imperial Japan, and Stalinist Russia—and the outbreak of World War Two in 1939—is a matter best left for speculation by historians.

Reservations are only a problem for multilateral treaties. If one party to a bilateral treaty attempts to later impose reservations as a condition for its ratification, that has much the same effect as a counter-offer in a contract negotiation. The two parties start the negotiations over; the "jilted" side will not be happy, but there are rarely any adverse legal consequences. With multilateral treaties, however, it is often logistically impossible to reconcile subsequent reservations, which have the potential of creating a patchwork-quilt of different obligations between the parties.

Before 1950, the traditional rule in these situations was that if a country made a reservation to a multilateral treaty, it had to be accepted by all parties. If it was not, the reserving State was totally excluded from the treaty regime. A new rule evolved at mid-century, impelled by the development of a new kind of international agreement: one that imposed duties on a State to protect the human rights of its own citizens (more on which in Chapter 9). A number of socialist nations had made debilitating reservations to the 1948 Genocide Convention, all but gutting its protections. The United Nations was not sure whether these countries' ratifications should even count toward the total to bring the Convention "into force" and legally binding. The U.N. requested an advisory opinion of the ICJ.[6] The World Court concluded that the best rule–especially in situations where there was no "perfect contractual balance between rights and duties" under the treaty—was to permit nations to make reservations, so long as they were not contrary to the "object and purpose" of the Convention.

That still left open many questions, including (a) what defines a reservation, (b) how does a country know if a reservation defeats the "object and purpose" of the treaty, (c) who will make this decision, and (d) what if a country still objects to the reservation? These were partially resolved in Articles 19 and 20 of the VCLT. For example, a reservation is anything that purports to change the legal effect of a treaty, and although many countries annex "declarations" and "interpretive statements" when they ratify treaties, these are not considered reservations.

Today, many treaties contain provisions specifying permissible grounds for reservation. These are, in essence, sanctioned "opt-out" clauses, where a State Party is free to choose to disable certain provisions of the agreement. On the other hand, some treaties are considered "package deals," and reservations are categorically barred. Parties are thus prohibited from "picking-and-choosing" the provisions they like and discarding the rest. (The 1982 U.N. Convention on the Law of the Sea, discussed at length in Chapter 11, was of this type.)

International tribunals and institutions have taken a more and more aggressive role in deciding whether a treaty party's reservation is compatible with the agreement's "object and purpose." Some try to bend-over-backwards to accommodate State interests, and thus accept rather dubious reservations. Other tribunals, including the European Court of Human Rights in the *Belilos* Case,[7] refused to allow Switzerland to reserve against what it regarded as a core provision protecting human rights. Although Switzerland was not forced to cease being a party to the European Convention on Human Rights, it did later modify the offending reservation. The United Nations Human Rights Committee has taken a similar position as to reservations to the International Covenant on Civil and Political Rights (ICCPR).

Ultimately, even multilateral treaties have a contractual flavor, and States may simply object to another nation's reservation, even if it is found not to offend the object and purpose of the treaty. In these circumstances, complex rules are triggered which might result in divergent treaty obligations running with different combina-

---

6. *Reservations to the Convention on Genocide*, 1951 I.C.J. 15.

7. 132 Eur. Ct. H.R. (ser. A) (1988).

tions of States Parties to the agreement. For these reasons, reservations are a significant complicating factor for treaty-based rules. It is essential, therefore, for international lawyers to check not only the relevant text of a treaty, but also to ascertain whether reservations are permitted, and whether a particular State has, in fact, lodged such a document. A country's obligations under a treaty might run only so far as its reservation.

D. Treaty Application and Interpretation

As for how treaties are applied and observed, it is worthwhile keeping in mind some basic default rules. First, international agreements are normally assumed to have only prospective effect. Retroactivity of treaty provisions is disfavored, so if the parties intend that a rule is to be applied to events occurring before the agreement is signed, they should so indicate. Likewise, it is normally assumed that a treaty will be applied throughout the territorial sovereignty of the State Party. If for some reason a country does not wish a particular treaty-based rule to be applied to part of its territory, it would have to so provide or make the necessary reservation (assuming a reservation was permitted on that score).

Aside from these issues of treaty application, the real difficulty in observance of international agreements arises from their interpretation. Just as it is impossible to draft a contract, will, or statute that is free from ambiguity, or the construction of which is doubtful in certain situations that had not been contemplated by the drafter, so, too, with international agreements. Indeed, if anything, treaties may be *more* vague, ambiguous, and otherwise difficult to interpret than other kinds of legal writings. The nature of many treaty texts as political or diplomatic compromises often means that contentious issues of application are deferred to a later day in order to win agreement in the here and now. It is essential in the smooth running of the international legal system that there be some established principles of treaty interpretation. It is especially important for international lawyers to understand the unique aspects of, and approaches to, construing treaties.

Interpretation of treaties is subject to the same dynamic struggle between international actors as with the formation of customary international law rules. States will actively "bid" and assert their particular constructions of difficult or contentious treaty provisions in order to win advantage in international relations. States will often oppose such interpretations, especially when they might conflict with their national interests. The important thing to realize is that, unless it protests, a State may later be found to have acquiesced in the acceptance of a particular treaty construction. International tribunals, institutions, and decision-makers are not obliged, however, to respect or privilege the interpretation made by one party to a treaty. Questions of treaty construction are thus resolved as often by dispute settlement as by negotiation.

There are three "schools" or approaches to treaty interpretation, and these correspond with methods for construction of any legal text—including constitutions, statute, and contracts. The first of these schools is *textualism*. All solid treaty interpretation begins with the words of a provision itself, as they are commonly understood. VCLT Article 31, in discussing treaty interpretation, calls for an examination of a text's "ordinary meaning." If words always had fixed and determinable meaning for every circumstance, then one would have no need for interpretation—nor for lawyers, for that matter. The trick is to be able to understand ambiguous or vague words or phrases in a treaty, in light of other clues the text has to offer. (Remember that many treaties are drafted in two or more languages, and it is vital to ascertain not only which languages are "authentic," but also that there may be different shades of meanings of terms in different languages.)

Two examples will suffice of this form of textualism. In 1958, the Austrian Constitutional Court was called upon to construe a provision of the Austrian State Treaty,[8] concluded after World War Two and which effectively neutralized that country. The provision in question imposed substantial restrictions on Austrian acquisition of airplanes of German or Japanese origin. It seems that an Austrian flying club wanted to purchase a glider from Germany, and such was blocked because of the prohibition. The flying club argued that the word "airplane" (as used in the German text of the treaty) did not include non-motorized gliders. The Constitutional Court rejected this literal interpretation, reasoning that the use of the broader phrase "air*craft*" elsewhere in the treaty suggested that the use of the word "air*plane*" was not to have the meaning suggested. The club thus had to buy its glider from elsewhere.

Textualism can be a form of cross-reading of different provisions in a treaty text, in order to reach a sensible result. Sometimes it is not that easy. Consider Article 3 of the 1919 International Labor Organization Convention on the Employment of Women During the Night: "Women without distinction of age shall not be employed during the night in any public or private undertaking, or in any branch thereof, other than an undertaking in which only members of the same family are employed." The proper meaning of this provision was challenged when a group of employers wanted the ability to employ women at night in managerial or supervisory

---

8. *Case on the Interpretation of the Austrian State Treaty* (Aust. Const. Ct. 1958), reprinted in, 86 JOURNAL DU DROIT INTERNATIONAL 835 (1959).

posts. The PCIJ gave an Advisory Opinion[9] and concluded that while it had never been intended to bar women managers from working at night, the text of Article 3 clearly extended beyond women working as manual laborers. Indeed, the provision carved-out just one exception: women who work in a business solely with other family-members. The World Court reluctantly agreed that while its interpretation of Article 3 may lead to a strange and counter-progressive result, it was obliged to follow the text.

Already one can see a tension between the text of a treaty provision and the intent of the drafters. But an *intentionalist* approach to treaty interpretation has never been popular in international law. Indeed, the VCLT relegates sources shedding light on the intent of the drafters—including the negotiating history (or *travaux préparatoires*) of a provision—to a secondary role. They can be used only where the text is "ambiguous or obscure," or the plain meaning of the text leads to a "manifestly absurd or unreasonable" result.

One reason that *travaux* may be somewhat disfavored in international law is the concern that some countries might sign a treaty long after it was negotiated and signed. Should these newcomers be bound not only to the text, but also the informal understandings of the drafters? This would unduly privilege the interpretive positions of the original signatories. Likewise, use of negotiating history—including earlier drafts of a treaty, reports and commentaries, and diplomatic statements—can be selective and manipulable. Despite these cautions, use of *travaux* has become a constant feature of interpretive disputes over treaties. It can be a two-edged sword. Especially in situations where one side or another has a negotiating advantage, tribunals will often insist that, in case of ambiguity, a treaty will be interpreted contrary to the interests of the drafting State (the *contra proferentem* canon). This rule requires that negotiators be up-front and candid about possible drafting ambiguities, and to have them resolved at the negotiations, rather than in any later dispute.

That leaves the third school of interpretation: seeking to effectuate the purpose of a treaty, rather than slavishly following the text or attempting to divine the intent of the drafters. Known in international law as a *teleological* approach, we might also call it purposivism. It is captured in the VCLT's requirement that treaties be construed in light of their "object and purpose" and in view of "relevant rules of international law." The idea here is to interpret a treaty in a way that gives scope to the fundamental reason or problem that an international agreement was supposed to address.

9. *Interpretation of the 1919 Convention Concerning Employment of Women*   *During the Night,* 1932 P.C.I.J., Ser. A/B, No. 50.

This approach is especially common with more "organic" or "constitutional" treaties, including those that establish international institutions (the United Nations Charter of 1945 is a good example of this) or that fashion a "framework" for further international legislation. There are limits to teleology in treaty construction, and interpreters cannot take the purpose of a treaty too far. For example, the ICJ has flatly rejected the notion of "maximum effectiveness," construing a treaty so as to give it fullest effect. In a 1950 Advisory Opinion,[10] the Court ruled that Peace Treaties concluded by eastern European States containing arbitration clauses could not be construed as to give the U.N. Secretary General the power to appoint arbitrators, if the States themselves had refused to do so.

An accomplished international lawyer thus uses a combination of textual, intentionalist, and teleological methods in interpreting a treaty text. The starting-point of any construction is the words of the agreement, but that must necessarily mean understanding the *entire* treaty, its structure and form. Where there is a background to the treaty—the diplomatic circumstances giving rise to the deliberations, the actual negotiating history, and *travaux préparatoires*—that should also be studied. Lastly, a skilled interpreter of a treaty recognizes that there is usually some fundamental object and purpose for an agreement, and even for its particular provisions.

E. Treaty Amendment, Invalidity and Termination

Having seen how treaties are born and how they live, now we come to how they change and how they die. Treaties, after all, are not meant to last forever, even though they are often framed in an idiom of ever-lasting obligation. There is a need for change in international law, and treaties would not be an effective source of international legal obligation if anachronistic rules were forever graven in stone. The critical point is how to balance expectations of faithful performance of treaties with a need to accommodate change.

The most obvious method of permitting treaty provisions to change in light on new conditions is to amend the agreement by the approval of all the parties. This is exceedingly common. In fact, many treaties are originally drafted with subsequent amendment procedures in mind. Some treaties, particularly in the areas of international environmental and economic law, have wonderfully

---

10. *Interpretation of Peace Treaties with Bulgaria, Hungary and Romania*   Opinion, 1950 I.C.J. 65, 221.

elaborate amendment procedures that allow for tacit and expedited approval of "technical" changes, while also requiring periodic meetings of the parties to update more substantive provisions. But care must be taken to ensure that all parties to an original treaty do, in fact, sign onto subsequent amendments. Difficult problems in treaty law arise when there is a disjunction between treaty obligations because one or more parties have not agreed to significant amendments.

Much more controversial than express amendment of treaties are more informal mechanisms of modification. Modification arises when some (but not all) of the parties to a treaty subsequently agree to a material change. VCLT Article 41 sets out an elaborate regime in which, as long as a treaty does not bar modification, selected States can give notice of a modification, provided the change does not derogate the rights of other parties and does not affect a provision the performance of which is essential. Interestingly, in drafting the VCLT, the International Law Commission (ILC) had included a provision recognizing that customary international law could modify the terms of a treaty. This provision was later dropped, however, as being inappropriate and problematic for treaty law.

The VCLT also has provisions concerning treaty invalidity. These are circumstances where, because of some defect in the formation of a treaty, it can later be abrogated. Such conditions include treaties entered into contrary to fundamental domestic constitutional limitations, error, fraud, corruption, and coercion. Needless to say, such circumstances are exceedingly rare in modern international relations. States are simply assumed not to commit mistakes of fact in making agreements. Nor is a claim that a treaty was compelled because of unequal political, military or economic power likely to succeed. Treaty invalidity was carefully limited in the VCLT, moreover. Obligations in invalid provisions can continue under other provisions of treaties or as custom. Invalid provisions can also be severed to save the rest of a treaty. Lastly, a State can lose the right to claim invalidity, if it has acquiesced in the operation of the treaty over a sufficient period of time.

The most contentious issue in treaty law arises, however, when one State purports to unilaterally suspend or terminate an obligation in an international agreement. A situation where this arises is when one party to a treaty believes that another State has breached the obligations of the agreement. The natural reaction in such circumstances is for the offended State to suspend or terminate the treaty. But as many lawyers know from circumstances of anticipatory breach in domestic commercial law, a party's first reaction to perceived bad behavior by a treaty partner is not often the best approach.

International law clearly recognizes the right of a State to terminate a treaty if another party has breached its obligations under the agreement. Customary international law and VCLT Article 60 has added an important caveat: a nation cannot terminate the treaty unless another party has *materially* breached a provision "essential to the accomplishment of the object or purpose of a treaty." In other words, a trivial or accidental breach of a treaty obligation does not give grounds for unilateral termination. Indeed, under this rule, if a party anticipatorily terminates a treaty, believing the other side has committed a material breach, but later finds it was wrong in that belief, then *it* will be regarded as the party in breach. Of course, just because a State believes a treaty partner has committed a material breach does not necessarily mean, in practice, that termination will be forthcoming. It might just spark a renewed round of diplomacy in order to heal the rift.

Another ground for termination of treaties is known as the doctrine of fundamental change of circumstances, or *rebus sic stantibus*. The idea here is that when the conditions which led to the conclusion of a treaty change so fundamentally, then one party or another can unilaterally terminate the agreement. Needless to say, such a doctrine has the potential of being utterly destructive of good faith and predictable observance of treaty obligations. It has nonetheless persisted in treaty law because of the need for a mechanism of peaceful alteration of treaty obligations that are no longer considered desirable. That may be because of changes in material facts which gave rise to the commitment or other transformations of international society,

One early example of an apparently legitimate invocation of the *rebus sic stantibus* doctrine was the United States' termination of the 1930 International Load Lines Convention. That treaty attempted to promote international shipping safety by imposing important restrictions on how much could be loaded on ships (overloading vessels can cause them to capsize). In July 1941, before the U.S. entry into World War Two, the U.S. Attorney General decided that the Load Lines treaty could be terminated because of changed circumstances.[11] The Attorney General reasoned that because most of the parties were at war, and because the treaty had been drafted with peacetime conditions in mind, it was reasonable to terminate the treaty on that ground.

The 1969 VCLT carefully sought to limit use of the doctrine by requiring the satisfaction of a multi-part test. Article 62 requires that (a) the change must be fundamental, (b) unforseen by the drafters, (c) the assumption of current circumstances must have been "an essential basis of the consent to bound by the treaty," (d)

---

11.   40 Op. Att'y Gen. 119 (1941).

the new circumstance must radically transform the obligation for the party seeking termination, (e) and obligations are yet to be performed under the treaty (and may not involve territorial boundaries). As one might suspect, no State has successfully justified a termination of a treaty for changed circumstances under the Article 62 standard.

Indeed, the only credible attempt to raise a *rebus sic stantibus* justification in the World Court failed miserably. Iceland had concluded in 1961 an Exchange of Notes with Britain, agreeing that it could claim a 12 nautical mile fishing zone, but that if Iceland wished to later increase that claim, the matter would have to be adjudicated in the ICJ. This proved to be a bad deal for Iceland. Later developments (discussed in Chapter 11) impelled States to later claim up to 200 mile zones. In 1971, Iceland unilaterally extended its zone to 50 miles, and Britain sued in the ICJ. Iceland protested that its acceptance of ICJ jurisdiction in the 1961 Notes was an unenforceable promise because of changed circumstances. The Court vigorously rejected this challenge to its jurisdiction,[12] ruling that while the change in the law of the sea may have been fundamental and unforseen, it really did not radically transform Iceland's obligation. Iceland was obliged to submit its increased zone to the Court, which subsequently rejected at least part of Iceland's claim.

If international law has sought to limit terminations of international agreements because of changed circumstances, it has also sought to preserve treaty obligations threatened by an outbreak of hostilities between the parties. The termination of treaties by war has always been a matter of customary international law. In fact, it still is; the VCLT is deliberately silent on this subject.

While there remains substantial controversy as to whether war cancels all treaty obligations, the better reasoned view is that an outbreak of hostilities only suspends those obligations the performance of which is incompatible with a state of conflict between the countries. For example, the New York Court of Appeals (Justice Cardozo writing) decided that a treaty provision giving rights of inheritance to foreigners was not affected by World War One.[13] One can imagine that certain kinds of treaties—especially those prescribing humanitarian rules of war (like protecting civilians and prisoners of war) (see Chapter 20)—would be precisely those that should *not* be terminated by war.

Whether the claimed reason of treaty termination is material breach, changed circumstances, or war, the possible "death" of obligations in agreements can spark some of the most serious

12. *Fisheries Jurisdiction* Case (U.K. v. Ice.), 1973 I.C.J. 3.

13. *See Techt v. Hughes*, 229 N.Y. 222 (1920).

disputes in international relations. Just as the law of treaties can merely prescribe general methods and approaches to interpreting treaties, it can only modestly structure certain cautionary rules that will make States and other international actors take pause before irrevocably terminating treaty obligations. In this sense, treaty law rules serve a critical purpose in preserving as many treaty obligations as possible, despite adverse circumstances. At the same time, there are also mechanisms in international law to amend, modify or (in extreme situations) terminate treaty obligations that become unreasonable or unfair. In this way, treaties as a source of international law are supposed to combine both certainty and flexibility.

Chapter 4

Other Sources and Evidences

We have now considered the three central sources of international legal obligation: general principles, custom, and treaties. What remains to discuss are any additional sources or evidences of international law, and then to integrate these into a coherent statement of the methods and sources of international law. I use "sources" and "evidences" as distinct terms, just as Article 38 of the ICJ Statute does. Remember, some material has only "subsidiary" significance and can be taken only as evidence of what a source of international law would declare to be a rule or norm of international obligation.

A.   Equity, Humanity and Other Values

A discussed in Chapter 1, there has been a constant tension in international law between natural and positive origins of international legal obligations. The sources of international law considered so far—general principles, custom, and treaties—are all positivist in the sense that international actors (primarily States) make the law through their own volition: whether through incorporation of domestic legal principles, State practice, or affirmative agreement. It would, however, be unwise for an international lawyer to categorically reject or substantially discount the role of natural law values in forming rules of international conduct.

For example, equity is often mentioned as a source of international law. To be sure, equity and fairness is a general principle of law recognized by all civilized legal systems, and would be incorporated into international law by that avenue. Many equitable principles have been vigorously employed in international dispute settlement. One such concept is "abuse of right," where an international actor is recognized as having the freedom to engage in certain conduct, but is otherwise barred from pursuing a course of action in certain circumstances or in a particular fashion.[1] Likewise, "unjust enrichment" has been used by international tribunals to give relief to an actor disadvantaged by a transaction, even though no formal contractual relationship existed. Finally, the World Court has in-

---

1. See *Cayuga Indians* Claim (Gr.   Awards 173 (U.S.-Brit. Arb. Trib. 1926).
Brit. v. U.S.), 6 U.N. Rep. Int'l Arb.

voked the doctrine of "clean hands"—a party that seeks equity must do equity. So in *The Diversion of Water from the River Meuse Case*,[2] the PCIJ rejected mutual claims by The Netherlands and Belgium that each had impermissibly altered the flow of their boundary waters.

There are two important caveats to the application of equitable or fairness doctrines in international law. The first is that equity does *not* mean reaching a result that is regarded as balanced: a judicial compromise. Such an outcome is the province of negotiation and mediation and is not regarded as being a legitimate application of a legal approach to dispute settlement. In recognition of this, Article 38 of the ICJ Statute expressly bars the Court from deciding cases "*ex aequo et bono* (based on what is just and good)," unless the parties expressly agree to that.

Similarly, equity does not mean equality. Despite strong efforts to fashion international law doctrines to serve the ends of distributional and social justice, international tribunals are not supposed to place judicial fingers on the scales in this fashion. One good example of this reluctance was the World Court's reaction to an argument made by a party to the *Libya-Tunisia Continental Shelf Case*.[3] The two countries were involved in a heated dispute regarding ownership of offshore oil and gas deposits, and Tunisia made the brazen suggestion that because it was poor, and Libya already rich with oil wealth, Tunisia should be given the benefit of some questionable methods of demarcating their respective continental shelf areas. This was stonily rejected by the World Court, which acidly commented (as it had in previous cases) that "equity cannot remake nature." In short, equity is a valuable and influential source of international law rules, but it has its limits, as the Tunisians discovered.

In a similar fashion, notions of humanity have also been central in the evolution of key areas of international law doctrine, including protection of human rights (see Chapter 9) and the laws of war (see Chapter 20). Indeed, the current emphasis on human values and interests (as distinct from those of States) is one of the hallmarks of modern international law. This trend accelerated after World War Two, and, indeed, the first World Court decision after that conflict marked precisely that transition. In the *Corfu Channel Case*,[4] the United Kingdom asserted that Albania had illegally mined certain straits used for international navigation. Even though no treaty was applicable and binding against Albania, the Court discerned "elementary considerations of humanity, even more exacting in peace than in war."

2. 1937 P.C.I.J. Ser. A/B, No. 70   **4.** 1949 I.C.J. 4 (U.K. v. Albania).
(Neth. v. Belg.).

3. 1982 I.C.J. 17.

Aside from fairness and humanity, other values have evolved in international law apart from the positive will of States and other international actors. It used to be that the law of nations was agnostic about the form of governments chosen by States; monarchies and totalitarian regimes were deemed as legitimate as democracies. A growing trend has been to consider representative democracy an affirmative value of international law, one that actually conditions the content of international law rules. In a similar way, stewardship and rational use of global resources (environmental, economic, and intellectual) are becoming recognized as an emerging ethic of international law.

Consideration of new, "natural" values in international law is a healthy development. And just as domestic lawyers need to keep in mind "policy" rationales and justifications for legal rules, an international lawyer would be wise to be sensible to these new sources. Concerns have been raised that when the sources of international law obligation are decoupled from the positive consent of international actors, then international law will lose what little predictability and legitimacy it has. One challenge for lawyering in the international arena will be to reconcile the need for new values with these traditional concerns.

B. U.N. Resolutions, Judicial Decisions and Publicists

In order to make the sources of international law more familiar to lawyers in the Anglo–American common law tradition, there has always been a tendency to inflate the role of such materials as court decisions, legislative enactments, and scholarly writings. Yet while these are recognized in ICJ Statute Article 38, it is only as a "subsidiary" means of establishing *evidence* of the content of international law norms. It is important to explain why this is so.

There is obviously no central legislator in international law, no World Parliament. It is true that some multilateral treaties, on certain subjects and with universal adherence, approach such a model. While there is a growing network of international institutions, producing a body of international regulatory schemes, these are all in the form of treaty regimes. Suggestions, therefore, that the resolutions of United Nations bodies (particularly the General Assembly, where each nation has one vote) constitute a binding source of international law are extravagant.

These intimations have been properly construed as an attempt to provide an easy way to make international law rules, apart from custom and treaty, and without States' consent to be bound. This is not to say, though, that the U.N. is powerless to make binding rules for its own operations, and in certain key respects (considered in Chapter 19), one U.N. organ—the Security Council—is the ultimate law-maker in international relations. The question, instead, is whether General Assembly resolutions, which are only "recommendations" under Article 10 of the U.N. Charter, can make law.

One point that has often been made by commentators is that General Assembly resolutions, precisely because they are recommendations, lack the necessary *opinio juris* for custom. This is so even though States may repeatedly vote for a resolution and profess their support for the legal rule it stands for. States, for example, overwhelmingly voted in the General Assembly for resolutions condemning State-sponsored torture, yet (as such groups as Amnesty International have reported) some of these same States actually engage in the torture of their own citizens. Which do we prefer to believe: the professed position of the State, or the empirical evidence of its actual conduct? In some instances, international lawyers and judges will take States' words at face value. For example, a U.S. court decided that torture constituted a violation of the "law of nations" for purposes of invoking the court's jurisdiction under the Alien Tort Claims Act (discussed further in Chapters 9(B) and 17).[5] In reaching that conclusion, the Second Circuit of the U.S. Court of Appeals relied on General Assembly resolutions, while properly noting that they constituted evidence only (but persuasive evidence) of State practice and *opinio juris*. The votes themselves, the court was careful to say, were not dispositive as a source of international legal obligation.

In a very different context, an international tribunal was obliged to deeply discount the legal effect of General Assembly resolutions. In the *TOPCO* Arbitration,[6] Libya had expropriated the oil concession of a United States company. When the company initiated binding arbitration under the concession contract, Libya countered that under customary international law it was not obliged to participate and that the tribunal had no jurisdiction. For this argument, Libya relied on three General Assembly resolutions. The sole arbitrator concluded, however, that none of these had been supported by a sufficiently wide cross-section of States. In fact, all economically-developed and capital-exporting countries (like the U.S.) had either abstained or voted "no." In essence, the arbitrator examined the *travaux préparatoires* of the resolutions in order to ascertain whether they could even qualify as evidence of a potential custom.

---

5. *Filartiga v. Peña-Irala*, 630 F.2d 876 (2d Cir. 1980).

6. *Texaco Overseas Petroleum Co. v. Libyan Arab Republic*, 17 Int'l Legal Materials 1 (Arb. 1978).

If international law has circumscribed the role of "legislative" enactments, like the resolutions of international organizations, how has it treated the decisions of international and domestic judicial tribunals? Citing such decisions is the stock-in-trade of international lawyers, and, happily, there is a wide body of case law from international tribunals (not to mention the decisions of *domestic* courts on international matters). Aside from the World Court (PCIJ and ICJ), which has decided a broad range of cases and issues, there have also been many specialized tribunals. Examples would include international claims tribunals, which for over 200 years have settled financial and property disputes between countries. There have also been decisions by international criminal courts (including the Nuremberg tribunal after World War Two and more recent institutions for Yugoslavia and Rwanda). After the Second World War there also developed human rights commissions and courts, the jurisprudence for which has become extensive. Lastly, there are economic and trade institutions (including the European Union, NAFTA, and World Trade Organization) which have adjunct judicial bodies resolving disputes.

This plethora of international tribunals—and international case law—is immensely gratifying for international lawyers. There is just one problem. The decisions of these tribunals are not, strictly speaking, binding precedent (or *stare decisis*), not even for the institution which issued the decision. This may come as a shock to a lawyer trained in the common law tradition, but in this respect international tribunals resemble more closely civil law jurisdictions (as in continental Europe) where the doctrine of *stare decisis* does not exist. Indeed, Article 59 of the ICJ Statute says emphatically that, except as between the parties to a dispute, a decision of the World Court has no binding effect.

Happily, the reality of judicial precedent does not coincide with the theory. The truth is that international tribunals almost invariably follow their precedents, especially on procedural issues, and it is very routine for international lawyers to rely heavily on judicial decisions to support their arguments. Yet, it would be a grievous mistake to assume that an international tribunal (just like a domestic court) is obliged to slavishly follow its precedents. Previous judicial decisions—whether from international tribunals or from domestic courts—are clearly a "subsidiary" means of establishing the content of international law norms.

That leaves one last kind of evidence, and this is a favorite of international law professors. The ICJ Statute specifically recognizes the "teachings of the most highly qualified publicists of the various nations" as evidence of rules of law. In short, the writings of international law academics and practitioners—"publicists" in the language of the Statute—can constitute evidence of international law. Just as attorneys know that it is always risky to support an argument on the thin-reed of a treatise, law review article, or even the more weighty *Restatement of Laws,* so too are international lawyers trained to use such materials sparingly.

There clearly is a hierarchy in the selection of publicists' writings. Before the 1900's, the preference was for the "classic" writers of international law, such figures as Grotius (Hugo de Groot), Samuel Pufendorf, Cornelius van Bynkershoek, and Emmerich de Vattel. Such gratuitous citations got tedious even for judges in the 1700's. One English judge remarked: "[T]here was something ridiculous in the decisive way each lawyer, as quoted, had given his opinion.... A pedantic man in the closet dictates the law of nations; everybody quotes, nobody minds him.... [A]nd who shall decide, when doctors [publicists] disagree?"[7]

Today, the most relied-upon secondary sources would probably include the reports prepared by the U.N. International Law Commission (ILC), in pursuance of its many codification projects, as well as those of such non-official groups as the International Law Association (ILA). Certain treatises have also been well-regarded. And for U.S. international lawyers, the *Restatement (Third) of Foreign Relations Law,* published in 1987 under the auspices of the American Law Institute (ALI), is a significant work, although one that must be used with caution, especially before an international tribunal or foreign court. Indeed, one must be careful in avoiding a parochial or biased view of international law by the selection of particular publicists' scholarship. The best way to use such material is to widely canvass writings from many individuals and many countries.

C. An Integrated View of Sources and Methods

It is important for every international lawyer to realize that there is a strong synergy between the various sources of international legal obligation. Understanding how these sources interact is vital to seeing how rules and doctrines evolve and change over time, and thus how decisions and outcomes are achieved in international relations.

To best illustrate this dynamic in the creation of international law, consider the formation of rules for international environmental law (considered in more detail in Chapter 12). Before the 1920's or 1930's there was simply no law on this subject. One would have looked in vain for State practice, treaties, case law, or even academic writings on this subject. Necessity is the mother of invention, and the exigency of creating law on this subject was impelled by a

---

7. *The RENARD,* Hay & M. 222, 165 Eng. Rep. 51(Adm. 1778) (U.K.).

single dispute: the 1941 *Trail Smelter* Arbitration between the U.S. and Canada.[8] This case featured a claim by the U.S. that an ore smelter in Trail, British Columbia, was causing such quantities of air pollution as to be causing substantial damage in Washington state. In the absence of any international law, the arbitrators were obliged to derive a rule from the domestic jurisprudence of States with federal systems (like the U.S. and Switzerland) that one entity should not use its territory in such a way as to injure the rights of another jurisdiction's territory. From this insight—a general principle of law recognized by a sufficient number of civilized nations— the arbitration concluded that Canada owed the United States a duty to prevent and minimize air pollution emanating from the smelter and to compensate for past damages.

From this kernel of a general principle grew the shoots of State practice, slowly at first, but then later with growing rapidity. Nations began to adjust more and more disputes regarding shared resources (including boundary lakes and rivers) or environmental concerns. In the 1950's, 1960's, and 1970's customary international law began to crystalize around a small group of rules of international environmental law: avoidance of transboundary pollution, liability and compensation for environmental damage, and substantive standards to protect wildlife and prevent harmful emissions. Indeed, this process was almost exclusively customary—there were exceedingly few treaties (either bilateral or multilateral) on this subject. At some point in this process there was a sufficient "critical mass" of State practice, combined with a realization that these norms had a binding and legal character (*opinio juris*) so that they were confirmed as customary international law.

Beginning in 1972, with the Stockholm Declaration on the Human Environment, treaty-making began slowly to occupy this field of international law. Again, the process began slowly as exclusively a manifestation of codification—organizing and rationalizing the body of customary norms. Codification did not, however, end the role of customary international law. Just as a tree that has been pruned continues to grow, so, too, a codified rule of custom will continue to be affected by subsequent State conduct. Indeed, customary practices might continue to exert an influence and change the treaty rule. That might occur through the development of new rules, or, more typically, through the process of treaty interpretation in which treaty provisions are gradually given certain well-established meanings.

8. *Trail Smelter* Case (U.S. v. Can.),
3 R.I.A.A. 1905 (1941), reprinted in 35
Am. J. Int'l L. 684 (1941).

Treaty-making in international environmental law quickly advanced from a footing of codifying custom to one of affirmatively legislating new rules of international conduct—"progressive development." The 1980's and 1990's saw a literal explosion in the number, variety, and complexity of treaties on international environmental law. Conventions were concluded on atmospheric issues, including ozone depletion, acid rain, and global warming. Many treaties were focused on habitat protection, rational management of common resources (like fisheries), preservation of wildlife and flora, and trade restrictions to promote these goals. Often these "legislative" treaties began as "framework conventions," merely sketching out the course of future negotiations. But, like much "soft" international law, vague guidelines hardened into explicit norms and then into elaborately-detailed regulatory regimes, with rules periodically updated by the parties through expedited or tacit amendment procedures. Some commentators have complained that international environmental law has become too "congested" with convention regimes and treaty-drafting, so that effective observance, compliance and enforcement of existing rules have been ignored.

In less than 60 years we have seen one very significant field in international law go from a literal vacuum (with no rules of international conduct *at all*) to incredibly sophisticated regimes featuring detailed rules of behavior and complex institutional machinery to enforce those rules. This would have been impossible without general principles "jump-starting" the process of international law formation (by effective borrowing from domestic legal systems), and the dynamic of customary international law (which allowed the quick accretion of State practice in response to pressing needs), and the processes of treaty-making (which permitted both the codification and progressive development of these rules).

It is this kind of synergy which explains the unique sources and methods of international law—and also the inherent strength of the international legal system. It also accounts for the special skills and aptitudes that an international lawyer must bring to bear in understanding the evolution of rules of international conduct, as well as constructing arguments and transactions on behalf of parties and clients.

PART TWO

SUBJECTS AND OBJECTS OF INTERNATIONAL LAW

Chapter 5

States: Identity, Recognition and Succession

This Part of the book examines the subjects and objects of international law. These two terms have caused substantial confusion among students and practitioners of international law (and even among scholars and judges), so careful definition is necessary. By a *subject* of international law, I mean an entity that bears international legal rights or duties. Subjects of international law are also known as "international legal persons," a phrase that is meant to convey the idea of full-fledged participation in the international legal system by entities that are capable of exercising rights and observing duties under international law. The subjects of international law are the actors, or players, on the international scene. In contrast, the *objects* of international law are the who, what and where that are being acted upon. The objects of international law are the legitimate topics of international legal regulation.

The distinction between "subjects" and "objects" of international legal regulation has been discussed and debated for centuries and can be traced back to the writings of Grotius and Pufendorf. Such distinctions are probably a bit anachronistic today. The reason is that the subjects and objects of international law have been radically transformed in the twentieth century. During the course of the last hundred years, international law became concerned with new issues that demanded international cooperation. The management of existing and emerging global commons and resources—such as rivers, polar regions and airspace (considered in Chapter 10), the oceans (discussed in Chapter 11), and the international environment (Chapter 12)—moved to the top of the global agenda. Likewise, the demands of a more and more integrated and interdependent global economy required the creation of rules that were regarded as a legitimate topic of international legal regulation (see Chapter 13). International law has come to involve virtually every aspect of human conduct, every kind of business transaction, and every type of social and cultural relationship that crosses national frontiers. International law has permeated every facet of international life.

At the same time, we have had a revolution in the subjects of international law. One of the most notable trends in modern international law has been the change in attitude towards the identity of international legal actors. It used to be that States were the only recognized subjects of international law, the only "real" players on the international scene. But, as has already been discussed, the subjects of international law have been broadened to include other kinds of actors. These include international organizations or institutions as collectivities of nations (discussed in Chapter 6) and, perhaps even more importantly, the growing role of individuals as holders of both international rights and duties (considered in Chapter 7).

As international legal actors have diversified and the legitimate topics of international legal regulation have expanded, the dividing line between "subjects" and "objects" has blurred. And that is probably for the best. But it remains essential for international lawyers to fully understand both the "roster" of international legal players, as well as the "playing field" that is the permissible range of international legal regulation. That is accomplished in this Part by first looking at international law actors (the subjects of international law), and then examining the topics of international law administration (the objects).

A.   State Identity, Sovereignty and Legitimacy

Despite what I have just said about the extraordinary transformations in international law in the last century, States remain the preeminent actors in international law. Barring a move toward World Government, nations will always be at the center of international law and international law-making. The essence of statehood is sovereignty, the principle that each nation answers only to its own domestic order and is not accountable to a larger international community, save only to the extent it has consented to do so. Sovereign states are thus conceived as hermetically-sealed units, atoms that spin around an international orbit, sometimes colliding, sometimes cooperating, but always separate and apart.

If statehood is considered a definite status, membership in the "family" or "community" of nations is highly desired. States are unqualifiedly entitled to the full panoply of rights and duties under international law. Among these is the capacity to enter into treaties, which is essential to the formation of consensual rules of international behavior. (States are also critical in the process of the formation of customary international law, although other types of international actors may also be involved in the process of developing new rules of conduct.) Likewise, only States are eligible to become full members of international organizations. Nations are also able to claim breaches of international law obligations and to seek redress. Other international actors (including individuals and transnational corporations) are often held to the same standards of conduct as States, even though their avenues for relief when their rights are violated may be more limited. States alone usually enjoy the full range of privileges and immunities from other nations' exercises of jurisdiction (including the significant right to claim sovereign immunity). Lastly, and most importantly, only nations (or insurgent groups aspiring to statehood) have the right under international law to engage in war or armed conflict as an instrument of policy, and even then under prescribed circumstances.

It is this bundle of rights that international lawyers regard as the core of sovereignty. Of course, there are concomitant duties imposed on States by international law, not the least of which is the responsibility not to violate the rights of other nations. All of this leads to the not so surprising conclusion that political entities aspire to statehood, and that such assertions of State identity can often lead to contentious legal disputes.

The classic statement of the elements of statehood under international law can be found in the 1933 Montevideo Convention. Article I of this treaty declared that "The state as a person of international law should possess the following qualifications: (a) a permanent population; (b) a defined territory; (c) government; and (d) capacity to enter into relations with other states." And although this formulation has been criticized, the dominant view is that this remains the customary international law standard of statehood.

Two of the four elements—territory and population—are fairly straight-forward and objective. Territory, which is the paradigmatic "object" of international law (something that is being *acted upon* by international legal players) is an obvious necessity for statehood. The Montevideo Convention requires only that a putative State's territory be "defined," but even this may not be a hard-and-fast requirement. A nation may have territorial disputes with its neighbors, thus its boundaries may not be fully demarcated, and yet that does not disqualify it from statehood. So long as a country's borders are sufficiently consistent, that will suffice. (These issues for territory will be further considered in Chapter 10).

That still begs two problems having to do with territory and statehood. One arises in the faintly comic circumstance when "nations" are created in some pretty outlandish ways. In two different cases—one arising in Germany and the other in the

United States[1]—some intrepid individuals purported to take over offshore platforms or submerged coral reefs, declare their own independence (calling their States "Atlantis, Isle of Gold" or the "Duchy of Sealand"), elect their own officials, and issue their own passports. This was ruled inadmissible under international law, since territory must be a naturally formed part of the Earth's surface to qualify. But, by the same token, international law has recognized a host of "micro-States," entities of exceedingly small size, like Monaco or the Vatican City (both less than 1 sq. mile) or Nauru (8 sq. miles). Whether such tiny entities can otherwise satisfy the criterion of statehood has sometimes been questioned, but the issue of size appears to be irrelevant.

Likewise, the fact that a putative nation's population is small or widely-dispersed has been disregarded for purposes of statehood. As long as a State's population is a group of persons leading a common life and forming a living community, then it qualifies. Under this standard, the officials and support staff of the Roman Catholic Church at the Vatican City qualify, while the fun-loving folk who created "Atlantis" or the "Duchy of Sealand" did not. But even where a population of an area is largely nomadic, and thus widely transitory, the World Court has indicated that may still suffice for purposes of "permanence."

Aside from the population and territory factors, the most contentious issues of State identity arise from the last two of the Montevideo elements: government and a capacity to enter into international relations. These are often combined into a single inquiry of whether an entity has sufficient independence to exercise international rights and to discharge international responsibilities. Some polities have delegated responsibility for the conduct of their international relations to other countries, and questions have arisen whether they can independently engage in international relations. The Principality of Liechtenstein, tucked away in the Austrian Alps, has assigned its foreign relations to Switzerland, and was thus disqualified from membership in the League of Nations, even though it was later allowed to sign the ICJ Statute (open only to States) and has, in fact, litigated cases before the World Court.

Entities that are in a position of dependence to other nations, whether as colonies or protectorates, are also notionally barred from statehood. Self-governing territories of metropolitan governments (think of Puerto Rico or French island colonies in the Caribbean) may not be regarded as States. Yet, entities that are in a position of "association" with other countries—and may have also

---

1. See *In re Citizenship of X*, 1978 Deutsches Verwaltungsblatt 510 (Admin. Ct. Cologne 1978) (Ger.); *United States v. Ray*, 423 F.2d 16 (5th Cir. 1970).

delegated substantial security functions to another nation—can be admitted to statehood. (One example of this is the Federated States of Micronesia, a former trust territory of the U.S. in the Pacific, which was admitted to United Nations membership.)

An ever-present problem for international law is what to do with entities that are created in violation of legal norms. This often arises from impermissible military conquests in which the victorious State declares a sham entity in order to gain some kind of political or diplomatic advantage. One notorious illustration of this was the creation by Japan of the "puppet" state of "Manchukuo" in northern China after the illegal Japanese invasion of that country in 1931. The League of Nations refused to accept Manchukuo as a State, and this incident prompted the United States to enunciate a principle (known as the Stimson Doctrine) that it would not accept the forcible creation of entities in violation of international law. This same principle motivated the United Nations to refuse to accept the membership applications of "Transkei," a black homeland or "bantustan" created by the white minority government in South Africa in the 1970's as a way to deflect criticism of that government's racist policies.

Finally, there are some *sui generis* or special political entities that do not aspire to statehood. International law has accepted the creation of a host of "internationalized territories," in which disputed areas are placed under the nominal sovereignty of one nation but with the actual supervision by an international organization. For example, the cities of Danzig and Memel were placed under an internationalized status by the old League of Nations. Tangier and Berlin were similarly treated by agreement of certain States. (Proposals are periodically made to place Jerusalem under such a scheme.) Although the status of these entities was litigated before the World Court, in no instance were any recognized as a full-fledged State, despite otherwise having the criteria of statehood. Likewise, the government of Taiwan has, to date, disclaimed any intention of asserting statehood, adhering instead to the fiction that there is but one China.

In all of this discussion of statehood, one thing to keep in mind is that the legitimacy of a State system based on sovereignty is the principle of self-determination. In order for nation-States to have any meaning and validity, they must be truly representative of peoples and of national aspirations. If international law is going to privilege States as the critical actor in international relations, then statehood had better mean that each State and its institutions are supported by some form of national consensus.

This does not currently mean that the government of each State must be supported by popular sovereignty or democratic principles in order to be legitimate under international law, although there may well be an emerging norm to that effect. Rather, self-determination is a principle related to the rights of peoples and distinct nationalities to have a State that is representative of their national aspirations. And as principles go, this has developed only since the early 1900's, accelerating in the aftermath of World Wars One and Two and the process of decolonization in the 1960's and 1970's.

Despite this customary international law norm of self-determination as an implicit qualification of statehood and sovereignty, there are many notable conflicts in the world today based on separatist and irredentist movements around the world. (Consider the Basques in Spain, the break-up of the former Yugoslavia, Québecois separatists in Canada, or the Kurds in the Middle East.) Likewise, international law has come to recognize a role for national liberation movements (like the Palestine Liberation Organization) as actors in international relations. Even so, international law remains conflicted because while it supports self-determination as a litmus test of State legitimacy, it also opposes the forcible dismemberment of existing States.

B. Recognition of States and Governments

There is, of course, an unspoken assumption in the criterion for statehood enunciated in the Montevideo Convention—that other nations are prepared to treat a particular entity as a member of the family of nations. Issues revolving around the recognition of States and the governments of States have proven to be some of the most contentious in international relations. Unfortunately, the international law on these topics has been unsatisfactory, to say the least. The doctrines surrounding recognition of political entities as States are distinct from the question of whether the government or particular leadership of a State should be dealt with diplomatically. For example, no one questions that Cuba is a State satisfying all the Montevideo qualifications, and yet the United States refuses to extend recognition to the Castro regime and to normalize diplomatic relations. Conversely, whether Palestine can be said to be a State has more to do with the nature of the political entity, its territory and people, rather than relations with a particular government or leader.

Recognition of States has been bedeviled by a theoretical construct that can fairly be described as arcane. At one extreme are those who believe recognition by other States is a requisite, or *constitutive*, of statehood. In other words, recognition should be added to the four Montevideo elements. But just because other nations will not work and play with a new political entity does not necessarily make it any less a State or its government any less effective. At the other extreme is a *declaratory* theory of State recognition that argues that statehood is purely objective—an entity has the criterion of being a State, or it does not. Under this theory, recognition is largely irrelevant. But in order for statehood to mean anything—to have international legal consequences—there must be some form of recognition.

The arid debate between constitutive and declaratory theories will never be resolved because, ultimately, the problem is one of politics. The political reality is that entities that can effectively act like States, are treated as States. With break-away or separatist entities, although most nations are skeptical about their chances of autonomy, when they actually achieve some measure of independence and the new nation is safely and permanently established, recognition should follow. This occurred for the revolutionary government in the United States, the former Spanish colonies in Latin America, and so forth in the history of the last two centuries. If anyone doubts the power and effect that recognizing new States has, just recall the break-up of the former Soviet Union and Yugoslavia and the subsequent conflicts that arose in those parts of the world.

Recognition of governments does, however, carry with it tricky legal consequences. On the international plane, changes in governments should not matter. As long as the identity of the State has remained unchanged and there has been no State succession (considered next in this Chapter), whether a State has elected a new President, or the government has been forcibly overthrown by a *coup d'état*, or the entire regime replaced by revolutionary means, should not matter for the international obligations of the State.

The best example of this was the *Tinoco Concessions* Arbitration.[2] A General Tinoco had come to power in Costa Rica via a coup and stayed in office for two years until he, in turn, was ousted. The leading powers, including Britain and the U.S., refused to recognize his government, and yet, during his rule, he gave valuable concessions to a number of British subjects. When Tinoco was deposed, the new government abrogated all of the contracts and concessions made earlier. The British government protested on behalf of its citizens and brought an international claim. The sole arbitrator, William Howard Taft (then serving also as Chief Justice of the United States), ruled that even though Britain had declined to recognize Tinoco, Tinoco's government was the *de facto* ruler of the country and his acts were presumptively valid, and if Costa Rica wanted then to cancel the contracts, it would have to pay damages.

2. (U.K. v. Costa Rica), 1 U.N. Rep. Int'l Arb. Awards 369 (1923).

On the surface, this seems patently unfair. Britain got the political advantage of *not* recognizing Tinoco and, yet, later could claim to protect its nationals' rights to contracts made by him. Arbitrator Taft's emphasis on the Tinoco government's *de facto* status was decisive. If Tinoco was actually in charge, his government's acts should be presumptively valid. A State will thus be held to a predecessor government's acts, unless that regime was actually a "puppet" of a foreign occupier. (For example, after World War Two, Yugoslavia was not held responsible for the conduct of the Nazi-supported government.) Likewise, States will be held responsible for the acts of insurgents or rebels who hold a sufficient amount of power.

Most of the consequences of non-recognition of governments operate on the level of domestic law, not international law. At the risk of anticipating some of the issues in Part Three, these need to be considered here. In the United States, at least, if a foreign government is not recognized by the President, there are two broad repercussions: (1) its access to U.S. courts is limited, and (2) the validity of its acts may be questioned.

Access to U.S. courts by non-recognized governments can be affected in two different ways. The first is that an unrecognized regime cannot sue as a plaintiff. The second is that an unrecognized government, if sued as a defendant, may not assert a defense of foreign sovereign immunity from the jurisdiction of the U.S. courts (see Chapter 17(A)). If this seems unfair—that an unrecognized foreign government is barred from suing as a plaintiff, but can be freely sued as a defendant—a host of caveats and exceptions have softened these effects on court access.

The first and foremost exception to the harsh rule is that the President (acting through the Executive branch) must affirmatively act to bar a government it does not recognize from suing in a U.S. court. The government's silence in these situations is sometimes construed as a tacit form of recognition. Just as often, though, the U.S. government will expressly allow an unrecognized foreign government to sue private parties in U.S. courts. (Even though the U.S. has not recognized the revolutionary government in Iran after 1979, it has still permitted the Iranian government to be a plaintiff in U.S. courts.) The bar against unrecognized governments as plaintiffs has also been evaded by substituting other parties as plaintiffs or assigning claims.

Very difficult problems arise when a particular government is *de*-recognized during the course of proceedings. For example, British courts ruled that when Italy conquered Ethiopia in 1936, and Britain shifted its recognition from the Ethiopian Emperor, Haile Sellasie, to the Italian regime, that acted as a retroactive termination of Sellasie's rights to moneys owed on a contract. He was thus barred as a plaintiff in that situation.[3] U.S. courts followed a similar rule in dismissing a suit brought by the government of South Vietnam after that country was conquered by North Vietnam.[4]

Another case involving Vietnam illustrates the exceptions available when an unrecognized government is sued as a defendant. A French businessman claimed money owed on a contract with a commercial representative of North Vietnam in Paris. North Vietnam was not recognized by the French government, although it still claimed sovereign immunity. This was granted by the French Court of Appeal of Paris on the theory that North Vietnam was a *de facto* regime.[5] Likewise, the Bolshevik government in the Soviet Union was allowed by New York courts to claim sovereign immunity as a defendant, although then unrecognized by the U.S. government.[6] A better statement of the rule of court access for unrecognized governments is that (1) if they are seeking to be a plaintiff in a case filed in a U.S. court, they must be affirmatively blocked by the Executive branch, and (2) if sued as a defendant, they will still be accorded foreign sovereign immunity so long as they are regarded as a *de facto* regime.

Likewise, the rule observed by domestic courts from most countries around the world is that the acts of an unrecognized government will still be given validity, so long as that government has *de facto* control of the State (or part thereof). The U.S. Supreme Court, after the Civil War, still recognized the official acts of the Confederacy (like the incorporation of businesses and celebration of marriages), as long as such acts were not, by their nature, hostile to the Union.[7] Furthermore, in the long-running litigation involving the expropriatory acts of the Soviet Union in the 1920's, a New York court ruled that as a *de facto* regime, Soviet nationalization acts would be recognized, at least for real property situated within Russia (although not for assets located outside the country).[8] There are exceptional cases where the acts of unrecognized governments have not been accorded validity by U.S. courts. These can as easily be explained by holdings suggesting that the foreign government had not achieved even *de facto* status, such as Pancho Villa's insurgent forces in Mexico in the 1910's.[9]

3. See *Haile Sellasie v. Cable & Wireless, Ltd. (No. 2)*, 1939 Ch. 182 (C.A.) (U.K.).

4. See *Republic of Vietnam v. Pfizer, Inc.*, 556 F.2d 892 (8th Cir. 1977).

5. See *Clerget v. Banque Commerciale*, 52 Int'l L. Rep. 310 (1979) (Cour d'Appel, Paris 1969) (Fr.).

6. See *Wulfsohn v. Russian Socialist Federated Soviet Republic*, 234 N.Y. 372 (1923).

7. See *United States v. Home Ins. Co.*, 89 U.S. (22 Wall.) 99 (1875).

8. See *Salimoff & Co. v. Standard Oil of New York*, 262 N.Y. 220 (1933).

9. See *Compania Minera Ygnacio Rodriguez Ramos, S.A. v. Bartlesville Zinc Co.*, 115 Tex. 21 (1925).

C. State Succession

That leaves one remaining topic on the nature of States in international law. State succession occurs when there has been a fundamental transformation in the identity of the State itself, not its government. Such a change of identity can occur in a broad range of circumstances. States can break apart or merge into a union. Former colonies can achieve their independence. Parts of the territory of one State can be sold or otherwise transferred to another nation. Characterizing the precise nature of the State succession is absolutely crucial for understanding the proper rule of international law to cover the situation.

The legal consequences of these various changes of identity are an area of international law that has been poorly understood and largely remains governed by customary international law (chiefly expressed through national court decisions and the positions of governments in response to various events). The U.N. International Law Commission has drafted two treaties which attempt to codify this area of law, but with little success. The 1978 Vienna Convention on State Succession in Respect to Treaties and the 1983 Vienna Convention on State Succession in Respect to State Property, Archives and Debts have drawn only a handful of adherents, and may not be a completely reliable guide to this area of international law.

The only sensible generalization that can be drawn on this subject is that the legal consequences of a succession depend on the nature of the change in State identity as well as the type of issue involved. Starting with State successions for treaties, an important nuance of international law is that a newly-independent State begins its life with a "clean-slate." In the case of decolonization, a new State can pick-and-choose the treaty obligations of its former colonial master (although accession to bilateral treaties in such a case requires the permission of the other treaty partner). Entities that have split or merged present far more difficult issues of continuing treaty obligations. Practically, these problems are worked-out by mutual agreement of the parties to various multilateral and bilateral instruments.

The public property and debts of entities subject to State succession reflect two sides of the same coin. The public property of a particular piece of ceded territory can be seen as the "assets" of the transaction, while the debts (perhaps for public infrastructure) are the "liabilities." Not surprisingly, international law links them together. The nationality of individuals (considered in Chapter 7) resident in territories subject to transfer or a change of State identity is also affected.

Much more controversially, international law relieves a successor State of liability for the tortious acts of a predecessor regime. For example, a U.S. citizen was injured by a denial of justice (more on which in Chapter 8) committed by the South African Republic in 1895, but before the claim was settled, the Boer War broke-out, and Britain conquered that nation. An arbitral tribunal held that the extinction of the perpetrator State terminated the international claim.[10] In other words, Britain did not succeed to the South African Republic's liabilities for international claims. Contractual relations made by a predecessor State have been given very uneven treatment in international decisions. Some courts or tribunals have ruled that a successor regime is under no obligation to respect the contracts or concessions entered into by the predecessor with private parties. (The British again took advantage of this after the Boer War to cancel valuable gold mining concessions.[11]) On the other hand, the World Court in a number of decisions has ruled that a successor State is obliged to pay compensation if it decides to cancel the private contracts entered into by a predecessor State.[12]

Issues of State succession are regarded as difficult even by international lawyers. They continue to perplex government counselors and practitioners, and in the past few decades it has been especially so. The re-emergence of the Baltic states (previously independent before Stalin's conquest in 1939), the dismemberment of the Soviet Union and Yugoslavia, the political divorce in Czechoslovakia, and the reunification of Germany and Yemen, all caused substantial difficulties. The question of which entity should succeed to the Soviet Union's permanent (veto-wielding) seat on the U.N. Security Council was decided in Russia's favor. Whether Serbia would be held to Yugoslavia's being bound to the Genocide Convention for its conduct in Bosnia and Kosovo was provisionally answered affirmatively (although proceedings are ongoing in the World Court on that issue). Issues of State succession—like those for recognition and the very criterion of statehood itself—will continue to be central to international law.

10. See *Brown* Claim (U.S. v. U.K.), 6 U.N. Rep. Int'l Arb. Awards 120 (1923).

11. See *West Rand Central Gold Mining Co. v. The King,* [1905] 2 K.B. 291 (U.K.).

12. See *Mavrommatis* Case, 1924 P.C.I.J. Ser. A, No. 2 (Gr. v. U.K.).

Chapter 6

International Organizations

Collectivities of nations, often called international organizations or "international institutions," have become a notable feature on the landscape of international relations. Even so, international law was rather slow in recognizing the legal status, or "international legal personality," of these entities. The story of this transformation in international law—recognizing an international actor other than States—not only presaged the revolutionary idea that individuals could carry international legal rights and duties, but was also a significant advance for functional cooperation among countries.

As already mentioned, positive developments in international law over the past four centuries have always followed bloody conflicts. In no respect is this more true than in the creation of international institutions. The first modern international organizations were created after the 1815 Final Act of Vienna, the peace treaty that ended 20 years of conflict after the French Revolution and Napoleon's conquests. The first such institution, the Central Commission for the Navigation of the Rhine, had very limited goals: the regulation of barge traffic along that major European river, the removal of obstructions, and the collection of uniform tolls.

That modest event sparked in the 1800's the creation of a host of "functional" international commissions and bureaus, designed to address specific problems of international cooperation. Such issues included the modalities of international communications, including the mail and telegraph. The Universal Postal Union and International Telegraph (now Telecommunications) Union, created in 1865 and 1875 respectively, exist to this day and make it possible to place a direct phone call to virtually any location on Earth or to mail a letter to any country without having to acquire foreign postage. Other functional institutions from this period had truly prosaic purposes: preventing diseases or epidemics, standardizing weights and measures, or operating lighthouses on lonely coasts.

The dream of a universal international organization, one that would aspire to garner global membership and to address a wide range of international problems, was only achieved with the creation of the League of Nations in 1919, after World War One. The League was unquestionably the brain-child of Woodrow Wilson, the U.S. president and former professor of government, and was intended to serve as a forum to resolve all international disputes. Its record in carrying-out its primary task—protecting international peace through a system of collective security—was severely compromised by a lack of political will in the face of serious acts of aggression by Japan, Italy and Germany. Nonetheless, the League was otherwise successful in addressing such issues as protection of the rights of minority populations in central and eastern Europe, adjusting disputes between smaller nations (especially in the Balkans and Latin America), advancing social services around the world (this despite the onset of the Depression in the 1930's), and codifying international law.

Moreover, the very institutional structure of the League was to provide the model for virtually every subsequent international organization. The League "organs" included an *Assembly*, where each member of the organization had one vote, and which set the general policies of the institution, adopted budgets, and was assigned specific tasks for debating issues of disarmament and economic cooperation. Counterpoised with the Assembly was the League *Council*, a much smaller body in which the great powers had permanent representation, along with rotating membership by other, smaller (but no less responsible) nations. This balance between "Great Power" realpolitik and a proto-"World Parliament" was significant. In addition to these organs was also the creation of a permanent staff for the League, led by the *Secretariat*. The idea for this was that the institution could rely on a professional, international civil-service that owed its primary loyalty to the League, not to individual countries of nationality. Lastly, a judicial entity, the *Permanent Court of International Justice*, was established in association with the League (although, technically speaking, a separate institution), that would provide neutral decisions on legal disputes.

When plans were made to launch a new international organization after the Second World War—the United Nations—the template and institutional design were already made. And, indeed, the U.N.'s organs closely tracked those of the League: a General Assembly, Security Council, Secretariat, and World Court (along with an Economic and Social Council and Trusteeship Council (the latter now defunct)). The United Nation's ability to manage conflict through its collective security mechanisms and prohibitions on aggressive war will be considered later in this volume (see Chapter 19). As with the League, the U.N.'s real successes have been in areas such as promoting human rights, spurring decolonization, facilitating aid and development, negotiating disarmament and arms control, and generally encouraging the rule of law in international relations.

It should also be recalled here that the U.N. stands in the center of a vast network of international institutions today. Known generically as "specialized agencies," these are the continuations of the functional bureaus and commissions created in the 1800's. For virtually every realm of human interaction—economic, social, and scientific—there is a specialized agency established (along the same plan of organs as the League and U.N.) to manage cooperation, prepare new treaties, and draft needed regulations. In the area of international banking and finance, the "Bretton Woods" institutions of the World Bank and International Monetary Fund (IMF) occupy a central position. In international transportation, such agencies as the International Maritime Organization (IMO) and International Civil Aviation Organization (ICAO) make possible safe shipments of crude oil by sea or smooth flight connections (the ICAO mandates, for example, that the international language of civil aviation be English). Likewise, institutions like the World Meteorlogical Organization (WMO) and World Heath Organization (WHO) coordinate vital weather-monitoring and disease-prevention initiatives. All of this is a veritable "alphabet-soup" of international cooperation across the broadest spectrum imaginable of global problems.

While emphasizing universal, or global, institutions, international lawyers must realize that regional integration has accelerated. Starting with the Pan American Union (now the Organization of American States) in the Western Hemisphere, such regional institutions have played a significant role in developing international law, especially in distinctive ways (you might recall the discussion of regional custom in Chapter 2). Of course, the leading example of this would be today's European Union (EU), formerly the European Community or Communities. Beginning as merely a coal and steel trading bloc, it has evolved into a comprehensive economic integration regime, granting extensive competence to central institutions (located in Brussels, Belgium) in virtually every facet of European economic, financial, labor, and social issues. The European single currency (euro) is here, as is growing political, diplomatic, and security coordination. Otherwise beyond the scope of this book, the EU illustrates how international institutions can shape the process of creating a real and effective union of disparate States.

Given the broad array of different international institutions, how does international law tend to distinguish them? There are three different types of international organizations. The first—what has been considered here so far—are "international public organizations," in which only States can be members. International lawyers have begun to realize that another type of institution, *nongovernmental* organizations (or NGOs), are gaining in importance. International NGOs have individual members or contingents from different countries around the world. Most of these are not international legal actors *per se*, although they may be extremely influential in the process of creating new rules or norms of international behavior. (In this category might be included NGO groups of international lawyers!) A handful of NGOs actually do have international legal status. The International Committee of the Red Cross (ICRC), based in Switzerland, is uniquely privileged under the laws of war (see Chapter 20) to further the humanitarian concerns arising from armed conflicts, including care of prisoners of war and civilians. It is precisely because of its non-government, unofficial status that ICRC is able to accomplish these goals. Lastly, and of some significance to international business lawyers, are quite a number of *multinational public enterprises* (MPEs) which are actually run by consortia of governments. Whether it is a commodity production cartel (like the Organization of Petroleum Exporting Countries (OPEC)), a regional airline, or a satellite communications operator, these MPEs may actually be treated more as international institutions than private-sector competitors.

What does it mean for an international organization to be a "subject" of international law, to have international legal personality? International public institutions and multinational public enterprises are the creation of States, and the formation of such institutions is usually accomplished by treaty or some other form of constituent instrument. The charters of international organizations are unique texts in international law, combining elements of public constitutions and articles of incorporation. Whether the charters are short or lengthy, magisterial in tone or pedestrian in detail, they all provide for organs through which the institution does its work. Lastly, and most importantly, the constituent text typically insures that the organization will be governed by international law, not the domestic law of one of the members. This combination of constituent texts, organs, and international law governance are at the core of a status for international institutions separate and distinct from its State members.

The seminal case recognizing the international legal personality of an international organization was the ICJ's 1949 decision in the *Reparation for Injuries Suffered in the Service of the United Nations* Advisory Opinion.[1] The very title of the Advisory Opinion, requested from the World Court by the U.N. General Assembly, is a masterful attempt at understatement. (The standing policy of the Court is to assign the most innocuously neutral titles possible to its decisions; thus, for example, a case concerning the flagrant shootdown by one nation of another country's aircraft would be antiseptically called "The Aerial Incident of September 5, 1990.") The "injuries" alluded to in the title of the Opinion referred to one of

1.   1949 I.C.J. 174.

the most extraordinary incidents in modern diplomatic history, and represented one of the gravest challenges to the fledgling institution of the United Nations (created in 1945).

In another stroke of irony, not a single word is written by the Court describing the circumstances which gave rise to the General Assembly's request for an Advisory Opinion. The facts, in a judicial manner common in European civil law nations, are assumed by the reader, but they are as follows. Just after World War Two, Jewish settlers in Palestine began a revolt against the mandate government of Great Britain. Jewish army units formed to fight the British, as well as to displace Arab populations. The British began a process of withdrawal, and into that political vacuum the new United Nations Organization dispatched a well-respected Swedish diplomat, Count Folke Bernadotte, to mediate between the Jewish and Arab groups. But radicals among both sides did not want a negotiated settlement, and Jewish extremists assassinated Bernadotte as he was leaving a Jerusalem hotel in 1948.

Needless to say, the international community was outraged and U.N. officials were particularly upset. (Recruitment of qualified international mediators, never an easy task, is certainly complicated if they are routinely murdered.) Calls began to emerge for the organization to bring an international claim against the parties responsible. The Jewish settlers had, after all, guaranteed Bernadotte's safety while he was in Jerusalem and had manifestly failed in that promise, and they seemed the obvious choice to receive an international claim. There was just one problem. At the time of the killing, the Jewish settlers had not yet declared the new State of Israel, and it was not yet a U.N. member.

There was another issue lurking here, one far more serious: did the U.N. even have legal standing to bring a claim for the assassination of one of its envoys? The ICJ was thus asked whether the U.N. had sufficient capacity to bring an international claim against Israel for Bernadotte's death. Or, in other words, did the U.N. have "international legal personality"—was it a subject of international law?

The answer from the Court was a resounding "yes." In a key passage, the Court addressed the question of whether States were the only subjects of international law:

> The subjects of law in any legal system are not necessarily identical in their nature or in the extent of their rights, and their nature depends upon the needs of the community. Throughout its history, the development of international law has been influenced by the requirements of international life, and the progressive increase in the collective activities of States

has already given rise to actions upon the international plane by certain entities which are not States.

With these words, in 1949, the Court declared an end to a conception of international law as merely a "law of nations," in which States were the only actors or players.

What followed in the Court's opinion was the conclusion that the U.N. had international legal personality, even though the U.N. Charter had not so provided. The ICJ relied on a teleological approach to interpreting the Charter (recall Chapter 3(D)) to give it real effectiveness. Key to the success of the organization, the Court reasoned, was an independent and loyal Secretariat, and if the U.N. lacked the capacity to bring claims on behalf of employees injured in its service, it would not attract top candidates. The ICJ went on to rule in the Opinion that the U.N. was free to bring an international claim for reparations (including money damages) for any employee injured in its service, even as against the nation of the staff-member's nationality. (Thus even if Bernadotte had been an Israeli citizen, the U.N. would have been entitled under this reasoning to claim against Israel.) Lastly, and of great consequence, the Court held that it did not matter that, at the time of incident, Israel was not a member of the U.N. and had not thus affirmatively recognized the legal personality of the organization. By its very nature, the United Nations had an "objective" character that was binding even on non-members.

Interestingly, the *Reparations* Opinion was not unanimous, and there was a significant dissent to key portions of its reasoning by none other than the U.S. judge on the Court, Green Hackworth. Judge Hackworth was concerned that the *Reparations* Opinion set a dangerous precedent by permitting an international organization to assert powers that were neither textually granted by its members in its Charter or constituent instrument, nor fairly implied from other provisions. Hackworth was dubious that an international institution should be granted "inherent" powers and was worried that an organization would quickly acquire a life of its own and depart from its intended "delegated and enumerated powers." Drawing on the idiom of American constitutionalism, and the actual language of such landmark cases as *McCulloch v. Maryland*, Hackworth feared giving international institutions potentially unlimited powers. An institution, driven by a majority of its members, could subvert its original purposes.

Not surprisingly, one of the major themes of the "constitutional law" of the United Nations and other organizations has been the issue of adjudicating charges that the organization has exceeded its intended role and has engaged in *ultra vires* acts. In a later case, the *Certain Expenses of the United Nations* Opinion,[2] the problem was framed starkly. In the 1960's, both France and the Soviet Union had objected to the deployment of U.N. peacekeeping forces in Africa and the Middle East. Both had refused to pay their share of the costs of these forces and were thus in arrears on their dues to the Organization. The question for the Court was whether the cost of these forces, deployed by the U.N. General Assembly (and not by the Security Council, as argued by the French and Soviets) was a proper "expense" of the U.N., within the meaning of the Charter.

The World Court decided that the costs of peacekeeping ordered by the General Assembly were a legitimate "expense" of the U.N., and thus France and the Soviet Union were obliged to pay their fair share. The Court rejected the "separation of powers" argument made by the two countries and ruled that peacekeeping was within the scope of the powers of the General Assembly, and was not exclusively within the authority of the Security Council (more on this in Chapter 19(C)). More importantly, the Court ruled, if organizational "dissenters" were unhappy with a decision made by the institution, their only recourse was to argue that the *ultra vires* act was contrary to the entire object and purpose of the organization, not that a certain decision should have been made by another organ within the institution. Thus, the ability of a minority to object to the conduct of an international institution was severely circumscribed. The World Court has, in a sequence of decisions, thereby expanded the legal personality of international institutions to permit them to take on a "life of their own," even in defiance of the will of a substantial number of their members.

It followed from the *Reparations* Opinion that international organizations, while not having the full bundle of rights and duties that States have under international law, certainly have many of the twigs. International institutions can conclude binding treaties not only with each other, but with States. (These instruments are governed by customary international law and a special, ILC-drafted Convention for that purpose.) International organizations often have standing before international tribunals, not only to raise claims for reparations when they have suffered some kind of loss, but also (more generally) to protect their interests. Institutions also have organic jurisdiction over internal matters (like employee discipline) that may not be interfered with by States.

That does, however, leave a number of unresolved issues regarding the prerogatives of international organizations. Some of these concern the privileges and immunities of institutions, and the ability of those organizations to avoid scrutiny, under domestic law mechanisms. This will be considered further in Chapter 17(C).

2.   1962 I.C.J. 151.

Perhaps more significantly, are the problems associated with what business lawyers would call "piercing the corporate veil." If, by acquiring international legal personality, an institution is establishing itself as a separate subject of international law, that can cause legal mischief and produce unfair results.

That was illustrated by the sad story of an international organization called the International Tin Council (ITC). The ITC was what was known as a "commodity stabilization agreement." The Council included members from both tin-producing and tin-consuming countries. The ITC worked to keep tin prices within an established and acceptable range. It did this by buying and selling vast stocks of tin. When prices were too low, the ITC would buy supplies to add to its buffer stock, driving prices up. When prices were too high, the Council would sell from its buffers, thus sending prices down. This is classic price-fixing and, if engaged in by any party other than an international organization, would clearly violate the antitrust laws of most nations around the world.

But in the late 1970's and early 1980's, the ITC's house-of-cards collapsed, as tin prices dropped and dropped, despite its intervention in purchasing all available supplies. The ITC quite literally ran out of funds and could not meet its obligations when it came time to pay for the tin it had purchased. The ITC thus became the first international institution to figuratively declare bankruptcy, leaving many creditors (including major banks in Australia and Britain) holding millions of dollars of bad promissory notes. Not surprisingly, the banks sued the ITC for contract breaches, and (realizing that the Council was an empty pocket) also impleaded the member States of the Council, arguing that they should be responsible for their agent's misdeeds.

The ITC's legal status and, more importantly, the ability of the banks to pierce the Council's corporate veil, were litigated in British courts applying both international and domestic law. In decisions issued in 1988 and 1989, Britain's highest court, the House of Lords, ruled that the ITC's member States were not responsible for the organization's bad debts.[3] The ITC had sufficiently separate legal personality, under both the English law of corporations and international institutional law, to prevent such a piercing. Interestingly, this holding was followed by U.S. courts, even though the United States was not a member of the Council (unlike Britain, which was) and thus was not obliged to respect its immunities or legal personality.

International institutions will grow in importance in both international relations and international commerce. The constitu-

---

3. See *J.H. Rayner Ltd. v. Dep't of Trade & Indus.*, [1989] 3 W.L.R. 969, [1990] 2 App. Cas. 418, 500, 81 Int'l L. Rep. 670 (H.L.) (U.K.).

tional law of the United Nations will remain central to the ability of the organization to manage international peace and security, while also resolving international disputes (both matters considered in Part Four). Essential to that evolving constitutional order for global international institutions is the concept of international legal personality. At the same time, multinational public enterprises may present even more contentious problems about the nature of international organization, especially as these entities enter into the international marketplace and conduct themselves as any private commercial operator would.

Chapter 7

Individuals in International Law

As has already been discussed, the real revolution in the subjects of international law has been in the recognition of individuals as capable of both exercising international rights and respecting international obligations. This development, standing alone, has been what has transformed a "law of nations"—the exclusive preserve of States, national interests and sovereignty—into the dynamic international law of today. Persons are no longer the passive "objects" of international legal action, things to be acted upon by States at their whim.

A. Nationality

Despite that observation, it is crucial to realize that States still remain the vehicle by which most individuals on the planet aspire to a legal ordering of their rights in various kinds of status relationships and transactions. Nations remain the potent instruments of popular will. Until we have some kind of World Government, there will be no such thing as "citizens of the world." It is critical then for international law to recognize and regulate the question of nationality—the essential relationship of loyalty and protection between a person and a State.

Most nations in the world recognize either of two bases for acquiring nationality, or some combination of them. One basis for nationality is known as *ius sanguinis*. Nationality is transmitted "by blood," from parents to children. The other basis is called *ius soli*, "by soil," depending on the place where one is born. United States nationality law, which is based on the Constitution's Fourteenth Amendment, is premised on the place of one's birth. That is why, for example, a child born in the United States of foreign tourists (or even illegal aliens) is regarded as a U.S. citizen. United States nationality law also recognizes as U.S. citizens—or U.S. nationals (there is a technical difference in the terms)—the children of U.S. parents, even if that child is born overseas.

Countries around the world have various nationality laws. Some are lax, freely granting citizenship with only minimum residency requirements. Other nations are quite strict in their nationality rules. It is possible, for example, in certain European nations and in Japan to live many years as a resident, and yet never be considered for citizenship. The laws of still other countries compulsorily impose nationality on foreign individuals who have either married citizens or who have been in residence for even a short time. Such an imposition can be involuntary—over the objection of the person affected. These compulsory nationality rules are intended to ensure the loyalty of all persons living within a national territory, or to legitimize the application of domestic laws to such people, or to frustrate the intervention of other nations on those persons' behalf.

In this continuum of various nationality laws, the United States finds itself at a happy median, reflective of its rich immigrant tradition. Permanent residence status for foreign nationals is difficult to achieve, but, once that is secured, an individual can usually become a citizen within five years. There is, however, no requirement of citizenship, even for long-standing residents of the United States.

What are the legal consequences of nationality? As already intimated, even in modern international law it is necessary to have an affiliation with a State. International travel would be impossible without the necessary travel documentation, including the indispensable passport (which is the ultimate proof of one's nationality). As will be considered further, most of the mechanisms for protecting and vindicating the rights of individuals under international law typically depend on a person having nationality.

That is why the condition known as "statelessness" is regarded as so horrific. Stateless persons are condemned to live in a perpetual legal limbo. They have no right of abode, no territory to assert as their home. They can claim no right of protection from any government. They may not legally travel, and if found in a particular jurisdiction may be detained or jailed. (One stateless individual "lived" at Paris' Charles de Gaulle Airport for *eleven years*, unable to sojourn, until European nations relented and he was granted travel documentation.)

Statelessness can be caused by a variety of circumstances. Gaps in domestic laws may not recognize someone as a national. An original country of nationality may have been absorbed or otherwise lost its identity as a matter of State succession. Migrations of people (precipitated by war or famine) can cause mass dislocations. The destruction of vital records may prevent someone from proving a place of birth or the nationality of one's parents.

Happily, international law has effectively sought to end the condition of statelessness. There are a variety of international conventions on the status of refugees and on reducing statelessness. States are, for example, prohibited now from terminating the nationality of persons (even for serious crimes like treason or espionage), if that would mean that the individual would thereby become stateless. Indeed, a right to nationality has come to be considered a fundamental human right. The American Convention on Human Rights (entered into by many nations in the Western Hemisphere, but not the United States) establishes this right, and the relevant provision has been interpreted by human rights institutions to limit the power of States to make constitutional changes to nationality rules.[1]

If statelessness (having no nationality) is a problem at one end of the spectrum, then one must also consider the difficulties of dual nationality (having too many citizenships). Dual nationality can arise in a number of situations. The most common is that a person has parents from one country, but is actually born in another. This combination of *ius sanguinis* and *ius soli* bases of nationality can easily result in dual citizenship—someone who has loyalties to two States. (It is not fanciful to imagine that someone might have three or more allegiances, depending on the vagaries of domestic nationality laws.) Dual nationality seems like the ultimate benefit in a jet-setting age, potentially granting the freedom to live and work in large parts of the world. (The combination of U.S. citizenship and nationality of a country in the European Union being most highly-prized.)

Dual nationality comes with a catch, a big one: having dual allegiances in the modern world can result in old-fashioned conflicts. The most obvious illustration of this occurs when a dual national finds that her two countries of citizenship are at war with each other. Taking sides, which is inevitable if a person is resident in one of the warring nations, will lead to charges of treason (and possible death) by the other. After World War Two, there were a number of cases in which U.S.-Japanese dual nationals who had sided with Japan's cause (including the notorious propagandist "Tokyo Rose" D'Aquino) were convicted of treason. Less fatal, but no less troublesome, drawbacks of dual nationality can include double-taxation by both countries (unless relieved by an international tax treaty concluded between the two States) and the inability to have an international claim brought on one's behalf (more on which in Chapter 8(B)).

One thing to keep in mind in this discussion is that there is an inherent tension between nationality questions and international law rights. As the 1930 Convention on Certain Questions Relating to the Conflict of Nationality Laws provided, "It is for each State to determine under its own law who are its nationals. This law shall be recognized by other States in so far as it is consistent with

---

1. See, e.g., *Re Amendments to the Naturalization Provisions of the Consti-* *tution of Costa Rica*, Doc. OC–4/84 (Inter-Am. Ct. H.R. 1984).

international conventions, international custom, and the principles of law generally recognised with regard to nationality." This statement begs the question of under what circumstances may a State refuse to recognize the grant of nationality made by another country?

This issue was squarely presented in the *Nottebohm* Case, decided by the International Court of Justice in 1955.[2] Frederic Nottebohm was born a German national in 1881, but he lived most of his life in Guatemala, becoming one of the largest land-owners in that nation and acquiring a vast fortune. Nottebohm was a savvy observer of international affairs. In the 1930's, after Hitler's rise to power in Germany, he realized that Germany would soon be embroiled in a war that would inevitably draw the United States and the Western Hemisphere into the conflict. Certainly, Nottebohm did not want to be considered a German national, and thus an "enemy alien," in the event that Guatemala declared war on Germany.

As a result, Nottebohm made a plan. At the invitation of his brother, who lived in the tiny—and traditionally neutral—Principality of Liechtenstein (see Chapter 5), he became a citizen of that country in 1939. But this proved too clever by half. Nottebohm had correctly predicted the chain of events that led the United States and Guatemala into war with Germany in 1941, but he had not counted on the fact that the U.S. and Guatemala would simply refuse to recognize his Liechtenstein nationality. (This was despite the fact that Guatemala had allowed Nottebohm to re-enter the country on his new passport, and his residency papers were changed to reflect his new citizenship.) In the end, his worst fears were realized: his properties were confiscated by Guatemala.

Liechtenstein sought later to bring a claim on Nottebohm's behalf, on principles of State Responsibility and diplomatic protection (discussed in the next Chapter). Yet the World Court refused, ruling that countries did not have complete discretion in granting nationality, and if certain limits were exceeded, other countries were not obliged to respect the grant of nationality. More specifically, the Court said that there must be a "real and effective" relationship between an individual and his State of citizenship, a "genuine link." The Court found as a factual matter that Nottebohm's links with Liechtenstein were too tenuous; he had never really resided in the principality, and his connections were ephemeral. The Court intimated that Nottebohm had duped Liechtenstein into participating in a clever fraud, and Guatemala was not under an international duty to respect it.

2. 1955 I.C.J. 4 (Liechtenstein v. Guatemala).

The *Nottebohm* decision's "genuine link" language has had important influences on many areas of international law that involve tracing a connection between non-State actors and nations. Whether it is establishing the place of incorporation for a business, or the proper State of registry for vessels or aircraft, a real—not fictional—connection is required. Questions of nationality also remain central to the rights and duties exercised by individuals in international affairs. As will be seen over the course of the next two Chapters, much of the international law of State Responsibility and of human rights is conditioned by determinations of nationality.

B. Duties of Persons Under International Law

Before individuals could acquire affirmative rights under international law, they first had to be burdened with obligations. In fact, this process of requiring individuals to conform their behavior to international norms—and directly punishing such persons (quite apart from their State of nationality) for infractions—has been ongoing for nearly 500 years. Even in the era of the "law of nations," where only States and national conduct mattered, individuals were recognized as subjects of international law duties and could be punished accordingly.

The clearest example of this is the international crime of piracy, the scourge of free navigation on the oceans for millennia. Piracy is the act of committing depredations on the high seas. (Although the mention of piracy summons-up images of Hollywood "B" movies and historic anachronism, it remains a problem in parts of the world's oceans even today.) Pirates are considered beyond the pale of protection by any nation, or, in the quaint (but historically inaccurate) phrase, *hostis humanis generis* ("the enemy of all mankind"). The international law consequence of committing an act of piracy is that such a person may be prosecuted by *any* nation which captures him or her.

There is a doctrinal link in international law between conduct that is considered to be a breach of an individual's duties to the international community—and thus an "international crime"—and the invoking of a wider jurisdiction to punish that crime. Sometimes that involves the availability of *universal jurisdiction*, meaning that any nation may prosecute. (This is discussed further in Chapter 16(B).) For other kinds of conduct, it means that nations other than the perpetrator's own State may punish the offender. Countries take very seriously their duty to punish offenses against international law committed by individuals. Indeed, the U.S. Constitution contains a specific provision granting Congress the power to "define and punish offenses against the law of nations."

The key moment for the imposition of international law duties on individuals was the Nuremberg trials of the top political and military leadership of the German Third Reich, held after the conclusion of the Second World War in 1945. This was not, despite popular belief, the first instance of trials of individuals charged with violations of the laws of war. Peter Hagenbach, a Burgundian knight was so tried in 1482, as was Captain Henry Wirtz, the notorious commandant of the Andersonville prison camp during the U.S. Civil War (and the only Confederate officer who was executed by the victorious Union). German submarine captains had also been prosecuted, but only lightly punished, at the Leipzig trials held after Germany's defeat in World War One.

The critical distinction of the Nuremberg trials was the legal order and regularity of the proceedings, something insisted upon by the victorious United States. (Winston Churchill and Josef Stalin had preferred that the Nazi leadership be summarily shot upon capture, but President Franklin Roosevelt's view prevailed.) A general indictment was issued by the Allied powers in 1942, known as the London Charter. The Charter specified a number of particular international crimes subject to the jurisdiction of any subsequently-created International Military Tribunal. The international crimes were:

(a) Crimes Against Peace: planning, preparation, initiation or waging a war of aggression, or a war in violation of international treaties, agreements or assurances, or participation in a common plan or conspiracy for [such]:

(b) War Crimes: violations of the laws or customs of war. Such violations shall include, but not be limited to, murder, ill-treatment or deportation to slave labor or for any other purpose of civilian population of or in occupied territory, murder or ill-treatment of prisoners of war or persons on the seas, killing of hostages, plunder of public or private property, wanton destruction of cities, towns or villages, or devastation not justified by military necessity:

(c) Crimes Against Humanity: murder, extermination, enslavement, deportation and other inhumane acts committed against any civilian population, before or during the war, or persecutions on political, racial or religious grounds in execution of or in connection with any crime within the jurisdiction of the Tribunal, whether or not in violation of the domestic law of the country where perpetrated.

After the complete victory of the Allies in Europe in 1944, specific indictments were handed-down for about 24 of the top German government, Nazi Party, and military leadership. The trials were conducted before a bench consisting of judges from the United

States, Britain, France and the Soviet Union.[3] The prosecution was led by Justice Robert Jackson, who took a nearly 2–year leave-of-absence from the U.S. Supreme Court.

The German defendants raised a number of substantive defenses to the charges, both at the Nuremberg trials themselves, as well as the subsequent prosecutions in the U.S.-occupied sector of Germany (these trials involved the financial, industrial and judicial leadership of the Third Reich). The first such defense was the contention that every action taken by the defendants was an "act of State," and the individuals were, therefore, immune under international law. The International Military Tribunal (IMT) made short work of this contention, as the London Charter had specifically provided that "The official position of the Defendants, whether as heads of State, or responsible officials in Government departments, shall not be considered as relieving them from responsibility, or mitigating punishment." In short, the IMT vindicated the notion of individual responsibility under international law.

The next defense raised by the Nuremberg defendants had also been anticipated by the London Charter. They argued that as military and political leaders they had been merely following Adolf Hitler's orders, and with Hitler conveniently dead (of suicide as Soviet forces entered Berlin), they were not culpable. The London Charter provided: "The fact that the Defendant acted pursuant to an order of his Government or of a superior shall not free him from responsibility, but may be considered in mitigation of punishment." This "superior orders" rule is now part of the military code of every nation on earth, and it, in essence, says that blind obedience to orders cannot be a defense to a charge of war crimes violations. A subordinate is thus under a legal duty to refuse an order if he reasonably believes it is unlawful.

Actually the most credible defense raised by the Nuremberg defendants concerned the *ex post facto* criminalization of one kind of conduct in international affairs. Recall that the London Charter specified the offense of "crimes against peace," or the initiation of aggressive war. It was doubtful whether this had been regarded, either in treaties or customary international law, as an international crime that could be committed by individuals prior to 1939 (the outbreak of World War II in Europe). Those defendants indicted on that count raised the *ex post facto* (or *nullum crimen sine lege*) defense, but it was rejected by the IMT on the theory that there had been sufficient notice given to the German defendants that waging aggressive war would be punished. Indeed, U.S. occupation courts in Germany ruled that international law might not even care

---

3. See International Military Tribunal (Nuremberg) Judgment and Sentences (Oct. 1, 1946), 41 Am. J. Int'l L. 172 (1947).

whether particular conduct was previously recognized as criminal. Nevertheless, in the parallel set of trials that were held in Tokyo for the Japanese war crimes defendants, one of the judges dissented on this point.

The Nuremberg and Tokyo war crimes trials have been criticized as "victor's justice." Most of the defendants were convicted and either executed or given long sentences. They were ably represented by German counsel, and, in one important instance, skilled lawyering won a relatively light prison sentence for a defendant (Admiral Dönitz, the commander of Germany's feared U-boat fleet), when all trial observers had predicted a trip to the gallows. The advocate had managed to secure a statement from Dönitz's American counterpart, Admiral Nimitz, that U.S. submarine operations in the Pacific had followed the same rules as the Germans had observed, thus blunting the charge that German practices had been unlawful. Three of the defendants at Nuremberg were acquitted entirely, and some of the charges for the others had to be dismissed because of a lack of evidence.

Nuremberg and Tokyo set an important precedent in demanding individual responsibility for violations of international norms. The trials were followed by the conclusion of the 1948 Genocide Convention, specifying the crime of targeting and destroying particular populations based on their ethnicity or religion, as the Nazis had done in the Holocaust. Elaboration of the Nuremberg precedent was also provided in Israel's prosecution of Adolf Eichmann, one of the architect's of Hitler's Final Solution.[4] Later attempts at defining the international crime of aggression, or of compiling a complete Code of Crimes Against the Peace and Security of Mankind, were less successful.

There is today a long list of acts that an individual can commit as a breach of international obligations. Many of these have been made the subject of particular treaty regimes, in which specific offenses are defined, and then States promise to either prosecute the suspect or to extradite the person to a country that will. This is known as the *ex dedere aux judicare* principle, meaning literally "hand-over or prosecute." Aircraft sabotage and hijacking are respectively the subject of two separate treaties, as are attacks on diplomats (or other internationally-protected persons), and hostage-taking. Most controversial of all has been the indication of terrorism as an international crime. (A good example of this is the prosecution of Libyans suspected in the bombing of a Pan Am flight over Lockerbie, Scotland, discussed in Chapter 19(C).)

4. See *Eichmann v. Attorney–General of Israel*, 36 Int'l L. Rep. 5, on appeal, 36 id. at 277 (1962) (Israel).

All of these efforts to create a broad structure of individual responsibility under international law and to eliminate the perceived impunity of war criminals culminated in efforts initiated after the genocides in Yugoslavia and Rwanda in the 1990's. The U.N. Security Council established *ad hoc* tribunals with jurisdiction to try persons suspected of genocide or crimes against humanity or grave breaches of the laws of war. These tribunals are currently operating and are developing a significant body of jurisprudence on this subject, especially as to questions of whether certain operations can ever be justified by military necessity, or how far command authority extends to higher-ranked officers, or whether mass rapes of civilian women constitute a form of genocide.

The temporary and political nature of these tribunals concerned many States and motivated suggestions for the creation of a permanent International Criminal Court (ICC). In July 1998, the Rome Statute of the ICC was signed by many nations (the United States did not and is continuing to review its possible participation with the Court). The critical innovation of the ICC is a permanent judicial institution and prosecutorial staff, standing available to commence investigations of suspected genocide, war crimes, and crimes against humanity (in essence, the original London Charter indictment counts). If a nation is unwilling or unable to initiate a prosecution against one of its own nationals, then the ICC's jurisdiction can be triggered. This was seen as preferable to a political decision made by the U.N. Security Council to initiate proceedings, especially given that the delicate make-up of the Council might frustrate such a vote.

The ICC has properly been regarded as the last element in establishing a rule of law for individual responsibility in international affairs. Although the ICC has many flaws that need to be addressed, it certainly represents the aspiration of the international community that individuals are endowed both with significant rights under international law, as well as important obligations.

C.   Rights of Individuals

Even so, substantial debate persists today as to exactly *how* individuals acquire rights under international law. Some commentators argue that, to have any real meaning, the source of rights for persons on the international plane must be States. This is a notion that people can only be given rights by the affirmative grant of sovereign States. This clearly conflicts with a view that individuals, because of their fundamental human dignity, are endowed with rights quite apart from the will of governments. This debate— which pits natural and positive sources of international law—is to a large degree irrelevant today. The fact is that persons *do* have rights under international law, and so speculating as to the philosophical source of those rights is, with a few exceptions, a theoretical distraction.

One thing is clear: people certainly do not have the same sets of rights as States do under a classic formulation of international law. Individuals cannot make treaties. Indeed, it is certainly doubtful in some situations whether certain kinds of contracts between persons (including business associations) and States are fully enforceable as a matter of international law. (This will be discussed further in Chapter 8(C).) Individuals certainly cannot acquire territory (just think of the denizens of Atlantis or Sealand). Lastly, persons cannot wage war in a way that will be recognized under international law, unless in such large aggregates as to constitute an insurgency or national liberation movement. As the World Court recognized in the *Reparations* Opinion, different subjects of international law possess various attributes and can claim only certain rights and duties.

One crucial qualification of the rights exercised by individuals in international affairs is that persons may not have available to them the full panoply of international law remedies that are open to States. We take it for granted under the domestic law of most nations that when a right is granted, so too is a remedy. It would be a nonsense to say that the law gives a right but denies an effective remedy for that right. In international law, that kind of paradox is more readily accepted. Persons may, for example, be given rights under treaties. (And, of course, such treaty-based rights are cited by the positivists in support of their assertion that all rights for people in international law must flow from States.) Only in exceptional cases are individuals (or corporations) given a direct right of access to international tribunals or institutions for the satisfaction and enforcement of those rights. Nevertheless, the World Court ruled as early as the 1920's that treaties can give rights to individuals that can be enforced in *domestic* courts. This matter is reflected in United States law, to the extent that treaties can sometimes provide a direct right of action to persons (considered in Chapter 15(B)).

The really critical question is whether the rights of individuals can be vindicated in a structure of international law that still, to a great degree, emphasizes States and sovereignty. Two broad mechanisms have been developed over time, and they will each be featured in the two following chapters.

The first avenue of redress for individual rights in international relations, and the first to be historically developed, was the international law of *diplomatic protection*. Diplomatic protection comes about when a nation asserts its right to protect the interests of a national by asserting an international claim against a State that has injured that person's rights or interests. The claim of the individual is being taken-up, or *espoused*, by his or her State of nationality. Whether the claim has any merit implicates the substantive international law of State Responsibility. All of this means that nationality remains a crucial concept for the protection of individual rights under international law, for if a person is stateless, no nation can espouse that person's claim. Moreover, if the State of nationality should for whatever reason be disinterested in the plight of its citizen, then no redress will be forthcoming. Actually, then, the right of diplomatic protection is only as strong as the political will of the individual's State to pursue the claim. In reality, most international tribunals are only open to adjudicate those individual claims that have been espoused by a government. (More recently, a handful of institutions—including the Iran–U.S. Claims Tribunal and some investment-dispute mechanisms—have been opened to individual claims without government sponsorship.)

The most serious drawback to the concept of diplomatic protection is the assumption that it will be a State, other than the country of nationality, which has injured the individual. It is true that persons traveling or conducting business in foreign countries are sometimes treated in ways that are contrary to the law of State Responsibility to aliens. Most often, however, it is one's own country that is the perpetrator of abuses, and the procedures of diplomatic protection and international claims have no relevance where an individual has a complaint against his *own* State of nationality.

That is why the *international law of human rights* was formed, beginning chiefly after the Second World War. This was the development that clearly placed the individual in a status of rough parity with States as subjects of international law. Originally, how a State treated its own citizens was of no concern to international law. Today, a vast body of global and regional standards has developed, along with an array of enforcement mechanisms to vindicate individual human rights. The combination of diplomatic protection and human rights approaches constitute a potent means for persons to hold and exercise rights under international law.

Chapter 8

State Responsibility and Diplomatic Protection

At the outset it should be noted that the doctrines of State Responsibility have broader application than the diplomatic protection of one State's nationals living in a foreign country. State Responsibility implicates the entirety of a nation's duty to respect the international law rights of other countries and, when it has violated those rights, to make proper amends and reparations. In this wider sense, State Responsibility is at the core of all modern international law, since it governs the manner in which entities enforce their rights under that law. These wider ramifications of State Responsibility will be considered in many particular contexts in the remainder of this volume: as an aspect of international environmental and economic laws (see Chapters 12 and 13), jurisdictional disputes (Chapter 16), and in the measures that States adopt to vindicate their rights, short of armed conflict (Chapter 18).

For the purposes of this Chapter, however, the focus is decidedly more narrow: the responsibility that States have to aliens living and working within their national territory. After discussion of some basic issues and concerns of State Responsibility, the essential elements of an international claim and the exercise of diplomatic protection will be reviewed. These conditions and procedural requisites for diplomatic protection are largely followed in the law of State Responsibility, even when the claims of individuals and companies are not involved. Lastly, this Chapter will discuss the nettlesome problem of expropriations and nationalizations of foreign property, as well as breach of contract claims against States.

A.   General Considerations and Problems

State Responsibility for injury to aliens is beset by a fundamental contradiction. It is a paradox that has challenged the legitimacy of this area of international law and greatly hampered its evolution. An individual who lives in a foreign country is expected to abide by the laws of the host State, yet, when that person is injured by the host government, she is free to seek diplomatic protection from her State of nationality. Foreigners thus appear to have the "best of both worlds"; they expect to travel and conduct business in other countries on conditions of equality, but when adverse events occur, they are free to seek their own nation's protection. This sense of unfair advantage to persons living in another country is why the international law of State Responsibility has been criticized as an instrument of coercion in the hands of nations engaging in new forms of economic imperialism.

Central to this debate are two competing visions of how a nation should treat foreigners living in its midst. One view is that a host government should, within recognized limits, treat aliens in the same way as it would treat its own nationals. This is the principle of *equality*. The other view is that there is an *international minimum standard* of treatment, a threshold below which no "civilized" nation should drop. These two ideals have collided in spectacular fashion.

Consider the simple, if sad, case of Harry Roberts. Roberts was a U.S. citizen who was arrested in Mexico on charges of armed robbery. He was thrown into a Mexican jail for 18 months awaiting trial. Roberts was confined in a small cell with about 35 other prisoners. The United States argued before a special claims commission, established to resolve disputes with Mexico, that the conditions of Roberts' incarceration violated Mexico's international responsibilities. Mexico rejoined that Roberts was entitled to the treatment afforded Mexican nationals; Mexican jails were overcrowded, but Roberts had not been singled-out for bad treatment. The General Claims Commission rejected this argument, holding that Mexico had violated the international law of State Responsibility. Roberts' treatment was depressingly substandard and the Commission articulated a universal test of "whether aliens are treated in accordance with ordinary standards of civilization."[1]

In another example, involving U.S.-Mexican economic relations in the 1930's, the United States protested Mexico's nationalization of privately-owned farmland, including tracts owned by Americans. In the famous Hull–Hay diplomatic correspondence,[2] the Mexican Foreign Minister defended the expropriations on the theory that the government takings affected Mexican nationals and foreigners equally. There was no illegal discrimination. Moreover, Minister Hay wrote that

> the foreigner who voluntarily moves to a country which is not his own, in search of a personal benefit, accepts in advance, together with the advantages he is going to enjoy, the risks to which he may find himself exposed. It would be unjust that he should aspire to a privileged position.

---

1. *Harry Roberts* Claim (U.S. v. Mex.), 4 U.N. Rep. Int'l Arb. Awards 77 (1926), reprinted in 21 Am. J. Int'l L. 357 (1927).

2. 19 DEP'T OF STATE, PRESS RELEASES 50–52, 136–44 (1938).

Secretary of State Cordell Hull responded, however, that U.S. citizens were still entitled to the full compensation of their confiscated property, even if Mexican nationals were not so permitted.

The dialectic between parity for foreigners and international minimum standards has yet to be resolved, and it has of late been transformed into a more subtle polemic about the relevant and appropriate sources for the international law of State Responsibility. One of the attractive aspects of lawyering in this area is that the familiar signposts of cases and decisional law are apparent here. One can read the decisions of international claims tribunals that date back as far as the 1790's (the Jay Treaty, concluded between the U.S. and Britain after the American Revolution, provided for two such claims commissions). Typically, international claims tribunals were instituted in conditions of political, military and economic inequality. Latin American nations (Mexico and Venezuela particularly) were often required to submit disputes with foreign residents to such tribunals. Taken together, this body of case law evolved by 1950 into a fairly comprehensive body of customary international law on diplomatic protection for aliens.

It was precisely because of the long association of State Responsibility law with colonial and imperial politics that it came under withering attack during the period of decolonization in the 1950's, 1960's, and 1970's. Newly-independent former colonies asserted that the then-existing customary international law of State Responsibility was not of their making, and they assertively bid to change it. The primary vehicle chosen for this transformation was a series of U.N. General Assembly Resolutions.

These were collectively known as the New International Economic Order (NIEO) and were an attempt at remaking the landscape of international economic relationships and their legal bases. The 1973 U.N. Declaration on Permanent Sovereignty over Natural Resources and the 1974 Charter on Economic Rights and Duties of States were drafted in order to propound new rules of customary international law. The key features of these resolutions were provisions allowing the expropriating State to establish the "appropriate" compensation to be paid and also (in case of a challenge by the foreign owner of the property) to have the disputes resolved only in domestic courts. Needless to say, these alterations to the prevailing customary international law rules were opposed by economically-developed, capital-exporting nations. (This lack of consensus was later noted by the arbitrator in the *TOPCO* Arbitration, discussed in Chapter 4(B).)

The NIEO initiative coincided with a time of rising commodity prices and wholesale expropriations of foreign businesses in the developing world (particularly in such extractive industries as mining and petroleum products). The pendulum, however, was bound to swing again, and, by the 1980's, commodity prices collapsed, and developing nations in South America, Africa and Asia were once again hungering for foreign investment. Having been once "burned" by host government expropriations of foreign properties, capital-exporting nations insisted on placing the law of State Responsibility toward aliens on a firmer footing. Since that time, such countries as the United States, Japan, and France negotiated bilateral Friendship, Commerce and Navigation (FCN) treaties with developing States, including specific provisions on the rights of foreign nationals to live and work in those countries. Additionally, a new form of international agreement, Bilateral Investment Treaties (BITs), have been created to address very particular issues of investment protection, including detailed rules for compensation in the event of expropriation or nationalization, as well as valuation of certain kinds of business assets (most notably, intellectual properties).

Bilateral instruments like FCNs have, to some degree, supplemented the traditional customary international law of protection of foreigners. They certainly have swept-aside any contention that the NIEO-era resolutions of the General Assembly are a valid statement of the relevant international law rules on this subject. Curiously, attempts to fashion a multilateral treaty on State Responsibility in general, and protection of foreign investment in particular, have had prodigious difficulties. The U.N. International Law Commission (ILC) articles on State Responsibility have been "in draft" for nearly 40 years, having literally outlived the countless Commission members who have labored over them. (A new set of Draft Articles are currently being considered by the ILC and will then be submitted to the U.N. and its member States.) An effort to create a Multilateral Agreement on Investment (MAI) was a spectacular failure, the negotiation disintegrating in diplomatic rancor and public outrage.

B. Substantive Conditions and Procedural Aspects

While fundamental sources and principles of the international law of State Responsibility remain fluid and dynamic, one can draw some general conclusions about the critical elements of international claims. Some of these are procedural in character and may be correctly regarded as the concern of the international law of diplomatic protection, particularly as applied to the claims of individual persons or business associations. The remainder of these elements are substantive in the sense that no assertion of State Responsibility can be made without them.

The following elements amount to a handy summary of the international law on this subject:

an international claim, (1) if otherwise admissible, arises when (2) an act or omission, (3) attributable to a State, (4) wrongfully violates a duty owed under international law to another State or its nationals, when (5) it is the cause of the claimant's injuries, and (6) there is no justification to excuse it.

Taking these elements in turn provides a complete overview of State Responsibility. If this framework for understanding international claims seems formulaic, that is intentional. International lawyers need to impose some analytic rigor on assertions of State liability. Just as a tort lawyer would never dream of drafting a complaint without researching the elements of the underlying actions, neither should international practitioners initiate claims without legally assessing all aspects of the dispute.

Admissibility. As already mentioned, an international claim is "owned" by the nation making, or *espousing*, the claim on behalf of its injured national (whether an individual or business). The espousing State controls the international litigation. It can choose whether or not to bring the claim, whether to subsequently settle or compromise it, or whether to hand-over the proceeds to the victim or pocket them for its own account. Although a handful of international claims commissions (including the U.S.-Mexican General Claims Commission, established in 1923, and the Iran–U.S. Claims Tribunal, created in 1981) have dispensed with the espousal requirement for claims, the vast majority insist on government sponsorship as an element of the claim. The first, and perhaps most difficult, aspect of admissibility in such cases is securing the agreement of one's own government to make an international claim against another State. This is no easy task and often involves the espousing government deciding that making the claim is worth any possible diminution in good relations with the State receiving the claim.

Once the issue of espousal is favorably resolved, the next major question to be addressed is usually the claimant's nationality. Remember, a State may only address a claim on behalf of its nationals. (There are some trivial exceptions to this rule, such as a State's ability to bring claims on behalf of any individual serving on its vessels or in its armed forces, or otherwise under its protection.) Surprisingly, problems of nationality of international claims have proven to be among the most fractious in the law of diplomatic protection.

For example, the rule used to be that individuals who were dual nationals (see the previous Chapter) could not bring a claim against *either* of their States of nationality. This harsh result was modified over time by international tribunals to embrace a test of dominant and effective nationality: a dual national *could* bring a claim against one of her States of nationality, *provided* it was not the dominant and effective one.[3] In an extremely contentious dispute decided by the Iran–United States Claims Tribunal, that institution ruled that dual Iranian–American nationals (almost all of which were associated with the hated regime of the Shah of Iran) could nevertheless bring claims against Iran for expropriated assets, so long as they could show that their dominant and effective nationality was that of the United States. They could make that showing by proof that the United States was their habitual residence, the center of their economic interests (and business assets), the locus of family ties and political participation (including voting), and also other evidence of attachment (particularly speaking English and being acclimated to American ways).[4]

If the claims of dual nationals have posed difficulties for international tribunals, those of business associations (including partnerships and corporations) have been particularly troublesome—so much so that this question received the attention of the World Court in the *Barcelona Traction* decision.[5] Barcelona Traction was a company that did business in Spain, supplying electricity to its namesake city. The company was incorporated in Canada, but a vast majority of its shareholders were Belgians. When the Spanish government expropriated the company, and Canada declined to espouse a claim on its behalf, Belgium sought to institute a case in the World Court.

The ICJ ruled that Belgium had no right to bring a claim on behalf of its shareholders holding stock in Barcelona Traction. The Court was concerned that to allow the claim would encourage multiple suits brought by many different countries on behalf of different groups of shareholders. In order to avoid this potential problem of "double-dipping," the State of incorporation for the business entity (in this instance, Canada) had the sole right to bring the claim. The Court recognized only one exception to this rule: if the State of incorporation and the respondent State were one in the same. In other words, had Barcelona Traction been chartered in *Spain*, the Belgian shareholders could institute an independent action because, after all, Spain was not likely to sue itself before an international tribunal.

The *Barcelona Traction* decision has been vociferously criticized by commentators, who have argued that as long as there is no

---

3. See *United States (Mergé) v. Italy,* 14 U.N. Rep. Int'l Arb. Awards 236 (Italy–U.S. Conciliation Comm'n 1955).

4. See *A/18* Case, 5 Iran–U.S. Claims Trib. Rep. 251 (1984).

5. *Case Concerning the Barcelona Traction, Light and Power Co., Ltd.* (Belgium v. Spain) (Second Phase), 1970 I.C.J. 3.

risk of double-recovery against a respondent State, shareholder claims can be brought by any State of nationality. Indeed, the Algiers Accords which created the Iran–U.S. Claims Tribunal in 1981 specifically adopted a different rule, allowing the U.S. to bring claims on behalf of any corporation in which U.S. nationals owned 50% or more of the capital stock. In addition, individual shareholders were permitted also to bring claims against Iran, if they had some form of controlling interest in an entity affected by the Iranian government's actions.

The Algiers Accords also rejected another principle of admissibility that had heretofore been regarded as an iron-clad restriction on claims: the exhaustion of local remedies rule. This was premised on the notion that injured aliens should at least seek redress from local courts before seeking satisfaction through their own government's espousal of the claim under international law. If a claimant had failed to exhaust local remedies offered by the respondent State, the claim was barred. There were, however, reasonable exceptions to this rule. Claimants were under no obligation to pursue local remedies if to do so would be clearly futile, or if the remedies offered were not adequate and effective for relief.[6] The World Court has consistently held over the last fifty years that the rule of exhaustion of local remedies remains alive and well, and unless the requirement has been explicitly disavowed by treaty (like the Algiers Accords), it will act to render a claim inadmissible. Nevertheless, the Court noted in the *Elettronica Sicula* Case,[7] that the burden of proof was on the State wishing to show that local remedies had *not* been exhausted. In that case, Italy was obliged to show that the American company had failed to fully exhaust the remedies afforded by Italian courts. The Court then ruled that Italy had not made that showing, and thus the claim was admissible.

The last ground for inadmissibility of international claims is *waivers of diplomatic protection* by individual claimants. Oftentimes host States will require, as a condition for accepting foreign investment, that the alien specifically disavow any rights to diplomatic protection, in the event of a later dispute. Known traditionally as "Calvo clauses" (named for the Argentine publicist, Carlos Calvo), such waivers were argued by countries in Latin America and Asia as conclusive bars to the admissibility of claims brought by foreigners. Tribunals have, however, given uneven effect to these clauses, often finding that while they might bar claims based on breach of *contract* between an alien and the host government, they cannot serve as a waiver of the claimant government's right to bring an

---

6. See *Finnish Shipowners* Claim (Finland v. U.K.), 3 U.N. Rep. Int'l Arb. Awards 1479 (1934); *Panevezys-Saldu-* *tiskis Ry.* Case (Estonia v. Lithuania), P.C.I.J. ser.A/B, No. 76 (1939).

7. 1989 I.C.J. 15 (U.S. v. It.).

international action for *tortious* injury of its citizen.[8] The Calvo doctrine has had a resurgence of late through "forum selection clauses" in which a foreign party to a contract agrees to the exclusive jurisdiction of the host State's courts. These will often be enforced by international tribunals.

Attribution. Assuming that a party can show that its claim is otherwise admissible, the question then becomes one of demonstrating that the respondent State is actually responsible for the act which gave rise to the claim. Such acts might include expropriations of foreign property or investments, regulatory interferences with foreign contracts, or denials of justice. (States are also liable for their omissions, such as the failure to protect an alien's property from depredation.) Whatever the underlying wrongful act or violation of a duty owed under international law (considered next), the question is whether that conduct is attributable, or imputable, to the respondent government.

The reason for the attribution requirement is that, under international law, host States cannot be the absolute guarantors of the safety of foreign visitors or the profitability of foreign business concerns. A tourist is mugged on the street by a bunch of thugs. While regrettable, that does not normally engage the responsibility of the State because the robbers' act cannot be properly attributable to the host government. A commercial competitor engages in "opposition research" (read "industrial espionage") in order to acquire a foreign company's valuable trade secrets. That act is not imputable to the State either.

But if a low-level government official extorts a gold watch or other valuables from a foreign visitor, or colludes with a business rival to acquire valuable intellectual property, his conduct *is* attributable to a respondent State. International tribunals have consistently ruled that when any government official or agent engages in an act affecting the rights of aliens, even if that conduct is illegal or *ultra vires* under the laws of the host State, it is still attributable to that government.[9] Likewise, even though the acts of mobs or rioters may not normally be imputable to a government, if it is manifest that police authorities failed to take reasonable measures to protect the lives and property of foreigners, then State Responsibility is engaged. In one notorious incident, the United States acknowledged responsibility for the lynching of Italian nationals in New Orleans in the 1800's.[10]

8. See *North American Dredging Co.* Claim (U.S. v. Mex.), 4 U.N. Rep. Int'l Arb. Awards 26 (1927).

9. See *Way* Claim (U.S. v. Mex.), 4 U.N. Rep. Int'l Arb. Awards 391 (1928).

10. See John Bassett Moore, DIGEST OF INTERNATIONAL LAW 837 (1906).

Indeed, when any person purports to act on behalf of the State, that individual's conduct is imputable for purposes of State Responsibility. When Iranian militants stormed the U.S. Embassy in Tehran and took hostage the American diplomats inside in 1979, despite the revolutionary government's attempt to disavow that activity, the World Court nevertheless attributed that conduct to the new Iranian government.[11] Revolutionary movements or insurrections that later come to power may also be held responsible for their earlier conduct.

Wrongfulness. Depending on the nature of the conduct affecting the rights of aliens, international law will impose different standards of care on host States. One historically common class of international claim went by the name "denials of justice." These claims arose in situations where the host State's law enforcement system or judiciary failed to operate properly, and, as a consequence, a foreigner's rights were affected. The *Harry Roberts* Claim, discussed above, was a denial of justice case. So, too, was the *B.E. Chattin* Claim, where the U.S.-Mexico General Claims Commission ruled that the procedural defects in the claimant's showtrial (including the failure to be informed of the charges, the lack of oaths for the witnesses, and the long delays) amounted to a denial of justice.[12] With the advent of definitive standards of criminal justice—often contained in international human rights instruments (discussed in the next Chapter)—there is almost a "strict liability" standard for a host State's failure to follow those rules.

At the opposite end of the spectrum of a host State's standard of care to foreigners are the failure to protect claims. Here, States are being charged with an omission. The standard adopted by most international tribunals is some form of due diligence: a State is required to exercise the same care in protecting foreigners as it would in protecting its own similarly-situated nationals. In the *William E. Chapman* Claim, for example, a claims commission ruled that Mexico had failed to grant the police protection for a U.S. consul (who had earlier been threatened by a private Mexican citizen) that it would for one of its own officials, and was therefore liable.[13] In a case before the Iran–U.S. Claims Tribunal, the plea of an Iranian national that he had been subjected to private harassment and threats by Californians was rejected under the due diligence standard.[14]

Some international law codifications–including the 1963 Vienna Convention on Consular Relations (VCCR)–establish substantive

---

11. See *United States Diplomatic and Consular Staff in Tehran* (U.S. v. Iran), 1980 I.C.J. 3.

12. 4 U.N. Rep. Int'l Arb. Awards 282 (1927).

13. 4 id. 632 (1927).

14. *Emanuel Too v. United States*, 23 Iran–U.S. Claims Trib. Rep. 378 (1989).

standards for treatment of foreigners by a host State. This might include the right of consular visit and access to aliens incarcerated in criminal proceedings. In some recent cases before the World Court, the United States has been charged with violations of such provisions.[15] Bilateral Friendship, Commerce and Navigation (FCN) treaties may also provide for very specific rights to be afforded to foreign nationals.

The remaining types of international claims—such as wrongful expulsion, contract breaches, and outright expropriations or regulatory takings (considered next)—are reviewed under more traditional tort standards of negligence or contractual forms of breach. Whatever standard is adopted by an international tribunal, the burden is on the claimant to show that the respondent State has acted in a manner inconsistent with international law.

Causation and Defenses. It should not be forgotten that international claims institutions will apply notions of causation to the cases under review. In short, there must be a causal link *between* the wrongful act or omission attributable to a respondent State *and* the injuries incurred by the claimant. Normally, such causation can be easy to prove, as when a host government takes foreign property or summarily expels aliens from its territory. In other cases, causation can be more subtle, and, at some point, a claims commission will cut short the inquiry.

Precisely such a result was reached by the U.N. Compensation Commission (UNCC), created after the Gulf War to conduct mass settlements of claims arising from Iraq's illegal invasion of Kuwait in August 1990. The UNCC quickly ruled that Iraq would be responsible for the expulsion of hundreds of thousands of individuals from Kuwait, the destruction of the Kuwaiti economy, and also the devastation of Kuwait's natural resources. There were also billions of dollars of claims by businesses that had contracts terminated by the United Nations' economic sanctions against Iraq (including a ban on oil exports), imposed just after the invasion (more on which in Chapter 19(C)). The UNCC ruled, as a categorical matter, that these injuries were not "directly caused" by the Iraqi invasion, and Iraq was not therefore responsible for them.

Lastly, affirmative defenses can play a role in the law of State Responsibility. Known generically as "circumstances precluding wrongfulness," these might include such favorites as comparative negligence and assumption of risk. (In international claims not involving individual persons or corporations, issues of waiver and abuse of right might also be implicated.) Causation and defenses,

---

15. Compare *Case Concerning the Vienna Convention on Consular Relations* (Paraguay v. U.S.), 1998 I.C.J. 248 and *LaGrand* Case (Ger. v. U.S.), 1999 I.C.J. 9; with *Breard v. Greene*, 523 U.S. 371 (1998).

along with determinations of attribution and wrongfulness, are the critical substantive elements of diplomatic protection and State Responsibility.

C. Expropriations and Contract Breaches

This leaves the most difficult and substantial issues of State Responsibility towards the rights of aliens. Those are the legal consequences of mass expropriations and nationalizations of foreign investment (often in key sectors of the national economies of the host States), as well as breaches of contracts or repudiations of debts entered into by the government and foreign investors or creditors. As already explained, the debate between rich, capital-exporting nations and poorer, developing States on this issue manifested itself as an attempted reworking of the sources of State Responsibility law. The current posture of international law on this subject can be regarded as an uneasy compromise between these two camps.

For starters, international law is fairly liberal in granting broad discretion to host States to expropriate or nationalize sectors of their economies, or to otherwise engage in significant economic "restructuring" or broad public regulation. This discretion is often called a "margin of appreciation" to the host State. And while some earlier decisions of the World Court attempted to impose a distinction between those expropriations that were for a "valid" public purpose, and those that were not, such a comparison is not often helpful. Virtually any nation, if counseled by sufficient numbers of skilled international lawyers, can provide a *post hoc* justification for an expropriation that will survive any subsequent scrutiny. Likewise, international law's categorical prohibition on expropriations that are facially discriminatory is rarely implicated, because host governments are usually smart enough not to single-out particular groups of foreigners for adverse treatment.

If international law does not impose any *per se* restrictions on a host State's right to expropriate foreign property, when exactly does a duty to compensate attach to a nation's action? In other words, when does a government action become a taking compensable under international law? Legally savvy States do not nowadays confiscate outright foreign property in their territory. Instead, they might engage in forms of "creeping" expropriation by limiting the ability of foreign investors to control their enterprises by restricting their ability to repatriate funds or accounts (often through foreign exchange controls). These kinds of restrictions, unless they accumulate to the point of an irreversible interference with the foreign investor's property rights, are often not regarded by themselves as compensable takings. States may also engage in what appear to be completely innocuous and unassailable forms of regulation—perhaps the imposition of taxes or of environmental protections—and these will not necessarily be regarded as expropriations requiring compensation under international law. An international tribunal early in the 1900's ruled that imposition of a series of license fees that had the effect of forcing the claimant to close a business were not an expropriation.[16] Nevertheless, recent decisions of institutions created by the North American Free Trade Agreement (NAFTA) and World Trade Organization (WTO) are revisiting this significant question of "regulatory takings" in international law.

As for the standard of compensation in the event of an expropriation or other government conduct amounting to a substantial interference with foreign property rights, the original assertion of the United States in the Hull–Hay correspondence of the 1930's appears to hold sway. Compensation must be "prompt, adequate and effective." Suggestions that host States need only pay "appropriate" compensation, at a deep discount, for mass nationalizations of property have been largely rejected *ex ante* in Bilateral Investment Treaties, or, after the fact, in decisions by such institutions as the Iran–U.S. Claims Tribunal or the International Center for the Settlement of Investment Disputes (ICSID).

That still leaves technical issues of how one is to value the property and investments held by foreign interests. This often turns on whether the foreign enterprise is a "going-concern," and thus should be compensated for its estimated future profits. This area of international law often implicates sophisticated accounting issues, business modeling, and current events. The Iran Claims Tribunal ruled in a series of cases that multi-billion dollar oil concessions held by American companies in Iran (and taken by that government) were to be compensated based on a fair market value test and discounted cash flows, based on contemporary estimates of oil prices, supplies and demand.[17]

As for contractual relations that are interfered with by respondent States, these disputes are usually only resolved if the private party had the foresight to insist on the inclusion of a provision for international arbitration and the application of a body of law other than that of the host State. Even so, international tribunals are split on whether a State can be properly ordered to render specific performance (or "restitution in kind") on a contract, or whether contract damages are the exclusive remedy. Lost profits are often included as a form of contract damage, although these are often attacked by respondent States as inappropriately speculative. Inter-

16. *Kügele v. Polish State*, 6 Annual Digest Int'l L. 69 (Upper Silesian Arb. Trib. 1930).

17. See *Philips Petroleum Co. v. Iran*, 21 Iran–U.S. Claims Trib. Rep. 79 (1989).

est on awards is more and more common, although grants of attorneys' fees or punitive (exemplary) damages are virtually unheard of.

Despite nearly two centuries of arbitral jurisprudence, along with a large body of bilateral instruments and a possibility of emerging multilateral codification, the international law of State Responsibility and diplomatic protection remains in flux. Perhaps it is because of the inherently contentious nature of such disputes. States are neither willing, nor happy, to admit liability for their international wrongs and to make reparations. To the extent that States are essential to the process of making the law of State Responsibility, establishing coherent standards in this area will be difficult. Nevertheless, substantial progress has been made in fashioning the general structure of elements—both procedural and substantive—for making and proving international claims.

The intrinsic limitations of this avenue for redress of individual rights must be recognized. Diplomatic protection is always within the firm discretion of the injured party's State of nationality and can never be exercised against that State's own interests. That is why we must turn next to the international law of Human Rights.

Chapter 9

Human Rights

Fully explicating the international law of human rights would take its own book. Indeed, human rights law has defined itself as a special aspect of international law—something more than a sub-discipline, but not quite a complete body of law in its own right. Heavily influenced by domestic principles of constitutionalism and civil rights, international human rights offers unique perspectives. The study of individuals' rights as against their own States of nationality is not, however, separate and apart from the wider sweep of international law. Basic elements of State identity and sovereignty, international organization, and the incorporation of international law into domestic law all factor into the practice of human rights. And, indeed, the best practitioners and advocates of international human rights are those with the strongest grounding in the "traditional" teachings of public international law.

Any intelligible discussion of international human rights law needs to make distinctions of two sorts. The first is between universal and regional standards that nations observe in the treatment of their own citizens. The second distinction is between those substantive rules of treatment and the procedural mechanisms for the enforcement of those rules. This Chapter will begin by tracing the evolution of substantive aspects of human rights law, in both universal regimes and in regional human rights systems. Then, I will characterize and assess the different models of enforcement of human rights norms.

A.   Substantive Aspects of Human Rights Law

So far in this volume, I have narrated a "traditional" view of international law—prevalent until the Second World War—that was utterly indifferent as to how nations treated their own citizens. Under this view, so long as a government did not interfere with the rights of neighboring countries (or of foreign nationals living within its territory), it could abuse its citizens in any way it wanted and never run afoul of international law strictures. It was certainly in this sense that individuals were regarded as "mere" objects of international legal rules, the playthings of sovereign neglect (or worse).

Examples of State practice indicating a contrary rule appeared in the late 1800's and typically arose in the context of European imperialism and colonialism. For example, the European "Great Powers" were much concerned with the manner in which the Ottoman Turkish Empire in the Balkans and Near East treated its Christian minority populations. Through a combination of diplomatic pressure, specific treaty provisions, and periodic military interventions, the Turks were compelled to moderate their internal policies towards these minority groups, including liberalization of rules that allowed these groups to maintain their ethnic and linguistic identity, as well as maintain a measure of political autonomy. In the same way, the European and American legal abolition of slavery and the slave trade affected the domestic practices of African and Middle Eastern polities.

The first authentic human rights regime was established by the Treaty of Versailles, which ended the First World War in 1919. Under the Treaty, the boundaries of Europe were extensively redrawn and substantial minority populations were displaced or found themselves under unfamiliar sovereigns. For example, the re-creation of the State of Poland left millions of ethnic Germans residing in its territory. New States created in the Balkans (including Yugoslavia and Hungary) also had substantial populations of people who did not share linguistic or ethnic identity with the dominant group. At the same time, it was recognized that a government's mistreatment of minorities could result in strife and be a potential cause for war. Needless to say, the minorities situation was a recipe for disaster.

The solution adopted in the Treaty of Versailles, and then subsequently enforced by the League of Nations and the Permanent Court of International Justice, was a series of guarantees entered into by States in central and eastern Europe to protect the rights of minority groups resident in their countries. Poland, Lithuania and Romania were particularly required to respect the rights of their respective German and Hungarian minority populations. In a broad sense, these agreements recognized and validated human rights, but only as exercised through groups and collectives. The rights guaranteed were those to educate minority children in special schools, or to continue to use the minority language, or to exercise special forms of political autonomy.

Predictably, these were incredibly contentious issues during the inter-War years, as "majority" groups chafed at what were perceived to be special rights granted to economically-affluent minorities. At the same time, Germany aggressively sought to protect the rights of its "diaspora" peoples. Nearly a third of all the litigation before the World Court between 1920 and 1939 involved some aspect of the protection of minority rights in Europe, with Germany suing Poland nearly a dozen times. Yet, despite the concern and involvement of the international community, the minorities issue was, of course, the ultimate ground cited by Nazi Germany for its invasion of Poland on September 1, 1939—the event that sparked World War II in Europe.

As already discussed, the Second World War marked the ultimate transition of international law from a system dedicated to State sovereignty to one also devoted to the protection of human dignity. This new paradigm was recognized in the Charter of the United Nations, signed by the victorious Allied powers in 1945. For the first time, an international agreement linked human rights with world order. Charter Article 55(c) called for "universal respect for, and observance of, human rights and fundamental freedoms for all without distinction as to race, sex, language or religion." The following article vested the U.N. with the power to "take joint and separate action" to accomplish that objective.

Articles 55 and 56 of the U.N. Charter have been regarded as "enabling" provisions, authorizing the Organization to proceed with developing human rights norms. The U.N. Charter has not itself been viewed as prescribing specific rules that States must follow in the treatment of their own citizens. For example, the Supreme Court of California concluded in 1952[1] that the Charter provisions lacked the necessary mandatory quality and definiteness that would indicate an intent to create enforceable rights in the United States. (That Court nevertheless struck down the state law at issue—prohibiting land ownership by aliens—on other grounds.) This interpretation of the Charter's human rights provisions has, at least implicitly, been endorsed by the U.S. Supreme Court.[2]

Shortly after 1945, the United Nations faced the task of pronouncing human rights norms. Its first effort produced one of the great documents of international law: the 1948 Universal Declaration of Human Rights. Drafted by a blue-ribbon panel of intellectuals and advocates (led by Eleanor Roosevelt), and with the input of national delegations, the Declaration is lucidly worded. Each provision rings with authority and certainty. Article 1 proclaims: "All human beings are born free and equal in dignity and rights. They are endowed with reason and conscience and should act towards one another in a spirit of brotherhood." Article 3 says simply and unqualifiedly: "Everyone has a right to life, liberty and security of person."

The thrust of the Universal Declaration was primarily the enunciation of civil and political rights—those freedoms necessary for individuals to operate within a polity. The Declaration proclaims such civil liberties as freedom from slavery and torture, the right to recognition and equality before the law, freedom from

---

1. See *Fujii v. California*, 38 Cal.2d 718 (1952).

2. See *Oyama v. California*, 332 U.S. 633 (1948).

arbitrary arrest and the guarantee of fair criminal procedures, and respect for rights of worship and expression. Also included are rights of participation in the political process. In addition to these "first generation" of civil and political rights, the Declaration also prescribes some "second generation" economic and social rights. These include the right to work, to rest and leisure, to education, and to participation in cultural life. Article 23(2) further mentions the right of everyone for "equal pay for equal work," the first mention of that concept in any document. Even though the Universal Declaration was adopted without dissent, it was not without controversy. Socialist countries were concerned about Article 17's enshrinement of the right to property. The United States was concerned about the First Amendment implications of Article 12's requirement that attacks of individual honor and reputation be barred.

The reason that the Declaration could be adopted by consensus, despite controversial provisions, was that it was understood by all that it was not a binding legal instrument. Perhaps the first recorded example of a multilateral "soft" law instrument, the Declaration specifically indicated in its preamble that it was "a common standard of achievement," something to be "strive[d]" for by national governments through "progressive measures." The United States issued a statement after the Declaration's adoption which noted: "It is not a treaty; it is not an international agreement. It does not purport to be a statement of law or legal obligation."[3]

As already noted, "soft" law has a tendency, over time, to harden into international legal obligation. Over fifty years later, virtually all of the provisions of the Universal Declaration concerning civil and political rights have come to be recognized as human rights norms in customary international law or in other multilateral instruments. Perhaps just as importantly, the high tone and moral authority of the Universal Declaration set an important benchmark in subsequent international discussions and negotiations about human rights.

It still remained, however, to turn the aspirations of the Universal Declaration into "real" and "binding" legal instruments. This process developed on two fronts: through global treaties establishing universal norms and through narrower regional regimes. Considering first the universal human rights treaties, the next major landmarks are the 1967 International Covenants. I use the plural here because although the original conception was to have a single instrument on human rights, this proved politically impossible. Certain authoritarian and totalitarian regimes (particularly in

---

3.   19 DEP'T STATE BULL. 751 (1948).

the socialist bloc) were opposed to binding rules granting enforce-able civil and political rights to their nationals. This "first genera-tion" of human rights was regarded as threatening to these coun-tries. By the same token, some Western nations, particularly the United States, were wary of the "second generation" economic, social and cultural rights. This requires some explanation. In the constitutional culture of the United States, the prevailing attitude was (and still is) that the purpose of rights is to insulate and protect people from government power. The only right that makes sense is one that places restrictions on government action against individuals. Second generation rights are, in essence, requirements that government *provide* certain benefits and services to the public (such as education, work, social security, or culture), and this was deemed incompatible with a system of ordered liberty. Govern-ments might (as a political necessity) provide such public goods, but they are not legally required to do so.

So it was that in 1967 the United Nations adopted two instru-ments: the International Covenant on Civil and Political Rights (ICCPR) and the International Covenant on Economic, Social and Cultural Rights (ICESCR). The decision to bifurcate these multilat-eral human rights instruments was fateful. The ICCPR has approx-imately 144 parties today; the ICESCR about 142. Even so, the record of observance and enforcement of these agreements has been mixed. The ICCPR has been regarded as the more specific in its obligations and the more burdensome for governments.

It took the United States until 1992 to complete ratification of the ICCPR. A number of provisions in the ICCPR were regarded as intensely controversial by subsequent administrations and the U.S. Senate (the role of which in the ratification process is discussed in Chapter 15). The United States thus took reservations to a number of provisions in the ICCPR.[4] Article 6(5)'s prohibition of the death penalty for those who commit crimes as juveniles was one such clause. The terms of Articles 17 and 20 (on reputational attacks and war propaganda) were deemed inconsistent with First Amendment speech rights and were also reserved. Some provisions were "inter-preted" by the United States as being co-extensive with rights already granted under the U.S. Constitution. Most problematical of all, the United States declared that the rights guaranteed under the ICCPR were not to be "self-executing," or directly enforceable, in U.S. courts. (This concept will be specifically considered in Chapter 15(B).) Although the international community has been critical of this type of reservation (and the matter is now before the U.N. Human Rights Committee), it has become a common way to modify the impact of human rights treaties. The United States' reserva-

---

4. See 138 CONG. REC. S4781 (April 2, 1992).

tions to the ICCPR made the international human rights exactly congruous to constitutional protections; to the extent that international rights actually *exceeded* domestic standards, they were repudiated.

All of this suggests that universal human rights standards are rather precarious when it comes to their incorporation into domestic legal systems. Those nations that have no intention of being legally bound to protect the rights of their nationals will simply not sign such treaties as the ICCPR. Those that have well-established legal cultures for protections of civil rights will recognize international duties, but only to a comfortable limit. Given the objections of the United States to the ICCPR, it is no wonder that it has categorically refused to ratify the ICESCR, what with its provisions enshrining the right to work (Articles 6 and 7), unionization (Article 8), social security (Article 9), and maternity leave (Article 10(2)).

In addition to the Covenants, there is also a body of universal human rights instruments dedicated to specific issues. The topic areas include the abolition of genocide, racial discrimination (including slavery and *apartheid*) and torture, forced labor and exploitation, the status of refugees, and the rights of women and children. These subject-matter conventions in essence overlap with the broader protections granted by the ICCPR. Thus many countries that have chosen not to become a party to ICCPR have consented to be bound to these specific treaties. By contrast, the United States has only ratified a handful of these instruments: the 1948 Genocide Convention, the 1926 Slavery Convention and its Protocols, the 1968 Status of Refugees Protocol, the 1984 Torture Convention, and the 1979 Convention on the Elimination of all forms of Discrimination Against Women (CEDAW). In addition to this list, the United States has ratified a number of treaties involving labor rights and practices, negotiated by the International Labor Organization (ILO), a U.N. specialized agency based in Geneva.

In all of this discussion of universal human rights treaties, it is easy to assume that customary international law has receded in significance. To do so would be a mistake. As already noted, many countries fail to ratify human rights instruments or take decades to do so. It has come to be regarded that those States which have engaged in a systematic policy of abusing the rights of their citizens—including genocide, extrajudicial killing, enslavement, torture, prolonged or arbitrary detention, or racial or gender discrimination—have committed a violation of customary international law norms. Likewise, as was discussed in Chapter 3, certain customary human rights norms (such as the prohibition against genocide, slavery and torture) have become *jus cogens* obligations which cannot be derogated by treaty.

Both treaty-based and customary human rights obligations carry with them some significant conceptual problems. What, for example, rises to a "systematic policy" of human rights abuse is a difficult question. So is the level of State action that violates human rights. If governmental authorities do not actively engage in racial discrimination, but, instead, countenance private actors that do so, does that violate customary or treaty rights of the victims? Just as the state action requirement under the Equal Protection clause of the Fourteenth Amendment has resulted in uneven enforcement of civil rights, international law faces the same conundrum.

These difficulties have only been partially resolved in regional human rights systems. Just as the end of the Second World War saw the advent of interest in universal human rights, so too were regional human rights bodies developed. The first of these was in Europe, with the creation of the Council of Europe in the late 1940's. The Council included as members all countries in Western Europe (even such micro-States as San Marino and Monaco). As the Cold War abated, the Council's membership came to embrace all of central and eastern Europe, the former Soviet Union (including some central Asian nations), and Turkey. In the Western Hemisphere, the Organization of American States (OAS), headquartered in Washington, D.C., developed a human rights regime starting in the 1950's. Last on the scene, the Organization for African Unity (OAU) fashioned a regional human rights system in the early 1980's.

The first and most obvious points about regional human rights systems is that they are only as strong and effective as the region's underlying unity and commitment to democracy and individual rights. Although international law (in general) and human rights (in particular) need not be tied to a particular political system, the reality is that human rights regimes can only flourish in representative democracies. Since domestic respect for the rule of law is the first line of defense for human rights, if this esteem is absent in a particular polity, then no measure of regional integration will help. As a general matter, the European experiment with regional human rights norms has been the most successful—in large measure attributable to common European attitudes toward the proper role of government in every-day life. The Inter–American system of human rights, by contrast, has had a much more difficult road to travel, especially during the 1970's and 1980's when many of the regimes in Latin America were dominated by the military, and authoritarian government (or worse) was rife. African attempts at creating human rights norms have been notable failures. East Asian and Middle Eastern nations have not even tried.

It would be mistaken to believe that regional human rights systems "compete" in some fashion with universal human rights norms. Nations that adhere to a regional system are more likely to ratify universal instruments, and, in a very concrete way, the two systems are mutually-enforcing. Regional human rights conventions can describe some human rights with a greater particularity and specificity than universal instruments. This is partly attributable to a more achievable consensus on regional values (think of the problem of canvassing general practices accepted by "civilized nations," discussed in Chapter 2). It might also reflect genuine regional differences as to certain rights. This, of course, raises a problem. Essential to the legitimacy of human rights is the notion that these are truly universal values, embodied in the spirit and inherent worth of all human beings. Accepting regional variations can also mean countenancing some moral relativity in the exercise of certain rights. Two examples might illustrate this.

Universal human rights instruments are chary of detailing property rights. They are mentioned in passing in the 1948 Universal Declaration; the ICCPR is utterly silent on the subject (the socialist bloc threatened objection if they were included). Nor are they described in the 1950 European Convention on Human Rights. But in the 1952 Protocol to that instrument, they are guaranteed in these terms:

> Every natural or legal person is entitled to the peaceful enjoyment of his possessions. No one shall be deprived of his possessions except in the public interest and subject to the conditions provided for by law and by the general principles of international law. [But this in no way impairs] the right of a State to enforce such laws as it deems necessary to control the use of property in accordance with the general interest or to secure payment of taxes or other contributions or penalties.

In spite of this language, European human rights institutions have given substantial discretion to governments—"margins of appreciation"—to take the property of their own nationals, with little or no compensation.[5] Nonetheless, European protection of property rights is stronger than anywhere else in the world, save for the United States (where it is enshrined as a constitutional value in the Fifth Amendment). The Inter–American Convention on Human Rights disclaims property rights in a variety of ways, not the least of which is by limiting the scope of its protection of property rights to "natural" persons and completely excluding "juridical" persons including corporations.

The other example of regional variance is also from the European human rights system. Protocol 6 to the European Convention bans the death penalty. Virtually all European nations have ratified that Protocol, the exceptions being the United Kingdom and Tur-

5. See *Lithgow v. United Kingdom*, 8 Eur. H.R. Rep. 329 (1986).

key (both of which are fighting insurgency movements and thus desire to reserve the right to impose death sentences against convicted terrorists). The jurisprudence of the European Court of Human Rights has tended to expand even further the ambit of rights granted under the treaty. A decision in one case graphically illustrated the conflict between different regional standards of human rights. In the *Soering* Case,[6] the petitioner was a German national who had been a college student in the United States. Jens Soering was suspected of aiding his girlfriend of murdering her parents in Virginia. They fled to England, were arrested on unrelated charges, and were sought for extradition by the Commonwealth of Virginia. The Commonwealth indicated that it would seek the death penalty for Soering. After futilely attempting to avoid extradition to Virginia by petitioning British authorities, Soering invoked the European Convention on Human Rights.

His argument was strikingly novel. He submitted that if he were extradited to Virginia, he would be subjected to "degrading treatment," prohibited under Article 3 of the Convention. The treatment Soering feared was *not* the carrying-out of a sentence of death. After all, Britain had never agreed to Protocol 6, so if the U.K. could have executed Soering for some crime, it could not be faulted for sending him somewhere he could be. Rather, the Court ruled that Soering would be subjected to the psychological debilitation (that is, "degrading treatment") of incarceration on Virginia's death row, waiting many years for his sentence to be carried out. The Court ruled that Britain was under an obligation not to remove an individual from the "protective zone" of the European Convention and not to send him somewhere he would be ill-treated in violation of the treaty. Britain was thus forced to choose between its participation in the European Convention and its bilateral extradition treaty with the U.S. (This was ultimately resolved by Virginia later indicating that it would not seek the death penalty in Soering's case.)

Aside from establishing a novel human right—freedom from a "death row phenomenon"—this case illustrates both the opportunities and dangers of free-form human rights jurisprudence, especially by regional systems. The *Soering* case stands for the proposition that regional human rights norms can have effects beyond the nations in the region. Soering's extradition to Virginia was blocked because of the Convention. At the same time, the creation of novel rights can have unintended consequences. Some national courts (in the Caribbean and Africa) have ruled that being too long in the shadow of the noose is itself a violation of human rights. If the concern is about the degrading treatment of long stays on death

---

6. *Soering v. United Kingdom,* 11 Eur. H.R. Rep. 439 (1989).

row, cannot these be resolved by simply decreasing the available appeals for capital prisoners? Indeed, that was precisely the basis for recent habeas reforms in the U.S., vastly cutting back on prisoner appeals. Sometimes no good deed goes unpunished in international law.

Nevertheless, a signal strength of human rights law is the regional human rights systems. The extensive jurisprudence generated by both the European and Inter–American institutions gives substantial content to the general language of the human rights treaties. This is particularly so in very high-profile cases (such as *Soering*), and in response to developments that are antithetical to democratic values and human dignity. The Inter–American Court took a strong stand against the use of "death squads" and the supposed impunity of authoritarian regimes during a dark time in that region's history.[7] At the same time, many regional institutions have been moving towards recognition of new classes of human rights. Among these are "third generation" rights to peace, development and environment—all recognized in the 1982 African Convention (Banjul Charter). In addition are "new" kinds of rights held by groups, and not individuals. Suggested protections for distinct ethnic groups and indigenous peoples harken back to the "minorities" conventions of the inter-War period in Europe. Lastly, some regional regimes link the rights of individuals in political society with distinct duties and loyalties owed by a person to their State. For example, the Banjul Charter requires that individuals observe a duty to preserve family institutions, not compromise national security, and to promote African unity.

One problem that is common to both universal and regional human rights systems is what to do when individual rights conflict with the perceived safety and well-being of the State. If human rights law reflects an accommodation between State sovereignty and individual dignity, how is that balance struck in times of crisis? This raises the problem of derogation of human rights instruments in emergency situations. A critical provision of the ICCPR is Article 4, which allows a party to depart from their obligations under the Convention, provided (1) it is a time of "public emergency which threatens the life of the nation," (2) the derogation is "strictly required by the exigencies of the situation," (3) that certain core rights (such as the right to life, the prohibition of torture and enslavement, and freedom of thought and conscience) be preserved, and (4) that notice of the derogation be communicated to other parties.

7. See *Velazquez-Rodriguez* Case, Inter–Am. C.H.R., OEA/ser.C./ Case 4 (1988), reprinted in 28 Int'l Legal Materials 291 (1989).

The derogation provision of Article 4 was essential for the passage of the ICCPR. States wanted to protect their freedom of action in times of emergency. (Indeed, even the U.S. Constitution contains a derogation provision—the suspension of habeas corpus—which was invoked during the Civil War and in Hawaii during World War II.) The ICCPR's provision was drawn from a regional human rights system: the 1950 European Convention, Article 15 of which is virtually identical. That clause has been construed by the European Court of Human Rights in a way that allows a "margin of appreciation" for governments to declare national emergencies but also imposes substantial restrictions on derogations. So in *Lawless v. Ireland*,[8] that Court ruled that Ireland was justified in declaring an emergency in the wake of Irish Republican Army attacks and that detention of suspects for limited periods without trial was "strictly required by the exigencies of the situation." The fact that these derogation provisions indicate that certain rights can never be violated—and these rights are comparable to *jus cogens* norms—is perhaps their most important aspect.

B. Enforcement of Human Rights Norms

International law has been quite successful in enunciating a large body of rules for how States should treat their own citizens. It has been rather less fortunate in developing truly effective enforcement of those norms. Nonetheless, substantial attempts have been made to fashion different sorts of enforcement mechanisms for human rights. It is worthwhile to review these models of human rights enforcement.

Model #1—The Slavery Conventions. Beginning in the 1820's, and culminating in the 1926 Convention, the international community banned slavery and the slave trade. The enforcement method selected in these multilateral instruments was to require all States to take measures to suppress slavery and slave institutions, to release persons found in bondage, and to prosecute those found to be engaged in these activities. In essence, these treaties imposed an international duty on all States and, at the same time, prescribed *universal jurisdiction* allowing any State to prosecute any individual suspected of being engaged in the slave trade, even if that person is a national of another State. This model, repeated for a handful of other offenses involving human rights obligations, depended solely on the commitment of States Parties to these conventions.

Model #2—The Genocide Convention. The 1948 Genocide Convention was the first multilateral human rights treaty concluded after the Second World War. Negotiated in the shadow of the

---

8. Eur. Ct. H.R., Ser. A, No. 1 (1961).

Holocaust, it recognized that State sovereignty and State power could be perverted to the ultimate evil: the wholesale murder and destruction of entire ethnic, linguistic or religious groups. The Genocide Convention replicated the formula of the slavery conventions by making genocide an international crime within a form of universal jurisdiction. States Parties to the Genocide Convention are required to pass domestic laws that will punish offenders. Some have done so irrespective of the perpetrator's country of nationality or the place where the crimes occurred. (The United States' implementation of the Genocide Convention[9] is limited to offenses occurring in the U.S. or the conduct of U.S. nationals.)

The Genocide Convention went on to specify two other mechanisms for enforcement. Recognizing that acts of genocide could be part of a broader pattern of aggressive conduct by States, or (at a minimum) indicative of a breakdown of international peace and security, Article 8 of the Convention allows for the referral of suspicions of genocide to the U.N. Security Council. The Council can then take whatever enforcement action (under Chapters 6 and 7 of the U.N. Charter) it deems best. The Council's track-record has been abysmal on this score—it took no action at all in the face of Pol Pot's genocide in Cambodia in the 1970's, nor any effective measures to counter "ethnic cleansing" in the former Yugoslavia or the Hutu massacres of Tutsis in Rwanda in the 1990's.

The other enforcement mechanism allowed in the Genocide Convention is Article 9's provision that the International Court of Justice will have jurisdiction over any cases brought which involve the responsibility of a State for genocide. This was not a popular provision, because it sanctioned litigation of State Responsibility in cases of genocide, and indeed even the United States reserved against the application of this provision. In the fifty years of the Genocide Convention, only one case has been filed in the ICJ on this ground: Bosnia–Herzegovina's and Croatia's litigation against the former Yugoslavia (Serbia) for the ethnic cleansing that occurred there. This case is still pending before the Court.

The Genocide Convention's model of enforcement, to the vast extent that it depends on Security Council action or an ICJ ruling, requires an extraordinary degree of international consensus in the face of genocidal conduct by other States. Such political will on the part of States has only rarely been evidenced. Because this is so, the Genocide Convention's dependence on these political institutions (shared by other human rights treaties) is bound to render enforcement ineffective.

Model #3—The International Civil and Political Rights Covenant. The 1967 ICCPR inaugurated a number of new approaches to

---

9.   18 U.S.C. § 1091.

the enforcement of human rights norms. One of these was Article 40's requirement that States Parties submit to the United Nations Human Rights Committee regular reports (every 5 years) of their compliance with the Covenant. This not only promotes "transparency" of what States are doing to protect human rights, but also provides an opportunity for what human rights advocates call the "mobilization of shame"—the systematic spotlighting of certain countries' human rights abuses, so as to pressure them to change. Although some have criticized Article 40 Reports as being long on rhetoric and short on specifics, they have recently been acknowledged as a modestly effective means to encourage openness and transparency about human rights practices.

ICCPR Article 41 established a procedure in which States could optionally allow for an interstate complaint process. Under that process, one Party could bring a request to a U.N. body to investigate the human rights practices of another Party. This would be submitted to a 5–member conciliation commission, that would then issue a report. Not surprisingly, only a handful of ICCPR Parties have allowed for this procedure, and it has not once been actually invoked. States are apparently cautious in casting the first stone.

Aside from the mixed success of Article 40 Reports and the total lack of Article 41 interstate complaints, the ICCPR was the first to develop, under a universal human rights regime, a method for individual complaints. Allowed under the ICCPR's 1966 Optional Protocol, which 95 nations have signed, this mechanism allows individuals to directly file human rights complaints with the U.N. Human Rights Committee. The procedural requirements of such filings are onerous however: individual victims must be identified (not anonymously or through human rights NGOs); there must be a violation of specific rights guaranteed under the ICCPR (without reservation by the States nor within a permissible derogation); and local remedies have to be exhausted. Despite these hurdles, a small number of complaints are substantively reviewed by the Human Rights Committee each year and are the subject of detailed reports critical of governments. Some of these have actually been influential in favorably effecting change in particular countries: persuading Uruguay not to arbitrarily detain political prisoners, for Mauritius to reform its nationality laws, for Canada (a perennial favorite for such complaints) to grant rights to indigenous peoples and prevent language discrimination.[10] Australia was recently required to reconsider its criminalization of certain consensual homosexual behavior.[11]

---

10. *Weinberger*, 1981 GAOR 36th Sess., Supp. 40, at 114; *Mauritian Women*, id. at 134; *Lovelace*, id. at 166.

11. *Toonen*, Communication No. 488/1992, UN Doc. CCPR/C/50/D/ 488 (1994).

The irony should not be lost that it is the countries that are least likely to be systematic human rights abusers that are the ones that are the subject of these Optional Protocol complaints. Nations with poor human rights track-records are not going to be parties to the ICCPR, and certainly not the Optional Protocol. The procedural limitations for individual complaints, as well as the lack of direct enforcement power by the United Nations, are obvious draw-backs to this model of human rights enforcement.

Model #4—European Convention on Human Rights. The European Convention has evolved the most sophisticated procedural mechanisms for adjudication of human rights disputes, at least under an international scheme. When created in 1950, the Convention institutions included (1) a Council of Ministers (a political body that conciliated disputes); (2) a Human Rights Commission (which served as an investigator and filter for human rights complaints); and (3) a Court of Human Rights (which actually adjudicated human rights cases). This structure has recently been streamlined to accelerate proceedings and to lessen the role of the Commission.

The European Convention institutions were given the power to hear inter-State complaints, as well as those brought by individuals against their own States of nationality. Unlike the experience under the ICCPR, inter-State complaints in the European system have been quite common, with a long-running series of cases (from the 1950's to 1970's) pitting Ireland and the United Kingdom in matters regarding human rights questions arising from Ulster. As a consequence, the case law of the European Court of Human Rights is vast, amounting to nearly a thousand decisions to date. The Court has explored virtually every aspect of criminal procedure in every European nation and has issued opinions on contentious issues of linguistic and ethnic rights, as well as privacy and free speech.

Most importantly of all, the decisions of these human rights institutions are now regarded as "self-executing" by European nations. (The United Kingdom was the last country to make this recognition.) That means that the decisions have automatic effect. European nations have complained bitterly about some decisions emanating from the Court's headquarters in Strasbourg (including recent rulings ordering that homosexuals be allowed to freely serve in military branches), but they have been obeyed. This is an enviable record, and one that has not been approached by any other regional human rights regime. Despite some structural similarities and a significant body of advisory opinions and case law, the Inter–American Commission and Court of Human Rights have not achieved such respect or prominence.

Model #5—Enforcement in National Courts. With all of this discussion of international and regional human rights institutions, it is easy to forget that the primary means of enforcing any human rights norm has to be through domestic legal institutions. To a surprising degree, many States have been slow to incorporate international human rights standards into their domestic law.

The United States has a mixed record on this score. Relying on its own domestic constitutional culture, the U.S. rarely acknowledges international law influences. One exception might be the tacit adoption of the United Nations' 1955 Standard Minimum Rules for the Treatment of Prisoners, which is sometimes cited in prisoners' rights litigation. In the same manner, the 1968 Protocol on the Status of Refugees has been invoked as part of U.S. immigration law.

Yet, despite this reluctance to use international human rights standards, the United States is the leading venue for private human rights litigation in the world. The vehicle for this is an obscure statute, passed by the First Congress in 1789, which provided that U.S. courts would have "jurisdiction of any civil action by an alien for a tort only, committed in violation of the law of nations or a treaty of the United States."[12] This is known as the Alien Tort Claims Act, or (more simply) the Alien Tort Statute (ATS).

After lying dormant for nearly 200 years, in a landmark case— *Filartiga v. Peña-Irala*[13]—it was interpreted to mean that if a foreign plaintiff can show an injury caused by a tort "committed in violation of the law of nations," then U.S. courts could provide relief. The plaintiffs in that case had been victims of State-sponsored torture in Paraguay. They fled from that country, settled in the United States, and later found their torturer as an illegal alien in America. In a bold gambit, the Filartigas' lawyers argued that because torture was recognized as a violation of international law, jurisdiction was proper in U.S. courts. The Filartigas later recovered civil damages from their tormentor.

Filartiga has spawned a wide body of human rights litigation in the United States, involving disputes as varied as Ferdinand Marcos' political abuses as former president of the Philippines, mass rapes committed by Bosnian–Serb forces in the former Yugoslavia, genocides in Rwanda, political oppression in Ethiopia, and arbitrary detentions of individuals in Bolivia and Haiti. What these all had in common was a showing that the underlying conduct violated international law. So long as personal jurisdiction can be acquired over the defendant, these human rights cases can proceed

---

12. 28 U.S.C. § 1350.   **13.** 630 F.2d 876 (2d Cir. 1980).

in U.S. courts. There is one notable exception, however (discussed further in Chapter 17): the ATS does not grant jurisdiction in suits brought against foreign States or sovereigns, only against individual defendants.

There have been suggestions, though, that the United States is not an appropriate forum for these human rights cases occurring in other countries, owing to domestic constitutional limitations on such litigation or because of American "arrogance" in applying its own standards to such cases. Nevertheless, the trend has been toward other countries opening their courts as well to such matters. In Europe, the approach adopted has been to allow criminal prosecutions for human rights abuses. The recent, well-publicized case brought by Spanish prosecutors against former Chilean head-of-State, Augusto Pinochet, was of this sort. In a very significant decision,[14] the British House of Lords ruled that Pinochet had no immunity from extradition and subsequent prosecution for human rights abuses committed by his government after Chile had agreed to be bound to particular human rights norms. (The British government later declined to extradite Pinochet to Spain, ostensibly on grounds of his ill-health.)

All indications are that domestic enforcement of human rights norms—even for conduct occurring outside the forum State and not otherwise involving its nationals—will increase. This enforcement model, combined with international criminal institutions (such as the Yugoslav and Rwanda War Crimes Tribunals, as well as the new International Criminal Court—discussed in Chapters 7 and 20), will have a deep impact on the vindication of human rights norms.

Model #6—Direct Action by States. Before leaving this subject, it is worth remembering that States unilaterally and collectively punish other countries involved in human rights abuses, often without recourse to international law institutions. This raises, of course, a key tension in international law: between enforcing human rights and protecting State sovereignty.

Some examples of unilateral human rights enforcement actions undertaken by States are fairly innocuous. A nation might decide to break-off diplomatic relations with a human rights offender, and periodically the United States has pursued such human rights "public diplomacy." Financial and economic restrictions might also be involved in these situations, including the nearly decade-long period when the U.S. imposed trade sanctions against the white-dominated government of South Africa.

14. *R. v. Bow Street Magistrate, Ex Parte Pinochet Ugarte* (No. 3), [1999] 2   W.L.R. 827 (H.L.) (U.K.).

But the real collision between a world public order based on human rights and one premised on State sovereignty arises with the phenomenon of humanitarian interventions. A humanitarian intervention occurs when one nation (or a group) unilaterally invades another country in order to alleviate or stop human rights abuses by that government. This matter will be discussed in some detail in Chapter 19(B), but the important point to be made now is that this is becoming an increasingly-used option in international affairs. Whether it was Vietnam's invasion of Cambodia in the 1970's, or Tanzania's 1979 effort to oust Idi Amin in Uganda, or (most recently) NATO's military action to expel marauding Serb forces from Kosovo, humanitarian interventions have captured the headlines and have also become a central issue of U.S. foreign policy.

How this ultimate enforcement mechanism of human rights norms (the physical invasion of the offending State and the removal of an abusive government) can be reconciled with other international law rules promoting international peace and security is perhaps an unsolvable riddle in international law today. Whether a doctrine of humanitarian intervention can be substantively defined (exactly how bad does the human rights situation have to be to warrant invasion?), whether it can be effectively limited to United Nations political action, and whether it actually produces favorable human rights conditions, remains to be seen.

What is certainly true is that, in very recent years, a "critical mass" of human rights enforcement models, along with a new international consensus on the need for effective implementation, may have finally created a favorable climate for human rights protections. It may be a combination of more effective international human rights institutions, more timely complaint processes, more vigorous domestic human rights litigation, or more muscular and forcible international insistence that States respect human dignity. Only time will tell.

Chapter 10

State Territory and Common Areas

We turn now to the objects of international law, the legitimate topics of international legal regulation. First among these objects (but yet often neglected in such discussions) is State territory. An international lawyer must at least have a passing familiarity with issues of acquisition and disposition of land territory in international law. Questions of asserting control over other kinds of common areas (rivers, polar regions, airspace and outer space) will also be considered in this Chapter. Matters dealing with ocean areas will be addressed in Chapter 11.

A. Territory

Territory is, in a sense, the ultimate object of international law. It is a necessary requisite for statehood (see Chapter 5). Control of territory is usually exclusively vested in one State or another, although it need not invariably be so (what with *condominia* regimes and servitudes). The exclusivity of territorial control is coupled under international law with a nation's correlate obligation to protect other States' interests as they might be affected from that territory.

Control of territory remains among the most contentious topics in international relations. Nations are quite prepared to resort to force in order to assert or defend claims to land territory, and although it seems outlandish that in the 21st century such territorial disputes can persist, they remain quite common. Within the last 20 years a number of notable wars (the Falkland/Malvinas conflict and the Gulf War to liberate Kuwait), along with countless border skirmishes, have been waged.

Over the past five centuries, the rules by which territory can be acquired have substantially changed. One of the most difficult legacies of international law's Eurocentric and colonialist past was the wholesale sanction given to European acquisition of land territories in the Americas, Africa and Asia. Under the legal doctrine established in the 1500's and 1600's, these areas were regarded by Europeans as *res nullius*, a literal "no-man's" land which was ripe for the picking. International law merely required that States engage in the symbolic act of "discovery," in order to perfect a territorial claim. The rights of indigenous peoples were utterly

110

ignored, even when such peoples were organized into well-integrated political entities (the Aztec and Incan empires in the Americas, as well as the numerous African kingdoms). Only a handful of polities (such as those in India, China and Japan) were able to withstand this colonial onslaught.

This mode for acquiring territory was forced to change by the 1800's and 1900's, and that alteration caused substantial difficulties for international law. This gave rise to the "problem" of *intertemporal law,* a phenomenon that has wide application even aside from territorial concerns. All of this was illustrated in the *Isle of Palmas* Case, an international arbitration decided in 1928.[1] At issue was sovereignty over an isolated island less than 2 square miles in size. The United States claimed title under an 1898 treaty in which Spain ceded the Philippines (this after the Spanish–American War). The U.S. argued that, through Spain, it could trace title back to the act of the original discovery of the islands in the early 1600's. The Netherlands claimed title by virtue of a series of contacts, beginning in 1648 and 1677, and culminating in a (more or less) intermittent trading presence in the late 1800's.

The arbitrator for this case (the Swiss publicist, Max Huber) was thus faced with a dilemma. Should he recognize Spanish (and thus American) title based on the discovery doctrine—the old rule of international law, in force in the early 1600's? Or, instead, should he apply what was universally recognized as the new rule: the principle of *effective occupation?* Under this new rule, States must exercise effective control of a land territory in order to maintain a claim of title; symbolic discovery, without more, was insufficient.

Huber's solution was elegant, although controversial. He applied the international law in force at the moment of what he regarded as the "critical date." For Huber that date was 1898, the year in which the United States acquired title, and thus metaphorically "stepped-into-the-shoes" of the former claimant, Spain. By 1898, the new customary international law of effective occupation was recognized, so that was the rule to be applied. By that year, the Netherlands—and not Spain—had taken more steps to effectively occupy the island. Holland, and not the U.S., was the owner.

Huber's decision raised a host of concerns. One relatively minor issue was how exactly does a State "effectively occupy" a small island? Is it sufficient, as the Dutch did, to come back to the island every few years to trade? In other arbitral decisions, tribunals have ruled that effective occupation may mean rather less when at issue are small, isolated islands or territories subjected to

---

1. 2 U.N. Rep. Int'l Arb. Awards (U.S. v. Neth.) (Perm. Ct. Arb. 1928).

harsh conditions (as in the Arctic).[2] On the other hand, effective occupation may require a higher degree of control for areas subject to fierce colonial competition (as in the African hinterland).

The more serious problem—and the one of wider relevance to international lawyers—is the choice of law implicit in Huber's decision. Does a decision-maker apply the law in force when a legally-significant act took place, or instead require that additional acts be taken, conformable with the law as it evolves? The first option would lock into place the legal consequences of acts that would today be regarded as invalid. The second option means that no international law claim is ever safe from challenge, because some party or other can assert that there has been a change in the law favorable to its position. Huber tried to soften the effect of this paradox by his selection of a "critical date" that made sense in the context of the arbitration.

Huber also relied on some notions of repose, at least with territorial acquisition. International law does recognize a form of adverse possession with territorial acquisition. If a State fails to make an effective protest of another nation's assertion of sovereignty over disputed territory, title in that territory will vest and may not later be challenged.[3] Furthermore, international law accepts another aspect of the colonial legacy: the (often) artificial boundaries that colonial powers in South America, Africa and Asia drew between administrative units or rival territories. Under this doctrine—*uti possidetis*—the modern States of Latin America are obliged to follow the original Spanish and Portuguese colonial boundaries (dating back to 1800), just as current African nations must follow the old English, French, German and Portuguese lines. Although there is a manifest contradiction between the principle of decolonization and the application of *uti possidetis*, the World Court has at least rationalized its use by observing that "maintenance of the territorial status quo ... is often seen as the wisest course ... [in order] to avoid a disruption [and promote] the essential requirement of stability."[4]

International law's emphasis on stability and security may readily account for the conservatism of doctrines surrounding acquisition and control of territory. For obvious reasons, title to territory based on military conquest is certainly not a legitimate ground today; however, what about lands acquired long ago by force? Likewise, certain transfers of territory made by treaty of

2. See *Clipperton Island* Case (Fr. v. Mex.), 2 U.N. Rep. Int'l Arb. Awards 1105 (1931); *Legal Status of Eastern Greenland* Case (Den. v. Nor.), 1933 P.C.I.J. Ser. A/B. No. 53.

3. See *Taba* Arbitration (Egypt v. Israel), 27 Int'l Legal Materials 1427 (1988).

4. *Case Concerning the Frontier Dispute* (Burkino Faso v. Mali), 1986 I.C.J. 554 (at ¶ 25).

cession still remain controversial. (Spain, for example, still disputes British control of Gibraltar, acquired by treaty in 1713, as does Cuba with U.S. title to Guantanamo Bay.)

States have also in the past voluntarily agreed to certain limitations on the use of their territory. These kinds of *servitudes* might include demilitarization of certain areas, or granting other States preferential rights (perhaps access through canals or waterways). These are certainly now quite exceptional. It should also be noted that some treaty regimes allow for more than one State to exercise control over the same land territory. (The Pacific islands of the New Hebrides were for a century jointly owned by France and Britain, until it became independent. The Canton and Enderbury Islands—also in the Pacific—are under joint British and American control.) Such *condominia* regimes are also quite rare.

Mention should also be made that a State's land territory includes also the air space above it. Although not an issue before the advent of manned flight in the last century, the security concerns incumbent in foreign intrusions into national air space have been a serious issue for international relations. International law allows States to regard such incursions as serious breaches of sovereignty, and to respond accordingly, as with the Soviet shoot-down of an American U–2 spy plane at the height of the Cold War.[5] (Many countries, including the United States, have established "Air Defense Identification Zones" (ADIZs), which require aircraft to identify themselves to authorities.) Destruction of intruding aircraft under these circumstances remains quite common, despite efforts by international organizations to develop rules that will avoid such incidents.

The use of national air space for civil aviation is governed by a complex network of multilateral and bilateral treaties. The 1944 Chicago Convention, aside from creating the International Civil Aviation Organization (ICAO), also established the basic freedoms of international air transport. An air carrier in one nation does not have the freedom to initiate scheduled flights to another country without that State's permission. These are granted in reciprocal Air Services Agreements, which regulate every aspect of commercial flights between the two nations. (One such Agreement will be featured in the discussion in Chapter 18.)

B.   International Common Spaces

The next major class of international law objects are international common areas. Known also as "global commons," these spaces implicate a variety of concerns for international affairs. The

---

5. See *Powers* Case, 30 Int'l L. Rep. 69 (U.S.S.R. S.Ct. 1960).

most fundamental of these is how the international community establishes rules to manage common resources. This is a pressing concern. Whether it is activities occurring on, or riches located in, the oceans (considered in the next Chapter), or the protection of the global environment (Chapter 12), States will vigorously compete for resources and to preserve perceived national interests. Failure properly to manage common resources can thus lead to conflict.

More than that, common resources lead to management challenges, precisely because the assets *are* held in common. Known as the "tragedy of the commons," this is the observation that things owned by everybody (say, a village green or mutual fishery) are conserved by nobody. No single actor has an incentive to foreswear adding extra sheep to graze on the green (and thus protect the grass) or to halt over-fishing. Under this theory, common resources are inevitably degraded and destroyed over time. There appear to be only two alternatives to this tragedy: divide-up the resources (and thus grant individual property interests in the asset) or rely on explicit institutions and rules to manage it.

International law has relied on variants of partition and management strategies for many international common resources. One of the first of such common areas to come under international legal management was international rivers; watercourses that run through two or more nations. Such rivers might be vital for navigation or trade, or for supplying drinking-water or irrigation, or for generating hydroelectric power. As might be recalled from Chapter 6, international institutions devoted to the management of international rivers and boundary waters were among the first to be developed.

As for navigation rights, international law today generally recognizes the rights of riparian States (those that border a river) and non-riparian nations alike to use a river for commerce. The one exception is that States may properly limit commercial traffic between two points on the river located within the same territory to the nationals of that State. This is the principle of *cabotage*, and it applies equally to river traffic as it does to commercial aviation and ocean shipping between two cities in the same country.

The more contentious issue is the *non*-navigational uses of international watercourses, including water rights, dam-building, and pollution prevention. In some parts of the world (most notably the Middle East), access to water literally means the difference between national life and death. International law has charted a middle course between extreme positions taken by States in these disputes. Imagine a scenario in which a river traverses two nations. The "upper riparian" (the State where the river begins) wants to build a dam for irrigation or power production. But that will cut the expected flow of water to the "lower riparian" farther downstream. Decisions from international tribunals[6] have indicated that in such situations neither State has automatic priority for their claims. Instead, there is "natural community of interest" in the river resource, and an equitable result should be worked-out through good-faith negotiations between the disputants.

International law has been relatively slow to add specific content to these general principles of river management. One significant step was the 1966 publication of the Helsinki Rules by the International Law Association (ILA),[7] a non-governmental organization of academic international lawyers. The Rules prescribed some specific criterion for balancing and weighing competing interests, such as (1) geography and hydrography of the river basin, (2) past utilization and economic needs of the riparians, and (3) the most efficient use of the water resources. These were later amplified in the official work of the U.N.'s International Law Commission, and Draft Articles on Non–Navigational Uses of International Watercourses are currently being reviewed by the international community. These codifications have already been applied by international tribunals.[8]

In the 20th century, human beings finally explored the polar regions of the Arctic (North Pole) and Antarctic (South Pole). The polar regions are significant not only as a platform for science, but also for geo-strategic reasons. Beginning in the 1910's and 1920's, States that bordered the Arctic Ocean (including Canada, Norway and the Soviet Union), as well as those nations that had ambitious scientific expeditions to the Antarctic, began to make actual territorial claims to these polar regions. These claims depended on assertions of discovery or more spurious notions of contiguity, but they were certainly not supported by any credible evidence of effective occupation. Indeed, aside from indigenous populations of Inuit, there are few permanent settlements in the high Arctic, and none at all on the Southern Continent (the number of scientists and tourists in Antarctica rarely exceeds 5,000 at any one time).

The way in which States have purported to perfect territorial claims in polar regions has a comic aspect. The Chilean and Argentine governments have flown pregnant women to Antarctica, had them deliver babies there, and then record in the childrens' passports the place of birth as their "Antarctic Territories"! The

6. See *International Commission of the River Oder* Opinion, 1929 P.C.I.J. Ser. A, No. 23 (1929); *Lac Lanoux* Case (Fr. v. Sp.), [1957] Int'l L. Rep. 101.

7. International Law Association, REPORT OF THE 52D CONFERENCE, Helsinki (1966).

8. See *Gabikovo-Nagymaros Project* Case (Hungary v. Slovakia), 1994 I.C.J. 151.

United States and Britain actually engaged in a 1934 diplomatic correspondence over the propriety of issuing postage stamps and operating a radio station in the Antarctic.[9] Canada has aggressively asserted its right to legislate anti-pollution restrictions in its claimed sector of the Arctic.

The practical solution for competing Antarctic claims was developed in the 1959 Antarctic Treaty which, for all intents and purposes, "froze" national claims to sectors on the Southern Continent. As long as that treaty remains in force, no nation can assert a territorial claim to Antarctica. At the same time, the Antarctic Treaty System demilitarized the region and established a unique form of condominium regime to manage activities and resources there. The Antarctic Treaty Consultative Parties (ATCPs), which includes all States that have a scientific presence in Antarctic, meets regularly to develop regulations for the safe and friendly use of the continent. These have included regimes for the management of fishing resources in the Southern Ocean, as well as a comprehensive environmental protection protocol (signed at Madrid in 1991). Similar forms of international cooperation are being developed for the Arctic region.

That leaves outer space, the final international frontier. Where a nation's air space ends, and outer space begins, can still be contentious. The usual rule-of-thumb is that a State's sovereignty over air space ends at the lowest altitude where a satellite can continually remain in orbit without disintegrating. The flight envelope of high-flying fixed-wing aircraft (such as the U.S. U–2 spy plane) is still considered to be in air space, while the Space Shuttle orbiter traverses outer space.

The resources of outer space include not only near-orbit locations and applications, but also the moon and other celestial bodies. As human technology is refined to use these resources, so too will international law be implicated. For example, substantial technology exists today for remote sensing of the earth's land areas by satellites in orbit. Sophisticated processing of raw telemetry from this sensing has either national security dimensions or vast commercial potential. A U.N. body has recommended some sort of accommodation between the proprietary rights of satellite-launching nations with the interests of those nations being sensed, particularly when the information being gathered involves natural resources or environmental harms.

An even more difficult dispute arose concerning the limited number of geostationary orbit slots—those locations over the equator where a satellite remains in a fixed location above the earth. These slots are essential for many forms of telecommunications

9. See 1 G. Hackworth, Digest of International Law 458 (1940).

satellites, and many developing nations located on the equator asserted in 1976 a form of territorial sovereignty or preference over these satellite "parking spaces." This matter was only resolved when an international institution—the International Telecommunications Union (ITU)—agreed to set-aside allocations for geostationary orbits for the future use of developing nations, rather than assigning them all to spacefaring nations now.

One significant aspect of international law's regulation of the uses of the moon and celestial bodies is the rule that these resources are the "common heritage of mankind." Both the 1967 Outer Space Treaty and the 1979 Moon Treaty use similar language to describe this concept. And while nations are comfortable in disclaiming title to territory on the moon, that does leave open the legal consequences of exploitation of resources on celestial bodies. Whether it is refining water on the moon, mining asteroids for rare minerals, or virtual tourism on Mars, these issues are likely to become more pressing. Does the common heritage principle mean that such activities must be under international control or that property rights derived from celestial objects are inadmissible? Until we have an authentic dispute raising such issues, such questions are, alas, academic.

One thing, though, that is not speculative is that uses of outer space pose real dangers to human safety, international security, and environmental protection. Although the common heritage principle was meant to ensure peaceful uses of outer space, the risk of military applications in near-orbit are quite real (including anti-ballistic missile (ABM) technologies). A handful of treaties pledge international cooperation in the safety and rescue of spacefarers. Environmental damage from space activities is addressed in a 1972 Convention on International Liability for Damage Caused by Space Objects. This instrument imposes absolute liability (no exceptions, no limits) on the State that launches an object into space. So in the 1978 crash of a Soviet satellite over Canada, and the 1979 disintegration of the U.S. SkyLab, the launching States acknowledged international responsibility for damage occurring on the Earth's surface.

The law of international common spaces has developed with the dual objectives of promoting opportunity and minimizing risk for the international community. The real challenge for international lawyers is not so much fashioning partition schemes for dividing-up common resources (although such an approach is sometimes necessary), as it is arranging continuing and enduring international cooperation. That certainly does not mean recourse to bland principles, such as equitable sharing or common heritage. Rather, concrete and specific systems of rules are the best way to head-off conflict, and, despite their failures, regimes like the Antarctic Treaty System offer the best hope for that cooperative future.

Chapter 11

Law of the Sea

The nearly 500 year history of the law of the sea reduces to a fairly simple dynamic: the conflict between nations with predominate maritime interests and those States that desire to secure access to maritime resources close to their shores. What has vastly complicated the law of the sea is that the identities of maritime powers and coastal States have changed over time, just as the range of possible (and permissible) ocean uses has vastly increased with technology and economic potential.

A. Ocean Resources and Law

Oceans cover three-fifths of the earth's surface. The original—and still prevalent—use of the oceans is as an avenue for trade and commerce. Maritime shipping still accounts for over two-thirds of the value of all goods transported internationally (think of the worth of crude oil shipped by sea). Maritime powers have traditionally asserted rights to freedom of navigation on the oceans, and this is certainly related to historic interests in security and naval power. The ability to "project" force over ocean areas remains one of the central tenets of military doctrine—for the United States, Russia, and all other Great Powers.

Ocean resources are obviously more than navigation and naval power. The seas provide critical products for the world community. Fisheries come in two varieties: coastal stocks located close to shore (and usually exploited by nationals of the closest State), and long-distance fisheries utilized by many countries. Even more important are the mineral resources of the oceans. Nearly one-quarter of the world's oil and gas reserves are located offshore. Drilled and produced from gigantic rigs and elaborate offshore facilities, the dollar value of these hydrocarbon resources is immense. New mineral resources (including so-called "manganese nodules" and "polymetallic sulfides") may also prove significant. Lastly, there is the significant role played by the oceans in directing the global environment and weather patterns. Pollution prevention has also become a vital "asset" in oceans management.

There is thus much at stake in the law of the sea. And, as already suggested, there has been a cyclical process in which the competing interests of maritime Powers and of coastal States have

118

manifested themselves in significant legal changes. One such period was from 1500–1650. At that time, the emerging colonial powers of Spain and Portugal were literally attempting to enclose vast areas of ocean spaces and to exclude such rival trading nations as Holland and England. In a pivotal case litigated in Amsterdam in the early 1600's, a young Dutch lawyer, Hugo de Groot (Grotius), wrote an impressive brief on the legal question of whether Portugal could legally exclude Dutch merchants from the East Indies, and, as a consequence, whether the Dutch capture of a Portuguese carrack, The SANTA CATARINA, was lawful. De Groot won his case, and his brief was later the basis for his tract, *Mare Liberum* (Freedom of the Seas).

By 1650, Grotius' position—that the seas were open to all and that coastal States could only exercise a narrow band of jurisdiction offshore—had completely won the day. In fact, this position held sway until the Second World War. Coastal States were allowed to exercise competence over a narrow "territorial sea," a scant 3 nautical miles from shore. (In case you were wondering, a nautical mile is slightly longer than a "statute" mile on land.) After 1945, the pendulum began to radically shift in favor of coastal State interests, in large measure because the world's leading naval power (the United States) also had the most to gain from asserting regulatory control over resources offshore. Coastal State assertions of various kinds of power out into the ocean exponentially increased.

All of these influences culminated in a series of diplomatic negotiations. In 1958 was the first U.N. Conference on the Law of the Sea (UNCLOS I), which produced four separate instruments (on territorial seas, continental shelves, high seas, and fisheries). Then followed UNCLOS II in 1960, which failed to produce a consensus on the breadth of the territorial sea. The 1960's and 1970's saw the explosion of coastal State claims, particularly by Latin American, Caribbean, and African nations. Some of these nations asserted control of ocean resources out to 200 nautical miles, or beyond. (This development was earlier mentioned (in Chapter 3(E)) in the context of the *Fisheries Jurisdiction* Case.) This precipitated a crisis with nautical Powers, which resulted in the convening of UNCLOS III in 1973.

UNCLOS III, conducted from 1973 to 1982, was the longest-running international law negotiation ever. Thousands of delegates, hundreds of meetings, dozens of coalitions and interest-groups, and a bewildering array of discrete issues vastly complicated the exercise. The ultimate goal was the drafting of a literal constitution for the oceans. This was finally achieved in the 1982 U.N. Convention on the Law of the Sea, or the Law of the Sea Treaty (LOST). This accord, now in force, is an incredibly long and detailed convention—

but it is not without its controversy. At the eleventh hour, the United States raised objections, and ultimately refused to sign the treaty. In the 1990's, the U.S. did sign, but has not completed the necessary ratification. The United States' position is that most (but not all) of the provisions of LOST reflect customary international law, and thus the U.S. need not move fast to become a party in order to take advantage of them. Other countries maintain that LOST is a "package deal," and the U.S. can only opt-out at its own peril.

The 1982 LOST did usher in an era of relative stability in the law of the sea. New coastal State demands for extended jurisdiction and power offshore have subsided. But predictions that the pendulum has swung back to maritime interests in the law of the sea are manifestly premature. This is an opportune time to take stock of the current features of the law of the sea, and international lawyers need to be familiar with this vast body of State practice and treaty law.

B. Maritime Zones

The law of the sea is amongst the most formalistic of international law fields. By that, I mean that many of the doctrines of law of the sea are structured around what may appear to be arbitrary and peculiar distinctions. Essential to understanding the contemporary law of the sea is recognizing the legal construction of maritime zones emanating out from shore. These zones *matter*; certain activities that are permitted by a coastal State within its territorial sea or contiguous zone (out to 24 nautical miles) are absolutely prohibited beyond that. So the legal outcome of a law of the sea dispute could very well turn on the precise location of certain critical events.

If these zones sound mystifying (and they are to most international lawyers), keep one simple point in mind. The closer to shore that a particular activity or resource is located, the more likely it will come under the control, jurisdiction, or regulatory authority of the nearest coastal State. Conversely, the farther one moves from shore, coastal State authority decreases until, presumably, one reaches a point (called the "high seas") where it ends and total freedom of the seas prevails. To understand the legal regime that operates in each of six maritime zones—internal waters (IW), territorial seas (TS), contiguous zones (CZ), exclusive economic zones (EEZ), continental shelves (CS), and high seas (HS)—imagine a journey for a legal actor that begins on a nation's shoreline.

Internal Waters (IW). Internal waters are bodies of water so closely connected with a coastal State's land territory that they are assimilated to that nation's full territorial sovereignty. All maritime zones are calculated from what are called "baselines." If all the coasts of the world were straight, that baseline would be the low-tide mark on the beach. Unfortunately, there is no such thing as a simple coastline. Bays might indent a coast. A landmass might have barrier or fringing islands. There might be manmade constructions, such as harbor facilities or lighthouses on rock outcrops. All of these can influence the drawing of baselines. Indeed, States with creative cartographers and lawyers will go to elaborate lengths to skew these baselines, in order to maximize a coastal State's claim to maritime real estate. (One such dispute was the straight baselines used in the *Norwegian Fisheries* Case, alluded to in Chapter 2(B).) Anything landward of these baselines is internal waters.

The legal regime of IW is straight-forward enough: internal waters are treated like the land territory. So whatever sovereignty a coastal State exercises in its territory, it may exert over incidents occurring on its IW. There are only two exceptions to this rule of absolute sovereignty over internal waters. The first, already mentioned (in Chapter 10), are servitudes created by treaty. These grant preferential rights to one State (or groups of States) over the internal waters of another nation. So, for example, the Kiel Canal which cuts across the northern part of Germany was, under the 1919 Treaty of Versailles, made an international waterway. (It was access to that canal that was the issue in the *Wimbledon* Case, discussed in Chapter 3(B).)

The other exception to coastal State sovereignty over IW is a principle of customary international law. That involves access to ports of one State by vessels of another. In times of peace, ports are left open, and access can only be restricted on a temporary basis, and only then in a non-discriminatory fashion. (Port States can, however, impose special restrictions on vessels carrying certain dangerous cargoes.) The corollary of States granting access to foreign vessels is restraint in the exercise of jurisdiction over them. In a number of cases, domestic courts have concluded that the coastal State cannot exercise either criminal jurisdiction over the crewmen of foreign vessels who commit crimes onboard the ship in harbor or otherwise apply domestic law to shipboard activities.[1] The only departure from this custom—when the crime is murder and offends the "peace of the port"—rather proves the rule. In all other situations, coastal nations defer to the flag State to exercise control over all aspects of life onboard the ship, including enforcing law and order.

---

1. See *Wildenhus' Case*, 120 U.S. 1   571 (1953).
(1887); *Lauritzen v. Larsen*, 345 U.S.

Territorial Seas (TS). Coastal States have exercised a narrow band of jurisdiction offshore for over 400 years. Known as "territorial waters," or territorial seas, the essential idea was that within this band of water, the coastal State asserted a form of sovereignty, qualified only by respect for the navigational rights of other nations. Historically, the breadth of the TS was narrow. Usually described as one marine "league" or 3 nautical miles, this was colorfully referred to as the "cannon-shot rule"—literally the distance lethal force could be projected from the shoreline.

Beginning after World War Two, the breadth of the TS began to expand. The 1958 Law of the Sea Conventions confirmed the limit at 3 nautical miles (although with an option for a 9 mile contiguous zone), but by the 1982 LOST, the distance was increased to 12 nautical miles. With the 1958 and 1982 Conventions also came rules that permitted coastal States to expansively draw baselines across bays, around fringing islands, and enclosing mid-ocean archipelagos. Under the 1982 LOST, vast areas of maritime real estate were newly placed under the regime of territorial seas.

This raised substantial concerns for the world's maritime Powers. The TS regime had always been qualified by the doctrine of *innocent passage*, which permitted foreign vessels to freely traverse the territorial waters of other States. As long as the passage was "continuous and expeditious," and provided the conduct of the vessel was "innocent," access was permitted. Moreover, coastal States were limited in their ability to exercise criminal or civil jurisdiction over foreign vessels engaged in innocent passage. International tribunals had ruled[2] that such jurisdiction could only be asserted when the passing vessel's activities had some connection with the coastal State or otherwise posed a substantial threat (as with drug trafficking), and this result was confirmed in the 1982 LOST. Coastal States were, moreover, limited in their ability to interfere with innocent passage, although reserving the power to suspend innocent passage for national security reasons. The 1982 LOST (in Article 19) defined with greater particularity a long list of activities that rendered passage *non*-innocent, including a variety of military-related functions that could be carried out by vessels. Beginning in the 1970's, some coastal States began to assert that they could categorically deny foreign warships access to their territorial seas. Needless to say, this did not make naval planners at the Pentagon, Kremlin, or Admiralty happy.

The maritime powers at UNCLOS III thus insisted that the *quid pro quo* for coastal State extension of territorial seas to 12

---

2. See *The DAVID*, [1933–34] Annual Digest Int'l L. 137 (U.S.–Panama Claims Comm'n 1933).

nautical miles would be the acceptance of further limits on coastal State authority to interfere with certain kinds of strategic naval movements. Thus was born the doctrine of *transit passage*. Transit passage applies only, however, in international straits—the strategic choke-points for maritime commerce and naval power (think of the Straits of Gibraltar, English Channel, or the entrance to the Persian Gulf). As long as a channel is used for international navigation (and the World Court had earlier held that that would be broadly construed[3]), then transit passage would apply. Under transit passage, the coastal State has virtually no right at all to interfere with civilian or military traffic, and under no circumstances can such passage be suspended by coastal States.

Disputes are likely to continue about the TS regime in the law of the sea. When one is speaking of the sovereignty that coastal States exercise within 12 nautical miles of shore, nations are likely to be prickly about any perceived security threats. Yet, at the same time, maritime Powers are adamant about freedom of movement of naval assets, especially in periods of international crisis. Delimitation disputes between countries' offshore claims can be particularly nasty if the States are in such close proximity that territorial seas have to be divided.

Contiguous Zones (CZ). Under today's law of the sea, once one moves beyond 12 nautical miles a subtle, but important, shift occurs in the nature of coastal State claims. No longer are coastal States asserting sovereignty (as they do in IW and TS). Instead, the basis of the claim is an assertion of control or jurisdiction over activities offshore, or (in the alternative) the avowal of sovereign rights to resources. Coastal State claims of control are usually made in the form of contiguous zones, which begin just where the TS ends.

The historic purpose of a CZ was as a remedy to the formalism of drawing fictional lines in the water. For example, in the early 1800's (a period of extremely high tariffs and import controls), smuggling was rife. Coastal States would routinely attempt to vigorously enforce revenue laws in their territorial seas. Would-be smugglers would simply park "mother ships" just beyond the 3 nautical mile line, wait for smaller boats to row out to the vessel and dart back in to shore, thus remaining beyond the reach of law enforcement. Exactly such tactics were used by "rum-runners" during the Prohibition era in the United States, and today by narcotics traffickers.

The solution to this problem has been the assertion, by coastal States, of certain kinds of regulatory authority beyond the TS, in order to prevent infringement of certain kinds of laws within its

3. See *Corfu Channel* Case (U.K. v. Alb.), 1949 I.C.J. 4.

territory or territorial waters. Known originally as "Hovering Acts" (evocatively describing the smuggler just "hovering" beyond reach), these quickly gained international acceptance. Indeed, Chief Justice John Marshall, in an early American decision,[4] noted that this aspect of the law of the sea reflected a struggle for law: if coastal State assertions of control were "such as unnecessarily vex and harass foreign lawful commerce, foreign nations will resist their exercise. If they are ... reasonable and necessary to secure their laws from violation, they will be submitted to."

Today's law of the sea permits coastal States to extend a CZ from 12 to 24 nautical miles from shore, and most nations have done so. (The United States declared its CZ in September 1999.) Under the 1958 and 1982 Conventions, the coastal State can only exercise customs, fiscal, immigration or sanitary regulations in the contiguous zone. The UNCLOS I and III negotiations specifically rejected coastal State bids to enforce security regulations in the CZ, although coastal States may exercise regulatory control over valuable sunken shipwrecks located within 24 nautical miles of shore.

Continental Shelves (CS) and Exclusive Economic Zones (EEZ). Even though they developed separately, it makes sense to consider the CS and EEZ regimes together since under the current law of the sea they are largely coextensive. The continental shelf describes the legal regime applied to the resources of, and activities affecting, the seabed and subsoil under the ocean. The EEZ regime governs resources and activities in the water column and ocean surface. Today, coastal States' continental shelves and EEZs can extend 200 nautical miles from shore (and, in certain circumstances, the CS can go out even farther).

As was mentioned in Chapter 3(B), the evolution of the continental shelf doctrine is probably one of the best examples we have of "instant custom." The origins of the doctrine can be traced to a single instance of State practice: President Harry Truman's 1945 Proclamation enunciating U.S. policy to regard "the natural resources of the subsoil and sea bed of the continental shelf beneath the high seas but contiguous to the coasts of the United States as appertaining to the United States, subject to its jurisdiction and control."[5] The Truman Proclamation was made after the United States' victory in World War Two, but in the midst of a surprising public panic that the country was running out of fuel. Oil reserves in the Gulf of Mexico, just offshore, were beckoning.

From this modest beginning, State practice blossomed and by the time of UNCLOS I (in 1958) there was a consensus among the international community that the CS doctrine had entered custom-

---

4. *Church v. Hubbart*, 6 U.S. (2 Cranch) 187 (1804).

5. 10 Fed. Reg. 12303 (Sept. 28, 1945).

ary international law. The 1958 Convention on the Continental Shelf codified the doctrine in six short articles. That treaty defined the CS as extending out to the 200–meter isobath (that point where the depth of the water was 200 meters), or "beyond that limit, to where the depth of the superjacent waters admits of the exploitation of the natural resources of said areas." The 1958 Convention thus acknowledged that as technology improved to drill for oil and gas, international law would adjust by allowing coastal States extensions of rights to the CS.

These provisions were incorporated into the 1982 LOST, but with the important qualification that the CS regime could be extended out to 200 nautical miles. If the geologic conditions are right, coastal States can apply to a U.N. body—the Commission on the Outer Limits of the Continental Shelf—to lengthen their continental shelves, but in no event beyond 350 nautical miles. And if oil and gas deposits are exploited on a nation's CS beyond 200 nautical miles, the LOST established an innovative profit-sharing scheme requiring that the coastal State remit a certain percentage of the proceeds to the U.N. Under these provisions, all economically-exploitable oil and gas resources offshore will be placed under some coastal State's jurisdiction. (How the continental shelves of two or more nations get divided will be considered at the end of this Chapter.)

Like the continental shelf, coastal States are given for their EEZs two kinds of authority: (1) *sovereign rights* over the natural resources of the water column (chiefly fish stocks); and (2) *jurisdiction* over activities affecting those resources, including offshore platforms and artificial islands, marine pollution prevention, and marine scientific research. Aside from this grant of rights under the 1982 Convention, all other high seas freedoms (discussed next) will apply in a coastal State's EEZ and on its CS. Reaching this accommodation took agonizing decades of conflict. As already noted, developing States made aggressive stakes to EEZs in the 1950's, 1960's, and 1970's. These assertions were typically made as territorial seas claims, often with substantial restrictions on free navigation. The primary object was to place certain high-value fish stocks under coastal State control.

The 1982 Convention's creation of 200 nautical mile EEZs sanctioned the largest territorial grab in history. Many nations (including the United States, which declared its EEZ in 1983) were big winners, while those States that were land-locked or had only a short coastline (what were called "zone-locked" or "geographically disadvantaged" nations) got little or nothing. Yet, ironically, disputes over fisheries have persisted. Such high-value stocks as tuna, salmon, and sea bass are routinely over-fished, often by illegal fishing vessels. One loophole—"straddling stocks" which range between one nation's EEZ and the high seas—was closed by a Special Agreement concluded in 1996. Spanish and Canadian vessels shot at each other in a recent incident in the North Atlantic, and arrests of fishing vessels are common. (Under LOST Article 73 these ships should be promptly released, and a special procedure is available before a new court, the International Tribunal for the Law of the Sea (ITLOS), to ensure that.[6]) The EEZ regime's restrictions on marine scientific research and oceanography have also proven cumbersome.

High Seas (HS). The high seas are all ocean areas beyond national jurisdiction. The high seas begin where States' EEZs end: at 200 nautical miles. Under Grotius' theory of *mare liberum*, complete freedom should reign on the high seas. This clearly is a myth; freedom of the seas is neither an unqualified virtue, nor practically desirable. The reason is that complete freedom from national controls or international rules usually means anarchy. Conflicting uses of ocean spaces go unresolved, or, even worse, truly bad activities go unregulated.

International law over the last 400 years has evolved a number of mechanisms to temper and manage freedom of the seas. One of these is the rule (like that of aircraft registry) requiring that all vessels have a State of registry, a "flag State." And as noted in the context of the *Nottebohm* Case (in Chapter 7(A)), there must be a "genuine link" between the vessel (its owners and operators) and that State of registry. The flag State is charged with the responsibility of overseeing and regulating all aspects of the ship's construction, design, equipment and manning (what are known as "CDEM" regulations), and ensuring that the vessel is in compliance with international standards. Most of these are set by the International Maritime Organization (IMO) in London. Despite the prevalence of such "open registries" or "flags of convenience" as Liberia, Panama and Honduras, international shipping safety is improving. Port States and coastal States have nevertheless sought to impose requirements on ocean-going vessels in excess of international standards, but this has been resisted.

Another mechanism for enforcement on the high seas is the *right of visit* exercised by warships. Certain activities are prohibited on the high seas and thus are grounds for stop and seizure. These include piracy and slave trading (discussed earlier in Chapter 7(B)), which are regarded as offenses within a universal jurisdiction. That means the warships of any nation may stop and prosecute individuals engaged in such international crimes. Piracy remains a serious

---

6. See *Saint Vincent & Grenadines v. Guinea (The M/V "Saiga")*, 37 Int'l Le-   gal Materials 360 (1998) (ITLOS 1997).

problem in the Caribbean and South China Sea, and the definition of piracy in LOST Article 101 leaves much to be desired (it fails to include terrorist acts taking place on a single vessel or incidents occurring in EEZs). Other grounds for visit under the law of the sea include a vessel being stateless (having no nation of registry), unauthorized broadcasting, and (in limited circumstances) narcotics trafficking.

Military and security issues raise the most difficult questions of high seas freedoms. The capture of belligerent and neutral vessels in wartime—the law of naval prize—was a perennial favorite for international law in the 1700's and 1800's, but less so recently (although that was the issue in The *PAQUETE HABANA* case, mentioned in Chapters 2 & 14). Seizure of American vessels by Britain was the *casus belli* of the War of 1812, and a similar incident nearly resulted in Britain entering the U.S. Civil War on the side of the Confederacy. Blockades of coastal States are regarded as hostile acts, whether denominated as "quarantine zones" (as with the 1961 Cuban Missile Crisis) or "exclusion zones" (declared by Germany in World Wars I and II, as well as by Britain and Argentina in the 1982 Falklands–Malvinas War). Today, the restrictions on high seas freedoms are as likely to be premised on environmental security (the prohibition of nuclear cargoes) or social emergencies (such as the U.S. interdiction of Haitian refugees).

The most extraordinary story of the 1982 Convention's handling of high seas freedoms involves fist-sized lumps of manganese, cobalt, nickel, and copper. Known as "manganese nodules," these are found on the deep seabed, under miles of water, and far from shore. Beginning with an innocuous enough speech by Malta's delegate, Arvid Pardo, before the U.N. General Assembly in 1967, the international community became entranced with these nuggets. Seeing a ready source of valuable, strategic minerals there for the taking, developing nations lobbied hard for the deep seabed minerals to be declared the "common heritage of mankind." What ensued at UNCLOS III were negotiations by delegates to fashion a set of international law rules to exploit this resource. And what a baroque regime it was: elaborate articles on production limits for seabed mining, complex regulatory systems including the creation of an international mining company (called "The Enterprise"), mandatory technology transfer requirements, and detailed institutional arrangements with the creation of a new, International Sea Bed Authority (ISBA).

There was just one problem with all of this. No technology existed—or has been developed—to recover manganese nodules from the deep seabed. (Robots and very, very long vacuum hoses have been proposed.) More importantly, the mineral economics are such that there has been absolutely no incentive to develop such proprietary technology, especially as the LOST required that such intellectual property be given away to the Enterprise. In short, the deep seabed mining provisions of Part XI of the LOST were a fiasco. They were, in large measure, the reason why the U.S. refused to sign the 1982 Convention. After the most offending features of Part XI were amended in a later "Implementation Agreement," the U.S. did sign (but has not yet ratified) the treaty. Preparations to initiate the work of the ISBA and Enterprise (headquartered in Jamaica) are under way.

The real lesson of the deep seabed mining regime is the dangers that come with internationalizing a resource. Although the common heritage principle sounds alluring, it is often impractical, especially when private sector initiative is stifled. The negotiations of Part XI also illustrate the absurdities of lawyers and diplomats negotiating ahead of the curve of science, technology and economics. The elaborate provisions of the LOST were utterly irrelevant and fanciful, and had to be later changed. While international lawyers should take pride in developing creative legal regimes, to do so in advance of practical certainties is folly.

C. Maritime Delimitation

The creation of maritime zones brings with it the need to demarcate these zones when nations dispute their boundaries. And with so much at stake—valuable fish stocks, critical oil fields, or strategic locations—the odds of nations being disposed to use force to assert their claims to maritime real estate vastly increase. The same principles that are implicated in territorial disputes also apply to maritime delimitation, although they are often amplified. For example, title to well-positioned islands has become a major issue for international relations. (The China–Vietnam–Philippines competition for the Spratley Islands in the South China Sea is but one example.) Control of a small island (for example, the Isle of Palmas, mentioned in the last Chapter) can generate hundreds of thousands of square miles of territorial seas, contiguous zones and EEZs. (The 1982 Convention tries to moderate this result somewhat by providing that rocks, incapable of supporting "economic life," cannot generate an EEZ.) Nevertheless, States will literally risk blood and treasure over specks of land no bigger than Gilligan's Island.

When coastal nations are in proximity to each other, either as *opposite* or *adjacent* States, real problems arise. Obviously, if less than 400 nautical miles separates two States, some form of delimitation is required. And the first rule of international law in such situations is that the States involved should negotiate in good faith to reach a result. As a consequence, there is large body of arranged marine delimitations. But negotiations often fail, and because of that, there is also a large set of arbitral and adjudicatory decisions. Indeed, this has become rather a cottage industry for both international lawyers and tribunals. (Marine delimitation disputes have accounted for nearly one-fifth of the ICJ's docket since 1969.)

As might be recalled from Chapter 3, these disputes have triggered difficult issues of customary and treaty law. The *North Sea Continental Shelf* Case[7] rejected the uncritical use of *equidistance*, the practice of drawing a delimitation line every point of which is an equal distance from each coastal State's shore. In certain situations, like the concave coast of Germany on the North Sea, it produces a distorted result—Germany got "zone-locked." Article 83 of the LOST stipulated an "equitable solution" for maritime delimitations of continental shelves and EEZs. This has meant in practice that an equidistance line might be the start of the process, but that line can be altered by "special circumstances."

What the appropriate special circumstances are, has been decided by international tribunals. These have included giving special treatment to islands, especially in circumstances where isles of one disputing nation are located right offshore the other State. (The Greek isles right-off the coast of Turkey, and Britain's Channel Islands off France,[8] are just two examples.) Historic rights to fish or to exploit resources in a particular area may be significant, as might be one nation's acquiescence in letting another State do so.[9] The legal significance of particular geological formations has been rejected, as has economic disparities between the two States.[10] Lastly, a principle of *proportionality* has been employed, in which the length of a State's coastline is compared with the amount of ocean real estate it has acquired under a delimitation. Together these special circumstances have been used by tribunals to produce equitable delimitations for coastal States. As long as ocean spaces and uses remain important for members of the international community, disputes over access to those resources will continue.

---

7. 1969 I.C.J. 3 (F.R.G. v. Den./ Neth.).

8. See *Delimitation of the Continental Shelf in the Western Approaches* (Gr. Brit. v. Fr.), 18 Int'l Legal Materials 397 (1978).

9. See *Gulf of Maine* Case (Can. v. U.S.), 1984 I.C.J. 247.

10. See *Libya-Tunisia Continental Shelf Case,* 1982 I.C.J. 17.

Chapter 12

International Environmental Law

International environmental law has emerged in the last few decades as a distinct specialty within international law, and to fully canvass this field would require its own volume. This area of international practice is starting to have an enormous impact on lawyers, policy-makers, and the public at large. The vibrant specialty of environmental law practiced in many nations is influencing the forms and content of international environmental regulation. Conversely, international environmental aspirations are sometimes galvanizing the adoption of stricter domestic standards.

The evolution of international environmental law was discussed in some detail in Chapter 4(C), as a paradigmatic example of the integration of general principles, customary and treaty sources of international law. There is no need to go over that ground again. Nor is it sensible to merely catalogue the astounding array of international environmental regimes that have been negotiated over the past twenty years. Instead, this Chapter will lay-out some of the broad frameworks for understanding this growing and dynamic area of international law.

International environmental law can best be understood as a group of many interlocking sets of general principles, theoretical assumptions, regulatory models, and enforcement mechanisms. Some of these evolved early in the history of the subject (as in the 1940's at the time of the *Trail Smelter* Arbitration), while others have emerged just recently. Many of these approaches to international environmental law are consistent and harmonious. A handful of them, though, are mutually contradictory, and carry with them the seeds of profound dissonance in effective international environmental management, or, at a minimum, pose the threat of causing substantial doctrinal mischief.

A. Guiding Principles

As was noted in Chapter 4, international environmental law began as a simple supposition, one that was intimately related to notions of State sovereignty: one nation should not use its territory to harm the interests of another nation in its territory. This was known as the *sic utere tuo ut alienum non laedas* principle (a notion that was significant also for the development of strict liability rules in Anglo–American law). In the context of the *Trail Smelter* Arbitration, the adoption of this principle pretty much dictated the result of the case, even though it was unprecedented in international law at that time.

But the "do no harm" principle, while useful for purposes of State Responsibility for trans-boundary harms, did not give much guidance for other forms of environmental damage. That is why international law enunciated in the 1970's the notion of "the *polluter pays*," an explicit recognition that environmental contamination was a type of "externality" that one nation could impose on another. The purpose of international law was thus to remove that artificial and unfair burdening. In this way, the international environment was seen as the ultimate international common space, a true global commons. After reports of nuclear fall-out or acid raid or a shrinking ozone layer, no country could hope to insulate itself from the effects of environmental degradation.

Yet all of this debate was focused on pollution and trans-boundary harms as being the only things worthy of regulation in international environmental law. By the 1980's, it was realized that other environmental risks and values had to be addressed. One of these was the proper way to plan human activities that had an affect on the environment. This gave rise to a procedural approach of mandating appropriate environmental impact assessment before certain activities were allowed to proceed. Modeled on the U.S. National Environmental Policy Act (NEPA), this has become a standard tool in international law. A contentious issue today is how to factor-in uncertainty in this process. If a planner is not sure whether a particular activity might be dangerous to the environment, should it be allowed to go forward and hope for the best? A number of international environmental instruments promote the use of the *precautionary principle* (or its less rigorous counterpart, the "precautionary approach"), which requires that, when in doubt, protective concerns should prevail and permission for the activity should be denied.

All of this enriched the central principled debate in international environmental law in the 1990's and today: the relationship between economic development and environmental protection. How far is international law prepared to go in sacrificing economic growth for a cleaner environment? Conservation may be a worthwhile virtue for the developed world of North America, Europe and Pacific Rim, regions that have already polluted their way to prosperity. For the developing world, economic growth and environmental protection may be inimical. The two have attempted to be reconciled in the notion of *sustainable development*, the idea of managing economic growth in a way that is consistent with long-term environmental health. Some countries, however, have been intensely skeptical that this is achievable.

That leads to the ultimate question for many international environmental lawyers: what is it that we wish to protect? For the drafters of the 1972 Stockholm Declaration on the Human Environment, the answer was that environmental protection was for the benefit of mankind. A cleaner environment was a better one for human beings. No mention was made in the Declaration that it was worthwhile to protect nature for nature's sake, or to preserve habitats for animals or plants, or just that human beings were custodians for the Earth's environment. The 1982 World Charter for Nature attempted to address this imbalance in thinking. At the same time, discussions about *inter-generational equity*—ensuring that the world's resources would be available to future generations—were also prevalent. The latest focus of thinking on the global environment, generated by the 1992 Rio Declaration on Environment and Development, has been to integrate anthropocentric ideas of environmental protection with concerns for nature's own integrity and cohesion.

B. Approaches to International Environmental Protection

If all of this discussion of theories and principles seems empty, you are not alone. One of the difficulties of international environmental law has not so much been the lack of State practice and government initiative to address pressing environmental concerns (there has been plenty of both), but a real paucity of political will and legal imagination in confronting those problems where there are hard choices to be made. The lack of a coherent theory or purpose to environmental protection complicates this task. Especially for a relatively new field of international law, this is a problem. International lawyers have contributed to these discussions by assisting in the adoption of a number of different approaches to manage environmental conflicts.

1. *Liability and Compensation Regimes.* The most obvious, and lawyerly, approach to international environmental management is to simply make all the questions turn on answers of State Responsibility. This tends to vindicate the adage: "If your only tool is a hammer, every problem looks like a nail." While the fashioning of liability regimes for environmental damage seems alluring as a mechanism to reduce those harms, it has proven most difficult in practice.

For starters, liability and compensation regimes are notoriously difficult to negotiate. States are obviously reluctant to make rules that will require themselves to pay for their environmental misdeeds. Nor have background rules of customary international law helped in this process. There is a substantial division in authority regarding the relevant standard of liability for environmental harms. Language in the *Trail Smelter* Arbitration is suggestive of a strict liability standard, provided that the damage is of "serious consequence" and the injury is established by "clear and convincing evidence."[1] The 1972 Stockholm Declaration was also indicative of a possible strict liability standard. But other sources, including the World Court's 1949 *Corfu Channel* Case,[2] might stand for the proposition that a State must be aware that it is causing environmental damage and fail to take steps to halt it. This would be more consistent with a fault, or negligence, standard of liability.

There have been a number of treaties creating liability and compensation regimes featuring strict liability. These have included conventions on oil pollution from tankers (the 1969 Civil Liability Convention for Oil Pollution Damage), nuclear power (the 1960 Paris Convention on Third–Party Liability for Nuclear Energy and the 1963 Vienna Convention on Civil Liability for Nuclear Damage), hazardous waste transport (the protocol to the 1989 Basle Convention on Control of Transboundary Movements of Hazardous Wastes and their Disposal), and a proposed scheme for genetically modified organisms (being negotiated pursuant to the Biodiversity Convention). These treaties have one thing in common: they all impose liability against private actors that are involved in these risky endeavors. States are not directly the subject of these regimes. Indeed, where State actors *can* be expected to have the greatest exposure to international liability, such regimes are unlikely to be negotiated. (Discussions to create a liability system for activities affecting the Antarctic environment have languished for years, as has the ILC's efforts to create a generic instrument on this subject.)

Quite apart from the standard of liability under these regimes, another aspect of many of these treaties is the establishment of compensation funds. Contributions are typically made to these funds by private entities engaged in the risky activity (for example, shipping oil or hazardous chemicals by sea). In the event of an environmental incident, there is a ready source of funds to compensate States and private actors that attempt to respond to the accident or that incur damages. Liability and compensation regimes also make use of insurance markets by requiring that entities engaging in high-risk activities carry sufficient coverage to compensate others in the event of an accident.

1. See 3 U.N. Rep. Int'l Arb. Awards   2. 1949 I.C.J. 4 (U.K. v. Alb.).
at 1965.

2. *Duties to Consult and Notify.* Closely related to the approach of imposing liability and ensuring compensation for environmental damage is the idea of creating a separate international duty for States to consult and notify other nations about environmental issues and emergencies. Such a duty has been inferred from general principles and customary international law for many years. The arbitral tribunal's 1957 decision in the *Lac Lanoux* Case[3] certainly emphasized the requirement of co-riparian States to consult and negotiate in good faith concerning their mutual water resources.

Some treaties have specifically codified this duty. After the Chernobyl atomic reactor disaster in April 1986, there was international outrage at the Soviet Union's failure to promptly notify European States of the impending nuclear fall-out. In what was probably a record of some sort, in *six months* the International Atomic Energy Agency (IAEA) in Vienna had concluded a Convention on the Early Notification of a Nuclear Accident. This treaty set forth the kinds of disclosure that are required with nuclear accidents, and also provided for the submission of disputes to the World Court.

If anything, the duty to consult and notify is part of a larger phenomenon in international environmental law-making: the international community is taking steps to address a problem only after an authentic disaster. This kind of "crisis" diplomacy and style of legal negotiation is not, however, an optimal way to proceed in making a cohesive body of international law.

3. *Qualitative Standards.* So far we have not discussed what is usually considered the defining characteristic of domestic environmental regulation: actual limits on pollutants or otherwise adverse activities. This approach assumes it is always easy to identify something as a "pollutant" and regulate accordingly. This is not always so. Taking one example, the international community has recently become concerned with the problem of "exotic species"—plants and animals that are accidentally or intentionally relocated from one part of the world to another. Without natural predators or a defined ecological niche, these species can propagate out of control. But is that pollution? (International agreements, including the 1982 Law of the Sea Treaty and the ILC's new convention on international watercourses, suggest it might be.)

Once the decision is made to identify something as pollution, and to control it, that is just the beginning of the battle. For at odds are two very different approaches to qualitative environmental standards. One is to set precise emission limits; for example, the tons of sulfur dioxide (SO^2) or nitrogen oxide (NO^x) belched by smokestack industry. The other tack is to set targets of environ-

---

3. 12 U.N. Rep. Int'l Arb. Awards
281 (Fr. v. Sp.) (1957).

mental quality. So if SO^2 causes "acid rain," then such a target might be to increase the amount of healthy forests which could otherwise be adversely affected by that kind of pollution. Both of these approaches have been employed in international environmental law.

In what is probably the most contentious cluster of issues for international environmental protection—preservation of the global atmosphere—emission controls are commonly used to combat acid rain (long-range air pollution), ozone depletion, and global warming (caused by carbon dioxide (CO^2) build-up). For each of these three problems, international action began tentatively. Usually the first step was the negotiation of a "framework accord," which articulated a basic set of goals, created the means of collecting scientific data, and established a rudimentary institutional structure (usually annual or biennial meetings of the Parties). Such agreements included the 1979 Convention on Long–Range Transboundary Air Pollution, the 1985 Vienna Convention on the Protection of the Ozone Layer, and the 1992 U.N. Framework Convention on Climate Change.

The next step in the process—usually within a few years—is the negotiation of precise emission reductions by States Parties. The 1987 Montreal Protocol directed reduction of ozone depleting chemicals (ODCs), substances that degraded the earth's protective layer of ozone (which blocks out harmful radiation from space). Likewise, the 1997 Kyoto Protocol set a 6 percent reduction by States of outputs of "greenhouse gases" (like emissions from automobiles, "dirty" industries, and other sources) from 1990 levels, this to be achieved by 2012. One point of controversy about these specific agreements (which have been subject to constant updating and amendment) is that the emission standards are unevenly applied. Known as a "double-standard," nations from the poorer, developing world are exempted from meeting the specified targets. Obviously, this was a critical concession made to win the approval of these nations, but it is part of a larger pattern in international environmental law-making that creates two tiers of obligations. The admonition that States take those measures as may be necessary, "to the extent practicable under the circumstances," is viewed as a license to simply ignore these standards.

4. *Permitting Schemes.* Closely analogous to qualitative standards for pollution prevention is the regulation of hazardous activities through permitting schemes. Typically an international convention would identify an activity (or range of activities) that might potentially have dangerous effects, classify those consequences, and then impose review and permission procedures. A paradigm of this approach was the 1972 London Dumping Convention which requires that States Parties scrutinize proposed ocean dumping of

different kinds of substances. Depending on whether the material is to be found on one of three lists—"black" (prohibited altogether), "grey" (allowed, but with substantial restrictions), or "white" (allowed, with few or no restrictions)—a permit would be granted.

This scheme has been recently followed in the 1989 Basle Convention on Transboundary Movements of Hazardous Wastes, as well the 2000 Cartagena Protocol on genetically modified organisms. There have also been proposals for a general regime requiring "prior-informed consent" (PIC) for shipments of a wide array of chemicals, pesticides and other substances. Permitting systems, especially when linked to environmental assessment (whether or not precautionary in thrust), can produce positive results.

The most ambitious plan of this ilk is to be found in the 1997 Kyoto Convention, which set forth a scheme for tradeable permits in greenhouse gases. Under this system, each nation would be allocated a set amount of "rights" to emit CO^2 and other gases. Those nations that quickly imposed domestic restrictions on energy consumption, or which grew more forests to counteract warming, or which developed new technologies to address these issues, would not use all of their rights. Such countries could then market their tradeable permits to more profligate States and reap the profits. Over time, the total number of rights would be decreased, thus moving the entire world into compliance with the internationally-set targets. How well this scheme will work remain to be seen. The exact modalities have yet to be negotiated, and there remains substantial objections from many developed States (including the United States) which produce most of the world's global warming gases.

All of this illustrates the obvious point that international environmental law-making will only be as strong and vibrant as domestic enforcement. State Responsibility mechanisms aside, international environmental protection is dependent on domestic monitoring, regulatory, and oversight capacities, far more than other areas of legal regulation. One example might be increased surveillance by flag States or port States to combat marine pollution from poorly-operated vessels. Almost all of the permitting schemes and environmental impact assessments contemplated by many treaties will be undertaken by the States whose nationals or corporations want to engage in certain activities.

5. *Habitat and Species Protection.* So far, the emphasis of this discussion has been on the role of international environmental law to reduce pollution and other forms of trans-boundary harms. Actually, a significant aspect of environmental protection has been species and habitat protection. Protecting wildlife has been a goal of international environmental law from its infancy. There have been

treaties on preventing poaching in Africa, whaling, and a host of species-specific accords (polar bears, Antarctic seals, and Andean vicuña have all merited their own conventions). With the alarming rate of habitat loss—through unchecked population growth, toppling tropical rainforests, and filling of wetlands—species extinction has accelerated.

International law has thus come to focus more and more on habitat protection. Beginning with the 1972 World Heritage Convention, States have been invited to establish internationally-recognized wildlife habitats. The Heritage Convention (along with the 1971 Ramsar Convention on Wetlands) has States Parties designate particular areas for international protection. These have been held by domestic courts to be binding on the host States. For example, the High Court of Australia ruled in 1983 that the listing of large areas of wilderness on the island of Tasmania, under the Heritage Convention, effectively blocked plans for a major hydroelectric dam project.[4]

Efforts to advance habitat protection reached their culmination in the 1992 U.N. Convention on Biological Diversity. (This instrument, along with the Framework Convention on Climate Change and a blueprint of international environmental action ("Agenda 21") were all signed at the 1992 Rio Conference on Environment and Development.) Negotiation of the Biodiversity Convention pitted States which are hosts for special ecosystems (tropical rainforest countries like Brazil, Costa Rica, Indonesia, and Congo) against "consumers" of those resources, countries dependent on tropical hardwoods or pharmaceutical products developed from native plants or indigenous peoples' knowledge. The Convention attempts to define "biological resources" as broadly covering any real or potential use of genetic information, organisms, populations or ecosystems.

The heart of the Biodiversity Convention's obligations is the duty of States, similar to that in the Heritage Convention, to protect biodiverse regions, species and ecosystems in place *("in-situ")*. Environmental impact assessments are mandated, and financial aid to biodiversity "source" countries is extended. The most controversial provisions of the Convention are those granting source States absolute sovereignty over genetic resources found in their biodiverse areas and those mandating forced technology transfers and surrender of intellectual property rights by nationals of other States who wish to gain access to those resources. The essence of these provisions is that if a nation's rainforest yields a

---

4. See *Commonwealth of Australia v.*   (H.C. 1983) (Austl.).
State of Tasmania, 57 Austl. L. Rep. 450

disease-resistant food crop or a cure for cancer, then that State should benefit.

This Convention (which the United States has signed, but not yet ratified) has thus been criticized as being generous in its grant of rights to source States of biodiversity, but deficient in its requirements that these nations take real steps to protect those resources. The intellectual property provisions of this Convention are, in essence, a partition strategy for this resource. By giving a property interest in the commercial value of species and genetic data derived from biodiverse regions, the hope is that host States will have an incentive to take better care of those resources, which will benefit them and all humanity. Variations of this plan have been used to promote many forms of wildlife protection. One such idea is giving "ownership" over elephants in Africa to particular tribes or villages, thus virtually eliminating the poaching that was common when herds were government-managed in nature reserves.

6. *Environment and Trade.* The most potent tool for protection of species, and of the entire environment, is linking enforcement mechanisms to the global trading order (discussed in the next Chapter). The first, path-breaking, international instrument to do this was the 1973 Convention on International Trade in Endangered Species (CITES). CITES' solution to the problem of rampant poaching of endangered animals and harvesting of rare plants was also economic—remove incentives for profit by eliminating the trade in these items. States Parties to CITES have adopted a form of permitting system discussed above. Depending on whether a species is currently threatened with extinction (Appendix I listing), or may be threatened in the future (Appendix II), or is simply subject to protection by one or more States (Appendix III), certain trade restrictions will apply. Appendix I is essentially a "black list," barring the movement of specimens of that species, except for specific research purposes. Appendix II and III restrictions are more modest, but each requires a high level of "transparency," in which importers of specimens are required to procure the necessary permits.

CITES has been hailed as an international law success story, and, indeed, it has managed to control some of the worst forms of abuse. Poaching of African elephants, for example, has dropped because the trade of ivory, irrespective of source, has been banned. This has caused problems, though, for the handful of countries that manage elephant herds on the proprietary model mentioned above. Villages that had been conserving herds, and expecting the proceeds from sales of ivory "harvested" from animals which die of natural causes, have been bitterly disappointed. In any event, CITES' trade strategy for environmental protection has been replicated in a vast network of agreements, ranging in subjects from sales of tropical timber to high seas fish stocks.

Today at least, the global trade regime has been bitterly criticized by environmental advocates who maintain that it unnecessarily punishes the unilateral acts of environmentally progressive nations. When the United States charged import restrictions on tuna caught by foreign fishermen with insufficient regard for the safety of dolphins (which swim with tuna and are often killed when nets are thrown), the affected nations sought relief before the institutions of the General Agreement on Tariffs and Trade (GATT) and, later, the World Trade Organization (WTO). In a series of decisions,[5] GATT/WTO panels have ruled that nations may not unilaterally impose trade restrictions on tuna caught with dolphin (or shrimp caught with turtles), nor may they unreasonably require heightened environmental protection as a condition for trading in their markets (such as rules against certain fuel additives or hormones in beef).

The difficulty of all this is that much recent international environmental law-making has been made by progressive States, with the international community following behind. WTO's requirement that environmental restrictions on trade can only be imposed *multilaterally* may delay some needed innovations. However, it will ensure that, once consensus is reached, effective international enforcement through global trade disciplines will be available.

7. *Environment and Human Rights.* An individual's right to a clean and healthy environment has been recognized as a "third-generation" right for some time (see Chapter 9(A)). But so far, at least, this approach to environmental protection remains relatively untested. With the exception of a handful of cases brought under the Alien Tort Statute in U.S. courts,[6] there have been virtually no opportunities for tribunals to rule on whether a government's wholesale destruction of habitat or general degradation of the environment rises to the level of an actionable human rights abuse.

A right to environment may, however, be a potent human rights claim for indigenous peoples. Given the practices of many developing nations of destroying large swathes of tropical rainforest or of impinging on native hunting grounds or religious sites, at least a few human rights institutions[7] have recognized this as a significant issue.

---

5. See *GATT Panel Decision—Restriction on Imports of Tuna*, 30 Int'l Legal Materials 1594 (1991); *United States—Import Prohibition of Certain Shrimp and Shrimp Products* (WTO App. Oct. 12, 1998), 38 id. 118, 174 (1999); *EC Measures Concerning Meat and Meat Products (Hormones)*, 1998 WL 25520 (W.T.O. App. Jan. 16, 1998).

6. See *Beanal v. Freeport–McMoran, Inc.*, 197 F.3d 161 (5th Cir. 1999); *Doe v. UNOCAL Corp.*, 963 F. Supp. 880 (C.D. Cal. 1997).

7. See *Yanomami Tribe* Case, No. 7615, Inter–Am. Comm. H.R. 24, OEA/ser.L.V./11.66 doc. 10, rev. 1 (1985).

The combination of traditional international law doctrines of State Responsibility and human rights—along with new forms of international environmental management (through qualitative standards, permitting schemes, and trade enforcement)—will continue to revolutionize international environmental practice. As a source of potential topics for international legal regulation, the global environment is virtually limitless. As the environment is the ultimate resource that the international community holds in common, international law offers a critical combination of law-making capacity, decision-making institutions, and enforcement mechanisms to manage this issue.

Chapter 13

International Economic Law

The last broad area of legitimate international legal regulation—our final "object" of international law—is the global economy. Although it might be peculiar to think of the international economy as a global "resource," it can certainly be regarded as a network of facilities and understandings promoting commerce and trade and, as such, is a central topic of international relations. The phrase "international economic law" subsumes a host of issues. At a minimum, it includes (1) the background rules of private international commerce, (2) the architecture of the global trading and monetary systems, and (3) the principles for international development and investment. These will be considered briefly in turn.

1. *International Commercial Law.* The traditional body of rules for transnational commerce by land and sea derived from the medieval *lex mercatoria* and *lex maritima*. In a sense, this may be the international law with the oldest pedigree today. Such rules were the product of expediency and necessity; merchants needed certainty in their operations and transactions across national frontiers. Today, this law has been developed through such public institutions as the U.N. Commission on International Trade Law (UNCITRAL), the Hague Conference on Private International Law, and the Rome International Institute for the Unification of Private International Law ("Unidroit"). Moreover, NGOs of merchants (and the lawyers who serve them) have exercised substantial influence in making transnational commercial law, including such institutions as the International Chamber of Commerce (ICC) and Comité Maritime International (CMI).

The critical documents of international commercial law today would probably include the 1980 U.N. Convention on Contracts for the International Sale of Goods (CISG). This was broadly conceived as an international version of Article 2 of the United States' Uniform Commercial Code (UCC), at least as applied to the sale of goods abroad. However, the CISG rules depart to an appreciable degree from those found in the UCC. Something every commercial lawyer in the United States should be aware of is that the CISG rules will prevail over those in the UCC for any contract made by an American party with someone from a CISG signatory, unless a contrary provision is made in the contract. (Other specific aspects

141

of rules in the CISG will usually be considered in courses and volumes on International Business Transactions.)

Another aspect of international commercial law is the manner of resolving disputes between merchants over the execution of contracts or transactions they have entered into. Thus was born the vibrant practice field of international commercial arbitration. Instead of depending on the vagaries of the judicial system of one of the contracting parties to resolve disputes, many contracts will select an international commercial arbitration institution that will serve as the forum for the dispute resolution. Such forums include the ICC in Paris, and arbitration centers in New York, London, Stockholm, and elsewhere. The availability of commercial arbitration for international disputes now makes it a necessity for any lawyer negotiating a contract with a foreign business entity to include a provision selecting one such institution in the event of a dispute, and, just as importantly, selecting a law to be applied by that arbitration.

The success of international commercial arbitration depends, however, on two factors: (1) the uniformity and predictability of procedures used in the arbitral proceedings, and (2) the availability of a certain means of enforcing arbitral awards and collection of judgments. International law has provided the answers to both these concerns. The first is in the form of the UNCITRAL Model Arbitration Rules. These have set the standard for what is considered procedural due process in arbitral settings, as well as providing rules on such nettlesome questions as evidence and burdens of proof. Although each international commercial arbitral institution has its own set of rules, each will typically follow the UNCITRAL model, which, for example, was adopted nearly verbatim by the Iran–U.S. Claims Tribunal.

As for the enforcement of international commercial arbitral awards, that was provided for in the 1958 New York Convention on the Recognition and Enforcement of Foreign Arbitral Awards. The New York Convention requires that arbitral awards rendered in one State Party to the Convention will be enforced by the courts of other Parties, with only certain, narrow exceptions. (Some countries have taken significant reservations to the New York Convention's obligations, which complicates enforcement in some situations.) This allows commercial entities to rely on arbitration around the world, with the confidence that the assets of the losing party will be available to pay any awards.

2. *International Trade and Monetary Law.* What makes the vast and growing network of private commercial relations across national boundaries possible is the global system of trade and monetary liberalization. This system is manifestly the domain of

public international law and has been the subject of treaties and custom for two centuries or more.

States have always competed in the global marketplace, and have attempted to seek legal advantages and benefits. The primary thrust of this competition has been in the area of *tariffs*—import taxes imposed on foreign goods in order to make them less attractive to domestic buyers. Along with *quotas* (quantitative limits on certain imports) and certain qualitative restrictions, tariffs are the main tool of trade protectionism. The United States, when it has been of a mind to reduce protection and promote free trade (and there have been many periods where it has not been so disposed), has relied on a network of Friendship, Commerce and Navigation (FCN) Treaties. These instruments (already mentioned in Chapter 8(A)), extend "national treatment" and certain trade benefits to the other Party, on the basis of mutuality and reciprocity. They were often combined with "most favored nation" (MFN) clauses, a promise that the United States would extend the same trade terms to the other Party that it was prepared to give our most favored trading partners.

After the experience of the global Depression of the 1930's, which was brought on in large measure by rampant trade protectionism in Europe and the United States, plans were made at the conclusion of the Second World War to create a new global trading regime. The original idea was to establish an International Trade Organization (ITO) that would serve as a central clearinghouse for the liberalization of import rules; that is, reduction of tariffs and quotas and other non-tariff trade barriers. Delegates met at the Bretton Woods Conference (in New Hampshire) in 1944, and were able to fashion the two other critical institutions of a new economic order: the International Monetary Fund (IMF) and the International Bank for Reconstruction and Development (World Bank). Additional negotiations occurred at Havana in 1948, but the third leg of this new regime, the ITO, was politically unacceptable for many nations (including the United States). Instead, an interim trade agreement was contemplated, which later came to be known as the General Agreement on Tariffs and Trade (GATT).

The GATT regime persisted for over 50 years, until 1994, when (at long last) the institutional framework originally contemplated for international trade regulation was achieved with the creation of the World Trade Organization (WTO). The reality is that the substantive trade rules of the new WTO are largely identical to those of the earlier GATT regime. That is why the world trade order is sometimes referred to as "GATT/WTO." The heart of the GATT system was simply a multilateral version of the U.S. most-favored nation clause—all GATT signatories got the advantage of the low tariffs and other rules concluded at the successive sets, or

"Rounds," of negotiations. (These took the name of a significant host or personage, hence the "Geneva," "Kennedy," "Tokyo" and "Uruguay" Rounds.) With the establishment of the WTO, these negotiations to reduce tariffs, quotas, subsidies, dumping, other trade barriers, and abusive practices are now held on a regular basis.

Again, the key elements of GATT/WTO are substantive trade equality and dispute settlement mechanisms. The MFN requirement of GATT Article I ensured a level-playing field for Parties. At the same time, GATT/WTO featured very precise rules on other subjects. Quantitative restrictions on imports (quotas) were banned under Article XI, although there were always lingering restrictions on products in the agriculture, textile, and national defense sectors. GATT/WTO features a number of provisions (including Article XVII) that attempt to treat developed and developing nations in different ways (this was the same problem of double-standards for environmental regulation, mentioned in the last Chapter). A Code adopted in 1979, for example, allowed developing nations to continue with government subsidies for export commodities or other products, a practice that would be impermissible for developed States. (A WTO dispute settlement panel ruled in 2000 that the United States' program of tax benefits for foreign sales corporations (FSCs) was in violation of GATT/WTO standards.) Lastly, GATT/WTO's rules against "dumping" (the practice of one nation temporarily selling goods at below cost in another State in order to later eliminate competition), have been unevenly applied to developed and developing nations. Controversies about dumping and subsidies (and their antidotes, countervailing and anti-dumping duties) have been among the most contentious under U.S. trade law.

There are a few areas where GATT/WTO does not purport to regulate. For example, nothing in the global trade regime is contrary to commodity agreements, where importer and exporter nations for a particular product consult and influence prices and supplies. (One such agreement, involving tin and the International Tin Council, raised an issue of international institutional liability, discussed in Chapter 6.) Also, Article XX of GATT/WTO allows trading nations some exercise of discretion for trade restrictions in certain areas or in accordance with special sorts of domestic legislation. (Article XX was invoked by the U.S. in support of its environmental legislation affecting tuna and shrimp imports, but this argument was rejected by WTO panels.) Finally, the current WTO regime (under Article XXIV) allows member States to form customs unions and free-trade areas. Under this provision, the European Union is considered a customs union, and North America (under NAFTA) a free-trade area. As long as these special trade regimes do not interfere with global goals of trade liberalization, they are permitted.

With the 1994 creation of the WTO came two new substantive initiatives for global trade, long-advocated by the United States and other advanced market nations. Traditionally, the emphasis of GATT had been products and commodities (from rolled steel to pigs feet). Starting in the 1970's, much of the global economy and of transnational commerce shifted to the service economy (including financial services, insurance, air transport, shipping, construction, telecommunications, information technology, and tourism). (In 1995, global exports amounted to $4.3 trillion, of which 60 percent was in manufactures, 19 percent in services, and the balance in mining and agriculture. Later figures suggest that the share of services has grown appreciably.) The General Agreement on Trade in Services (GATS) was intended to address this area of global trade, although it may be too early to evaluate its performance. Likewise, concerns regarding rampant piracy of patents, copyrights, and trademarks held by developed-nation entities galvanized the negotiations on an Agreement on Trade–Related Aspects of Intellectual Property Rights (TRIPS). TRIPS integrates trade mechanisms for protecting established IP rights under various international conventions (such as the 1971 Berne Convention and those negotiated by the World Intellectual Property Organization (WIPO) in Geneva).

The ultimate feature of GATT/WTO is its ability to fairly resolve trade disputes. This had been a constant criticism of the old GATT system, as trade abusers were often able to avoid sanctions. Indeed, to the extent that GATT attempted to avoid unilateral trade retaliations and sanctions, it was often unsuccessful. The new WTO has some institutional machinery to resolve this problem. Dispute settlement panels are available for expeditious trade litigation, with an appellate review process. The panel decisions are now self-executing and do not require political approval by the Ministerial Conference (where, previously, the trade malefactor could simply veto sanctions against itself).

Where WTO has not been successful is in the transparency of its rule-making and dispute-settlement processes. The virtual entirety of WTO proceedings are closed to public view. NGOs have almost no access, and decisions are often presented as a *fait accompli*. Recent protests over WTO actions (as with the demonstrations at the Ministerial Conference in Seattle) are as much about the perceived threats of globalization to national economies (and impacts on jobs and State regulatory power) as they are about the lack of openness and political accountability of WTO conduct.

The activities of the International Monetary Fund (IMF) have been no less controversial in their own way. The IMF's charge, under the Bretton Woods Agreement, is to provide structural guidance to the world economy by providing a multilateral system of payments between member nations and to eliminate currency controls and exchange rate regulations. The IMF successfully nudged national economies from fixed to floating exchange rates for convertible currencies. (This is what makes it possible to conduct most international business with a reduced concern for exchange rate fluctuations.) The IMF ensures monetary liquidity of its members by accounting for their available reserves, expressed in an artificial unit of currency known as Special Drawing Rights (SDRs). The permissibility of certain forms of exchange restrictions have proven vexatious, and have been challenged in U.S. courts.[1]

But the most controversial role for the IMF is its involvement in international balance-of-payment emergencies, when a State can no longer meet its debt obligations or required payment schedules. In such circumstances, the Fund will offer facilities and arrangements for credit. But this comes with a catch. Known as "conditionality," the IMF may insist on a currency devaluation (which will make exports more attractive, but will be ruinous for importers and for wages) or other structural economic reforms. Although these conditions for loans are legally unenforceable, recipient States dare not defy them for fear of being refused loans or facilities in the future.

3. *International Development and Investment.* The ultimate goal of international economic law should be the raising of standards of living for all peoples in all countries. International law attempts to achieve this goal through a number of very different mechanisms.

As has already been mentioned, a third-generation human "right" to development can probably only be charitably described as inchoate. Despite calls for a New International Economic Order in the 1960's and 1970's, as well as a host of U.N. General Assembly Resolutions—including the 1974 Charter of Economic Rights and Duties—it would be inaccurate to believe that developed States regard themselves as being under an international legal obligation to transfer wealth to the Third World. Nevertheless, there are a host of international development agreements. These include bilateral agreements for foreign aid. There are also multilateral schemes for assistance, import preferences, and technology transfer. (The series of Lomé Agreements made between the European Union and African, Caribbean, and Pacific nations is one

1. See *Banco Frances e Brasileiro SA v. Doe,* 36 N.Y.2d 592 (1975); *Libra Bank Ltd. v. Banco Nacional de Costa Rica,* 570 F. Supp. 870 (S.D.N.Y. 1983).

example of this.) There are also a bevy of U.N. agencies committed to development issues.

Another approach is institutional. The World Bank—the last of the contemplated triad of Bretton Woods international economic organizations—is the leader in this regard. After World War II, the lending thrust of the Bank was reconstruction; today, it is granting loans to developing nations for infrastructure projects. The World Bank Group actually consists of three separate entities: the World Bank proper (which makes loans to countries in good debt standing and under precise lending conditions), the International Finance Corporation (IFC) (which provides venture capital to private businesses), and the International Development Association (IDA) (which gives concessionary loans to the world's poorest countries). Using forms of government guarantees, the Bank attempts to find private lenders at attractive interest rates.

The Word Bank's policies, like those of the IMF, have been controversial. Just as the IMF's conditionality requirements have engendered resentment, so too have the World Bank's rules of "surveillance" as part of the loan packages. More than that, there have been criticisms—especially from human rights and environmental advocates—that many of the projects that have received World Bank financing have been ill-conceived, or worse. In response to this criticism, the World Bank created in 1993 an Inspection Panel charged with hearing complaints about Bank projects and raising them with Bank management. The Panel also monitors whether the projects the Bank finances are actually consistent with its policies. Although still in its nascent stages, Panel decisions[2] allow for increased input by NGOs into the secretive lending and development practices of multilateral financial institutions.

Issues surrounding the promotion and protection of international investment flows are very much part of the international economic law of development. They have already been intensively considered in the context of State Responsibility and diplomatic protection for foreign investment in a host country (see Chapter 8). As was already noted, the substantive standards of compensation for host State expropriations or nationalizations have shifted over time. We have today returned to a form of the prompt, adequate and effective compensation standard enunciated by the United States in the early part of the 20th century. It is important to realize that there has been no multilateral codification of this principle of investment protection, although it has been enshrined in various FCNs, as well as Bilateral Investment Treaties (BITs).

---

2. See, e.g., Inspection Panel, Request for Inspection—Bangladesh: Jute Sector Adjustment Credit 2567–BD, Panel Report and Recommendation, World Bank Doc. INSP/R97–3 (Mar. 20, 1997).

Some international economic institutions and facilities are available for the promotion of foreign investment. Perhaps the most important of these is the practice of investment guarantees. This is a form of "political risk" insurance which is underwritten at the time an investment is made in a host country against the risks that the investment will later be nationalized (expropriation coverage), or that the proceeds of the investment cannot be repatriated (inconvertibility coverage), or that the investment will otherwise be affected by negative political developments in that host State. Investment guarantees can be offered through private insurers (Lloyd's of London, for example), by multilateral institutions (the Multilateral Investment Guarantee Agency (MIGA) of the World Bank), or by domestic governmental units (the Overseas Private Investment Corporation (OPIC) in the United States). Although political risk insurance premiums are not cheap, an international lawyer would always counsel a client making a foreign investment to carefully consider such coverage.

Another institution that is available to promote investment is a centralized forum for the resolution of investment disputes. Created by the World Bank in 1965, the International Centre for the Settlement of Investment Disputes (ICSID) in Washington remains a favored choice by both foreign investors and host nations. Its jurisdiction is often invoked in forum selection clauses found in overseas investment or infrastructure contracts. Its growing use indicates a desire by investment host nations to provide regular and predictable dispute settlement. Although some ICSID panel decisions have been controversial,[3] it remains a respected forum. ICSID is currently used as the facility for investment disputes under NAFTA and other free trade regimes.

The multi-faceted aspects of international economic law will continue to preoccupy international lawyers. Whether it is structuring profitable international commercial transactions for their clients, or arbitrating disputes arising from those contracts, or litigating trade disputes on behalf of aggrieved trade associations or governments, or negotiating sovereign debt, or underwriting guarantees for foreign investment, the practice opportunities may be limitless. International law may, indeed, have the greatest potential for progress and effectiveness in this field. It remains to be seen, however, whether the primary institutions of international economic law can overcome their historic tendency for a lack of transparency, and whether a new openness will mean better law and procedures for the global trading, financial, monetary and investment regimes.

3. See *AGIP v. Popular Republic of the Congo,* 21 Int'l Legal Materials 726 (1982) (ICSID 1979); *Benvenuti et Bonfant v. People's Republic of the Congo,* 21 id. 740 (ICSID 1982); *AMCO Asia Corp. v. Republic of Indonesia,* 25 id. 1439 (1986) (ICSID 1986).

PART THREE

INTERNATIONAL LAW AND U.S. LAW

Chapter 14

International Law and Domestic Law

The relationship between domestic law (sometimes called "municipal law" in European nations) and international law is subtle and complex. As has already been suggested in this volume, much of international law depends for its success on enforcement through national legal systems. International environmental standards, for example, are often actuated through domestic regulation. International human rights aspirations are practically enforced through municipal civil rights laws.

This Part of the volume examines the intricate connection between international and domestic law. After some introductory material in this Chapter, the focus shifts to very specific aspects of the role of international law rules in the United States. This is sometimes referred to as the "Foreign Relations Law" of the United States, but it is really part and parcel of the broad sweep of international legal studies.

Among the issues considered in this Part are the hierarchy of international law sources (particularly custom and treaties) in relation to established principles of constitutional, statutory, administrative, and judicial law-making. Next to be reviewed, in Chapter 15, will be aspects of treaty-making and domestic enforcement of obligations contained in international agreements concluded by the United States. Then, the manner in which the United States asserts jurisdiction over various kinds of persons, entities, status relationships, transactions, and occurrences will be discussed (see Chapter 16). Lastly, the many ways that international law creates immunities to a domestic legal system's assertion of jurisdiction (such as foreign sovereign immunity and diplomatic immunity) will be reviewed (Chapter 17). Again, while the thrust of the discussion in this Part is United States' practice, some examples will be drawn from that of other countries in order to provide a well-rounded understanding of the practical integration of international law rules in domestic legal systems.

A. Domestic Law in International Law

Before turning to these issues, it needs to be borne in mind that international law is substantially influenced by domestic law. That predisposition might be manifested by the elevation of general principles of national law "recognized by civilized nations" as a source of international legal obligation (see Chapter 2(A)). Precise rules of domestic law may be interpreted and applied by international tribunals in disputes between States. In other words, the relationship between international law and domestic law is a "two-way street." International law's use of municipal law is, however, constrained by a number of important principles.

The first of these is that a State typically may not invoke a provision of national law as the basis for refusing to perform an international legal obligation. As U.S. Secretary of State Bayard observed in 1887, "if a Government could set up its own municipal laws as the final test of its international rights and obligations, then the rules of international law would be but the shadow of a name and would afford no protection either to States or individuals."[1] Many international tribunals have emphatically rejected the arguments of litigant States that their domestic laws somehow "trump" international law.[2] Many international courts have likewise declined to follow an "authoritative" interpretation of a custom or treaty, made by one of the disputants (and supported by a decision of a domestic court), preferring to independently construe the practice or agreement. (In one famous example of this, an international arbitration refused to follow the U.S. Supreme Court's rulings condemning certain British vessels as prize during the Civil War.[3])

International law recognizes only a handful of instances where a State may rely on its internal law as a basis for refusing to comply with an ostensible international law obligation. Article 46 of the Vienna Convention on the Law of Treaties (VCLT) provides that when one Party's ratification of an agreement has been made in a way that violates its domestic constitutional law, and such violation was manifest to the other Party or Parties, the treaty is null and void. In a sense, this exception proves the rule that States may not rely on their own national law as a way to evade international legal obligations.

1. [1887] U.S. Foreign Rel. 751.

2. See, e.g., *Case Concerning Certain German Interests in Polish Upper Silesia* (Ger. v. Pol.) (Merits), 1926 P.C.I.J. Ser. A, No. 17; *Case Concerning the Rights of Nationals of the United States of Amer-* *ica in Morocco* (Fr. v. U.S.), 1952 I.C.J. 176.

3. See 4 John Bassett Moore, INTERNATIONAL ARBITRATIONS TO WHICH THE UNITED STATES HAS BEEN A PARTY 3902–3950 (1898).

A second important principle at work on this topic is that international tribunals are free to apply and interpret national law as relevant to the international disputes that come before them. For example, the World Court in the *Brazilian Loans* Case[4] was obliged to rule on that nation's default on certain loans that were supposed to be repaid in French francs. A significant question was the meaning and effect of French legislation governing the payment of debts in gold or gold value. (The case arose just before the global Depression, and many countries were taking their currencies off a gold standard, which obviously affected the value of any debt repayments.) The PCIJ observed that to the extent the Loan Agreement with Brazil made French law binding on this point, the Court was obliged to ascertain what that law was.

Obviously, and this is the point raised just beforehand, an international tribunal will reject a ruling of a domestic court if it is self-serving, fraudulent or erroneous. It should be noted that some international tribunals will go to elaborate lengths to avoid making a decisive ruling in a case based on the national law of one of the disputants. The Iran–United States Claims Tribunal, established after the Iranian Revolution and Hostage Crisis (which began in 1979), was called-upon to resolve many commercial disputes arising from those events. Even though many of the contracts at issue in those cases may have designated Iranian law or the law of a U.S. jurisdiction, the Tribunal typically attempted to derive general principles of international commercial practice (a *lex mercatoria*, mentioned in the last Chapter) and apply those instead. This not only had the affect of avoiding the appearance of the Tribunal applying a source of law that would be distasteful to the losing Party, but also indicating that the basic rules for commercial transactions were common the world around.

B.   International Law in Domestic Law

It must be kept in mind that the international legal system is really indifferent as to *how* international legal obligations are enforced in municipal law, provided they effectively are implemented. There has long been a debate about the incorporation of international law into domestic law. The two sides in this polemic have been given the unfortunate names of *monists* and *dualists*. Reduced to its essentials, *monism* is the idea that international law and domestic law are parts of the same legal system, but that international law is higher in prescriptive value that national law. *Dualism* is the position that international law and municipal law are separate and distinct legal systems which operate on different

4.   1929 P.C.I.J. Ser. A, No. 21 (Fr. v. Braz.).

levels, and that international law can only be enforced in national law if it is incorporated or transformed.

Although the monism/dualism argument is a favorite topic of cocktail conversation among international law academics, it is vital for every international lawyer to understand the significance—and limits—of this discussion. For starters, this debate only matters on the domestic law plane. As I just observed, international law simply does not care how a rule of international law is applied in internal law. International law just assumes that all international obligations are carried out in good faith and that State Responsibility attaches for the failure to observe a rule of custom or treaty. The monism/dualism divide matters only for a particular nation's domestic "housekeeping" for recognizing and applying international law rules.

When framed in that way, this insight is immensely significant. Many international law rules can only be effectively enforced through domestic law mechanisms. It may well matter whether a domestic constitution or statute can "trump" a customary international law or treaty obligation. Today, for example, the chief proponents of the monist position (a direct inclusion of international law rules into domestic legal systems) are human rights advocates. They take this position in the belief that States may otherwise be reluctant to accept into their own law rules that limit their ability to mistreat their own citizens. As I have already suggested (see Chapter 1(B)), the dominant position remains the dualist one, and this is particularly true (as will be seen shortly) for the United States.

Indeed, one would have to look hard for a country that embraces a pure monist posture. The closest may be The Netherlands, the Constitution of which (in Articles 93 and 94) appears to allow international treaties to automatically preempt domestic statutes, and (some have suggested) the Constitution itself. But, interestingly enough, the Dutch Constitution does not allow direct incorporation of customary international law rules. In contrast, a number of constitutions of other European nations allow "general rules of public international law" to take precedence over domestic laws. The German Constitution has such a provision (Article 25), as does Italy's (Article 10(1)) and Austria's (Article 9). So, even for those monist nations, there can be a divide between "treaty monism" (like Holland) and "custom monism" (like that in Germany).

When one looks at the United Kingdom—the paradigm of all common law jurisdictions under a Parliamentary form of democracy—the position radically changes to a dualist one. Although originally British courts recognized that the customary law of nations was "part of the law of England,"[5] by the early 20th century these same courts were declining to incorporate customary principles as a rule of decision, absent clear instructions from Parliament to do so.[6] As for treaty obligations, the British position (often called the "Ponsonby Rule") is that no international agreement has binding effect unless it is implemented into domestic law by an Act of Parliament.

The United States' position on the domestic incorporation of international law is dualist, but differs in many respects from that in Britain. The remainder of this Chapter will explore the general place of international law sources in the hierarchy of United States law. The best way to develop this discussion is to answer four seemingly simple, straight-forward questions.

Question #1—Does international law prevail over the Constitution? The answer to this is an emphatic "no," and for this reason alone the United States qualifies as a dualist nation. Even so, this answer requires some elaboration. For starters, the U.S. Constitution is certainly not silent on matters of international law and foreign relations. Treaty-making powers are allocated, and the effect of international agreements is provided for (to be discussed in the next Chapter). Congress is even granted the power to "define and punish offenses against the law of nations," just as it is permitted to legislate on matters of foreign commerce. The President is given the authority to receive and send ambassadors (necessary for recognition, considered in Chapter 5(B)), as well as being commander-in-chief of the armed forces, even though Congress is given the power to "declare war." Lastly, the federal Judiciary is seemingly given the authority to resolve disputes involving international questions, and is explicitly granted jurisdiction over admiralty and maritime disputes as well as those involving foreign ambassadors.

It is now well-established that neither a rule of customary international law nor a provision of a treaty can abrogate a right granted under the Constitution. In the first such case raising this point, a U.S. court of appeals ruled that a treaty with France giving testimonial immunity to its consuls in U.S. courts had to give way to a criminal defendant's Sixth Amendment rights to confront witnesses.[7] In the leading case, *Reid v. Covert*,[8] the U.S. Supreme Court made in 1957 a ruling concerning an agreement governing the status of U.S. armed forces and their dependents stationed in occupied Germany after World War Two. The treaty provided that

---

5. See *Triquet and Others v. Bath*, 3 Burr. 1478, 97 Eng. Rep. 936 (K.B. 1764) (U.K.).

6. See *Mortensen v. Peters*, 8 Sess. Cas. (5th Ser.) 93 (Scot. 1906) (U.K.).

7. See *In re Dillon*, 7 F. Cas. 710 (C.C.N.D. Cal. 1854) (No. 3,914).

8. 354 U.S. 1 (1957).

the dependents of army personnel were subject to court martial for any crimes committed in Germany. The Supreme Court held that just because this was allowed for in a treaty it could not abrogate the defendants' Sixth Amendment right to a regular jury trial by their peers, not a military court. More recently, the Supreme Court ruled on the status of customary international law and treaty obligations requiring host States to protect the "dignity" of foreign embassies. The Court held that such an international rule (assuming it even existed), could not justify an ordinance that prohibited speech critical of a foreign State within 500 feet of its Washington, D.C. embassy, but that allowed complimentary speech. Such an ordinance violated protesters' free speech rights under the First Amendment.[9]

It is vital to observe, however, that just because the U.S. Supreme Court might rule that a treaty obligation or rule of custom is unconstitutional does *not* necessarily mean that the United States is relieved of its international obligations to fulfill that treaty or custom. The United States' *international* obligations will continue to persist until the custom is changed or the treaty is terminated, but the rule will have no domestic effect. That is a key aspect of practicing international law in a dualist jurisdiction: a particular obligation may be binding on the State in its international relations, and yet have no force in its internal law.

Question #2—Is customary international law part of federal common law or state common law? As posited, this question only concerns the status of customary international law in U.S. law. Under the Supremacy Clause of Article VI of the Constitution, treaties are unambiguously regarded as part of federal law (this will be considered further in the next Chapter). Because the Supremacy Clause does not mention customary international law, doubts continually have been raised as to whether custom is part of federal law or the law of the individual states.[10] This may not appear to be significant until one recalls that if an issue is a matter of state law, federal courts should apply that state law, and not a supposed federal general common law.[11] Moreover, whether customary international law is state law may also affect the jurisdiction of federal courts in hearing such matters.

Two theories have been propounded for the status of customary international law and its incorporation into American law. One notion is that the process of incorporation was through the states, as former colonies of Great Britain, at the time of independence in

---

9. See *Boos v. Barry*, 485 U.S. 312 (1988).

10. Henceforth, in the next two Chapters, when "state" is used without

a capital "S," I mean a state of the United States.

11. This is the rule of *Erie R.R. Co. v. Tompkins*, 304 U.S. 64 (1938).

1776.[12] The other mechanism was by virtue of the creation of the national government of the United States (first under the 1781 Articles of Confederation and then under the Constitution) and the creation of a national sovereignty.[13] While the Constitution did grant to Congress some power to incorporate customary international law (the Define and Punish Clause, for example), that may not be dispositive on this question.

Nevertheless, the better-held view today is that customary international law is federal law. This means, at a minimum, that cases involving claims to exclusively customary international law rights and duties (some kinds of diplomatic immunities or law of the sea privileges, for example) are to be decided by the federal courts.[14] Whether this conclusion also extends a grant to the federal courts of a power to make a judge-made federal general common law of foreign relations may be more doubtful, and it will have to be settled by future litigation.

Question #3—If customary international law is part of federal law, are states obliged to observe it? Again, this problem arises from the fact that the Constitution's Supremacy Clause does not specifically mention customary international law as a source of law that preempts contrary state law. It sometimes has been asserted that even if customary international law is *federal* law, it does not necessarily follow that states of the Union are obliged to obey it. Indeed, there have been some notable disputes between states and the national government. One of the earliest, in 1841, was New York's prosecution of a Canadian citizen for murder on charges arising from a British invasion.[15] The British protested that the prosecution violated customary international law. The United States government agreed, but said it was powerless to intervene in the New York proceedings. A serious diplomatic dispute was only averted when the defendant was acquitted on the charges.

Over a hundred years later, the U.S. Supreme Court ruled that an Oregon statute discriminating against foreigners in inheritance matters violated both treaty law and custom.[16] In that case, the Court appeared to sanction a principle that state laws are preempted to the extent they interfere with a foreign relations interest of the United States, even in the absence of an explicit Act of Congress. This matter is intensely controversial and has been the subject of a number of recent Supreme Court decisions which have

---

12. See, e.g., *Respublica v. De Longchamps*, 1 Dall. 120 (Pa. Oyer & Terminer 1784).

13. See *The NEREIDE*, 13 U.S. (9 Cranch) 388 (1815).

14. See *Bergman v. De Sieyes*, 170 F.2d 360 (2d Cir. 1948).

15. See *People v. McLeod*, 25 Wend. 483 (N.Y. Sup. Ct. 1841).

16. See *Zschernig v. Miller*, 389 U.S. 429 (1968).

appeared to uphold a federal foreign affairs interest as against the states.[17]

Question #4—Can customary international law be "trumped" by federal statutes and Executive determinations? The final question to be addressed is the precise status of customary international law in relation to other sources of *federal* law. (The answers to the earlier questions concern whether custom is superior to *state* law. Moreover, custom has to be inferior to the Constitution.) Once again, there are two prevalent theories that describe this relationship.

One idea is that customary international law is co-equal with treaties and statutes. That would mean that a later rule of custom will take precedence over an earlier treaty obligation or an earlier Congressional statute. (The precise operation of a "last-in-time" rule will be discussed in the next Chapter.) Although this has been propounded by some noted scholars, there are real difficulties with this suggestion. The most notable problem is the method by which custom is confirmed in U.S. practice. Custom is not legislated. Instead, it is often simply accepted in U.S. practice by statements made by the President acting through the Executive Branch. It cannot thereby be seriously suggested that a Presidential statement as to the existence or content of a rule of customary international law could cancel a prior statute. Difficulties also arise that since custom is always renewing itself through State practice and *opinio juris* (see Chapter 2(B)), it could conceivably always be in the position of ousting prior statutes and treaties.

The better-argued view is that customary international law rule cannot take precedence over a contrary statute or treaty, at least in U.S. domestic law. Nevertheless, treaties or statutes should be interpreted and applied in view of more recent developments in custom. Moreover, an old rule contained in a statute or international agreement could well be changed by a new law or treaty which codifies a later change in custom. But where there is *no* statute or treaty "on-point," U.S. courts are obliged to follow rules of customary international law. This point was ably made by Justice Gray in 1900 in *The PAQUETE HABANA* case (discussed in Chapter 2(B)), when he observed:

> International law is part of our law, and must be ascertained and administered by the courts of justice of appropriate jurisdiction as often as questions of right depending upon it are duly presented for their determination. For this purpose, where there is no treaty and no controlling executive or legislative act

---

17. See *United States v. Locke*, 120 S.Ct. 1135 (2000); *Crosby v. National* *Foreign Trade Council*, 120 S.Ct. 2288 (2000).

or judicial decision, resort must be had to the customs and usages of civilized nations. . . . [18]

This formulation has caused mischief in at least one respect. Can the President unilaterally decide to violate customary international law? Court decisions are mixed on this point.[19] In any event, while the Executive Branch should not be allowed to willfully violate customary international law that is clearly applicable and binding upon it, courts will often extend substantial deference to Executive Branch positions as to the content of that law. In very exceptional cases courts may decline to rule on the merits of cases involving customary international law, for fear of answering a "political question," although the Supreme Court has indicated that foreign relations issues are fair game for the courts.[20] Courts are allowed, however, to take judicial notice of international law, and decide for themselves whether the President's position as to a rule of custom is justified or not.

As has been suggested by the foregoing, the relationship between international law and internal law in any domestic legal system is complex. The United States is no exception in this regard. Although U.S. constitutional jurisprudence squarely puts it in the dualist camp, there are key qualifications on the role of customary international law as providing a rule of decision contrary to the law of the several states, or even of ill-conceived Executive Branch positions. Perhaps what is most surprising, many critical questions concerning the hierarchy of international law sources in U.S. law have yet to be definitively settled, even after over two centuries of experience under the Constitution.

18.   175 U.S. at 700.

19.   Compare *Garcia-Mir v. Meese*, 788 F.2d 1446 (11th Cir. 1986); with *Fernandez v. Wilkinson*, 505 F. Supp. 787 (D. Kan. 1980).

20.   See *Japan Whaling Ass'n v. American Cetacean Soc'y*, 478 U.S. 221 (1986).

Chapter 15

International Agreements in U.S. Law

A vital aspect of practicing international law today in the United States is the proper appreciation of the role of international agreements in making law for various individuals, transactions, status relationships, and incidents. Treaties—and the rights and obligations they contain—are no longer the exclusive concern of government lawyers. Whether it is litigating an air crash under the Warsaw Convention, or perfecting service of process by the Hague Convention, or vindicating a human right granted by the ICCPR, the essential question becomes one of appropriately using a treaty as a source of binding legal obligation in proceedings in the United States.

As was noted in Chapter 3, the legal terminology used by the United States to describe international agreements is markedly different from that employed elsewhere. Under the U.S. Constitution, the term "treaty" has a particular meaning—an agreement made by the President with the advise and consent of the Senate. This Chapter will consider the scope of the treaty-making power granted by the Constitution, as well as the status of treaties as part of the "law of the land," and thus binding on states and also directly enforceable through court proceedings. Treaties are not the exclusive mechanism by which the United States government can enter into international obligations, and this Chapter will also review the two sorts of so-called "Executive Agreements" and assess their status.

A. The Treaty Power

The Constitution has two clauses concerning treaties. Article II, section 2 provides that the President "shall have the Power, by and with the Advice and Consent of the Senate, to make Treaties, provided two-thirds of the Senators present concur." Article VI, section 2 (also known as the Supremacy Clause), requires that

> This Constitution, and the Laws of the United States which shall be made in Pursuance thereof; and all Treaties made, or which shall be made, under the Authority of the United States, shall be the supreme Law of the Land; and the Judges in every State shall be bound thereby, any Thing in the Constitution or Laws of any State to the Contrary notwithstanding.

These two clauses together establish the mechanism for treaties to be adopted and their consequent effect as law. Even so, many questions remain about the nature and limits of the treaty power.

A few points of clarification need to be made. In popular parlance, the Senate "ratifies" treaties that are presented by the President. That is a misnomer; the Senate actually "advises and consents" to a treaty (the actual language of the Constitution). The President then has the discretion to later "proclaim" the treaty and conclude the ratification process. The Senate can condition its advice and consent on the attachment of various reservations, understandings, and declarations ("RUDs") of the treaty. Although only reservations purport to change the legal effect of a treaty (see Chapter 3(C)), Senatorial understandings and interpretations may also be regarded as contentious and unwelcome by the Executive Branch. There have been legal disputes about the permissible scope of certain reservations, and at least one court has ruled that the Senate cannot condition its advice and consent on a reservation that has nothing to do with the international legal obligations contained in the treaty.[1]

It is exceedingly rare for the Senate to outright refuse to advise and consent to a treaty. Indeed, in the entire history of the Republic this has occurred only 21 times (the last occasion was the 1999 rejection of the Comprehensive Nuclear Test Ban Treaty). The disapproval of the Treaty of Versailles, including the Covenant of the League of Nations, in 1920 was certainly the most serious example of this. More typically, the Senate will simply refuse action on controversial treaties, and many such pacts have languished in the Senate for decades.

There has always been a perceived need to restrain or cabin the treaty power. Perhaps this derives from a sense that a source of law which is made exclusively by the President and the upper chamber of Congress (the Senate) is somehow undemocratic to the extent that it excludes the House of Representatives from the process. One limit on the treaty power has certainly been recognized: treaties may not abrogate an individual liberty granted under the Bill of Rights (the first ten amendments to the Constitution). That was certainly the ruling in the *Reid v. Covert* decision, discussed in the last Chapter, and was the closest the Supreme Court has come to ruling a treaty unconstitutional. Other limits on the treaty power have been poorly understood and even after centuries of speculation remain potentially divisive.

---

1. See *Power Authority of New York v. Federal Power Comm'n*, 247 F.2d 538   (D.C. Cir. 1957).

One such limitation is federalism, the proper allocation of power between the national and state governments. The key question raised by federalism concerns is whether a treaty can legislate in a field reserved, by the structural clauses of the Constitution, to the states. The leading case on this subject remains the Supreme Court's 1920 decision in *Missouri v. Holland*.[2] The case arose concerning an unexpected—and one would have thought, uncontroversial—area of regulation: protection of migratory birds. It was originally unquestioned that wildlife management was a matter for state action. But early in the 1900's, Congress adopted legislation that placed some aspects of that issue under the control of the federal government. That legislation was subsequently attacked as exceeding Congress' powers under Article I of the Constitution to regulate interstate or foreign commerce. Several lower courts found the legislation unconstitutional.

Undeterred by those decisions, in 1916 the United States entered into a Convention, known as the Migratory Bird Treaty (MBT), with Great Britain and Canada. Two years later, the MBT was implemented into federal law by the Migratory Bird Treaty Act (MBTA). After a federal game warden attempted to enforce the MBTA (and Department of Agriculture regulations issued under the Act) in Missouri, that state sued, asserting the MBT and MBTA were unconstitutional. Missouri's argument was breathtakingly simple: if the original legislation federalizing bird protection was unconstitutional, how could concluding a treaty with a foreign nation authorizing such regulation, make it permissible? In other words, how could a treaty grant to Congress a power that was denied to it under the Constitution?

In a short, delphic opinion, Justice Holmes ruled in favor of the federal interest and held that the MBT did not violate any federalism limits on the treaty power. At the outset, it is important to realize what Holmes' decision did *not* say. Holmes could have ruled that migratory bird regulation was within Congress' Article I powers, and thus there was no need for the MBT or MBTA to "cure" the earlier constitutional deficiency of the original legislation. But the Court did not make that ruling, and one might suppose there were insufficient votes for that conclusion.

Likewise, Holmes could have ruled that the treaty power is totally unrestrained. In dictum, Holmes did observe that the Supremacy Clause required only that "Treaties [be] made, or which shall be made, under the Authority of the United States." That is different from that Clause's requirement that statutes "be made in Pursuance" of the Constitution. It might be argued that while acts of Congress must be consistent with the Constitution, treaties do

---

2.   252 U.S. 416 (1920).

not, and therefore Missouri's argument of a federalism restraint on the treaty power would fail. The proper reading, however, of the Supremacy Clause is that the Framers did not wish to discredit those international agreements that had been concluded by the United States *prior* to 1787 (including treaties of alliance with France and Holland and the peace treaty with Britain), and so they offered the language of "under the Authority of the United States." In any event, the idea that treaties could be unconstitutional was definitively rejected later in *Reid v. Covert.*

Instead of these solutions (one unachievable for lack of votes, the other plainly wrong), Holmes adopted a difficult middle course. He observed that "it is obvious that there may be matters of the sharpest exigency for the national well being that an act of Congress could not deal with but that a treaty followed by such an act could." Since "the treaty in question does not contravene any prohibitory words to be found in the Constitution," the Court ruled that it was not barred by the Tenth Amendment or other federalism clauses. Holmes ruled that if a treaty was (1) motivated by exigency and great national interests, and (2) did not violate an express constitutional prohibition, then it could grant to Congress law-making authority it did not otherwise have under Article I of the Constitution.

There was one attempt to override the *Missouri v. Holland* decision by constitutional amendment in the 1950's. The proposed Bricker Amendment said that "a treaty shall become effective as internal law in the United States through legislation that would be valid in the absence of a treaty." The amendment was never approved by Congress. The issue of federalism restraints on the treaty power receded over time, particularly as the Supreme Court consistently ruled that virtually every form of legislation was permitted under the Commerce Clause of Article I. Although there was speculation that a treaty could not legislate in a "forbidden zone" of authority granted to the states (such as state boundaries or state militias), this was never tested. Now that the Supreme Court has come to impose new limits on Congress' power under the Commerce Clause—and has struck down some statutes as violating those limits—the issue raised in *Missouri v. Holland* may return to the fore.

Other suggested grounds for limiting the treaty power have posed fewer difficulties. The idea that treaties have to be limited in subject-matter to topics of "international concern," although mooted by Chief Justice Charles Evans Hughes in some unguarded remarks before the American Society of International Law in 1929,[3] has been rejected. Under such a theory, the United States could not

---

3. See 23 Am. Soc'y Int'l L. Proc. 194 (1929).

conclude human rights treaties which impacted the rights of U.S. citizens. It has also been argued that treaties which require legislative action on the part of the United States may be impermissible to the extent that such action requires a vote by the House of Representatives. For example, a treaty which constituted a declaration of war would be unconstitutional, since the House must vote on such a declaration. Likewise, no treaty may automatically be regarded as authorization to spend moneys, since that too requires House action. A contention that the 1977 Panama Canal Treaty was unconstitutional because it violated the House of Representative's right to vote on dispositions of U.S. property was rejected,[4] since the Property Clause (like most other constitutional provisions) did not vest the House of Representatives with specific decision-making authority.

The scope of the treaty power thus remains vast, and apart from some very specific qualifications (such as a narrow ambit of states' rights and House prerogatives), there are few federalism or separation-of-powers limits. Except where a treaty affirmatively violates an individual liberty (whether it be trial process, free speech, or property rights), it will usually be held to be constitutional. Clearly, the critical limit on the treaty power is a purely political one: the requirement of a two-thirds approval in the Senate for advice and consent.

B. Treaties as the Law of the Land

Now that the constitutional contours of the treaty power are better marked, it remains to understand how treaties are actually enforced as part of the "Law of the Land" under the Supremacy Clause of Article VI of the Constitution. This matter resolves itself into three separate inquiries: (1) the distinction between self-executing and non-self-executing treaties, (2) the operation of the "last-in-time" rule when a statute contradicts a treaty, and (3) concerns arising from the termination of treaties. Each of these issues will be reviewed in turn.

Although the Supremacy Clause does not appear to contemplate distinctions between treaties to be given automatic force in U.S. domestic law and those that are not, just such a differentiation was soon made after the founding of the Republic. The 1829 case of *Foster and Elam v. Neilson*[5] concerned the application of an 1819 treaty with Spain which (among other provisions) transferred title to Florida to the U.S. The question presented was whether the treaty acted to confirm a land grant previously made by the

---

4. See *Edwards v. Carter*, 580 F.2d 1055 (D.C. Cir. 1978).   **5.** 27 U.S. (2 Pet.) 253 (1829).

Spanish crown. The Supreme Court concluded that the treaty had no such direct effect on the property rights of private claimants. Writing for the Court, Chief Justice John Marshall introduced into U.S. law a distinction between treaties that were to have immediate application without the necessity of implementing legislation by Congress ("self-executing treaties") and those agreements that needed a subsequent Act in order to have binding effect domestically ("non-self-executing treaties"). The Court concluded that while the rest of the 1819 treaty was self-executing, Article 8 required additional implementing legislation. (Ironically, the Court later reversed itself on this point,[6] realizing that it had failed to understand a nuance of the Spanish version of the treaty.)

From the *Foster and Elam* case came the self-executing/non-self-executing treaty distinction, although Chief Justice Marshall was decidedly vague about how to make the determination in practice. His observation that those treaties with more of a "contractual" flavor should be regarded as non-self-executing is of little help. Despite some recent scholarly revisionism on this point, it appears that the presumption behind the Supremacy Clause and Marshall's decision was that most treaties would be regarded as having self-executing effect on U.S. law, without the need for further legislative action by Congress.

One of the difficulties of this inquiry is that it usually requires careful analysis of the treaty provision in question. Some clauses in a treaty may be regarded as self-executing, while others are not. Some good rules of thumb are that if a treaty provision contemplates further legislative action, then it is non-self-executing; that provision will not be "the Law of the Land" until a subsequent Act of Congress. This is especially so if the subsequent action involves something that requires action by the House of Representatives (making an appropriation of money or declaring war). Another good rule is that treaties which provide that "certain acts shall not be done, or that certain limitations or restrictions shall not be disregarded or exceeded" by the Parties, will be regarded as self-executing.[7] Perhaps the best guide is whether the treaty provision is specific enough in content and clearly manifests an intent by the Parties to be binding in U.S. law without further implementing legislation. If so, it is self-executing; if not, it is non-self-executing.

Problems of self-execution are particularly acute when the issue is whether an individual can directly claim a right under a treaty. Although this may be an analytically distinct question from self-execution, the two are often conflated. In large measure, this is a new problem that reflects a growing trend that treaties are

---

6. See *United States v. Percheman*, 32 U.S. (7 Pet.) 51 (1833).

7. *Commonwealth v. Hawes*, 76 Ky. (13 Bush) 697, 702–03 (1878).

intended not only to adjust relations between nations, but also to facilitate commerce, promote human rights, protect the environment, and allow for greater individual contacts between nations. U.S. courts have tended to find no "private right of action" under a treaty where the agreement is too vague (such as the U.N. Charter's human rights provisions[8]) or simply does not provide for such a right (like the peace treaties concluded with Germany after World War II[9]). In a similar way, courts have ruled that many of the critical conventions for the law of the sea (discussed in Chapter 11) and the laws of war (Chapter 20) are non-self-executing. At the same time, courts have generally held that extradition treaties (considered in the next Chapter), and critical private international law instruments (including the 1929 Warsaw Convention on airline liability and various Hague Conventions on international civil procedure) are self-executing.

In the vast majority of these cases, judges use methods of treaty interpretation to decide the combined questions of self-execution and private right of action. One court[10] looked at a number of factors: the object and purpose of the treaty provision, the existence of alternative domestic procedures for implementation and enforcement, and whether our treaty partners recognize the private right of action. In a growing trend, the Administration which proposes a treaty (and the Senate which advises and consents to it) will explicitly provide whether the treaty is to be regarded as self-executing. Although this raises tricky questions of good faith enforcement of international agreements, especially for human rights treaties (which the U.S. routinely denies self-executing effect), it is one promising piece of evidence for lawyers and courts to consider in making this determination.

Once it is decided whether a treaty provision is self-executing, that resolves many problems of its binding effect. If it is, the provision is part of the "Law of the Land" under the Supremacy Clause, and can be directly applied in domestic proceedings. If it is non-self-executing, the parties will have to look to subsequent implementing legislation by Congress. If there is no such Act, the treaty has no domestic force. If there is, then that statute will be applied and interpreted, consistent with the original treaty. That leads to situations where a statute conflicts with an earlier treaty, and vice versa.

Where a later treaty conflicts with an earlier statute, which prevails depends on self-execution.[11] If the later treaty is self-

8. See *Sei Fujii v. California*, 38 Cal.2d 718 (1952).

9. See *Dreyfus v. Von Finck*, 534 F.2d 24 (2d Cir. 1976); *Iwanowa v. Ford Motor Co.*, 67 F. Supp.2d 424 (D.N.J. 1999).

10. See *United States v. Postal*, 589 F.2d 862 (5th Cir. 1979).

11. See *Whitney v. Robertson*, 124

executing, then the earlier statute is considered abrogated to the extent it actually conflicts with the new international agreement. This is known as the "last-in-time" rule. However, if the new treaty is non-self-executing, then there is no preemption until such time as Congress gets around to implementing the treaty through domestic legislation. (And, of course, a later statute always trumps a contrary, earlier Act.)

The more difficult question is raised when a later statute conflicts with an earlier international agreement of the United States. Here, the assumption is that Congress is free to override or abrogate the domestic effect of the United States' treaty obligations.[12] Of course, such action has absolutely no effect on the United States' international duties. The treaty continues to have force on the international plane (until terminated on its own terms or in accordance with the law of treaties) but may not be enforceable by domestic courts or administrative authorities.

There are, however, some qualifications to this application of the "last-in-time" principle. The first is narrow and technical. A later statute that abrogates an earlier treaty cannot eliminate any rights that had vested under that agreement. The second consideration is positively crucial. It is the notion that "an Act of Congress ought never to be construed to violate the law of nations if any other possible construction" is possible. This is known as the canon of *The CHARMING BETSY* case,[13] and it remains a significant principle of statutory construction to this day. (The underlying case concerned a confiscation of a vessel suspected of trading with the French during the undeclared naval war with that country.) It means, at a minimum, that a statute will not be allowed to abrogate an earlier treaty (or rule of custom, for that matter), unless the Congressional intent to override that obligation is clear and manifest. This is obviously intended as an antidote to possible legislative inadvertence, but it also requires a high level of political resolve from Congress to enact bills in conflict with international law. Periodically, *The CHARMING BETSY* rule has saved the United States from profound diplomatic embarrassment, as with the attempted shut-down in 1987 of the U.N. observer mission of the Palestine Liberation Organization (PLO).[14]

The last point to be considered about the binding legal effect of treaties is what happens when an agreement is purportedly terminated. For starters, this decision is firmly committed to the political branches of the U.S. government. Private parties may not argue

U.S. 190 (1888).

12. See *Chae Chan Ping v. United States*, 130 U.S. 581 (1889).

13. 6 U.S. (2 Cranch) 64, 118 (1804).

14. See *United States v. Palestine Liberation Organization*, 695 F. Supp. 1456 (S.D.N.Y. 1988).

before a court that a treaty cannot be applied because our treaty partners have breached it.[15] The Executive Branch can decide whether the treaty remains in force, and until it takes action to terminate or suspend the agreement, U.S. courts are obliged to continue to give it domestic effect as part of the "Law of the Land."

When viewed as a separation of powers problem, treaty termination remains a contentious—and unresolved—issue. It has been presumed that the President, acting alone, can initiate the needed action to end the United States' treaty obligations under international law, and thus to end an agreement's domestic effect as well. Some have suggested that if it requires the President and the Senate acting together to *enter into* a treaty, then surely the same combination is required for action to *end* the agreement. Although this issue has reached the Supreme Court at least once—with President Carter's unilateral termination of a Mutual Defense Treaty with Taiwan in 1979—it still remains unsettled because the High Court refused to rule because it was a "political question."[16] One can imagine, though, that this issue will assuredly have to be elucidated at some juncture.

C. Executive Agreements

Treaties are not the exclusive means by which the United States can enter into legally-binding arrangements with other nations under international law. In fact, the number of treaties submitted to the Senate for advice and consent has dwindled, while alternative forms of agreement (called "executive agreements") have flourished. As of the 1990's, the United States had concluded less than 1500 treaties, while it had entered into over 10,000 executive agreements. In terms of sheer volume, executive agreements have assumed a degree of substantial importance.

As always with such matters, it is exceedingly important to be precise in one's use of terms. That is because there are *two* types of executive agreements—(1) Congressional–Executive Agreements, and (2) sole Executive Agreements. Congressional–Executive Agreements are simply Acts of Congress, ordinary legislation which enacts an international obligation by a majority vote of the House and Senate, with the President's signature. Often, a Congressional–Executive Agreement is resorted to as a matter of political expediency. It may be that there is a "blocking-third" of Senators (all it takes is 34) who are prepared to "veto" advice and consent on a treaty. It may also be that a President prefers to submit an

15. See *Charlton v. Kelly*, 229 U.S. 447 (1913).

16. See *Goldwater v. Carter*, 444 U.S. 996 (1979).

important international initiative to both chambers of Congress for maximum political effect.

Although Congressional–Executive Agreements were first invoked relatively recently (in the administration of Franklin Roosevelt to pass lend-lease aide to Britain over the objection of a neutralist faction in the Senate), they have come to be acknowledged as a complete—and constitutional—alternative to the treaty power under Article II of the Constitution. Two recent Congressional–Executive Agreements—enacting U.S. participation in the North America Free Trade Agreement (NAFTA) and World Trade Organization (WTO)—have raised objections that the original scheme of the Constitution requires that important international obligations be submitted to the Senate and be subject to the super-majority vote requirement there. So far, however, no court has accepted such a challenge against Congressional–Executive Agreements.[17]

The second type of executive agreement—sole Executive Agreements—do raise substantial constitutional concerns, because (as their name suggests) they are concluded on the single authority of the President. Obviously this form of agreement-making raises the specter of unrestrained Executive power. The ability of the President, on his own authority, to enter into international agreements with binding domestic effect can be derived in a number of different ways. These have been specified in State Department Circular Number 175, first issued in 1955 (and since updated), and have been qualified by the requirement that no matter what authority a sole Executive Agreement is made under, it must be promptly reported to Congress.[18]

For example, an earlier statute or treaty (which would have been subject to Congressional or Senatorial approval) might authorize the President to enter into subsequent agreements, clarifying the details of an international arrangement. This raises relatively few concerns, as Congress is giving advance authorization for the sole Executive Agreement, and (in a sense) is delegating to the Executive Branch the power to make it. This would be no different from a Congressional delegation of regulatory authority to an administrative agency. Likewise, the President is relatively free to make sole Executive Agreements if those pacts are *non*-self-executing, and thus will require later Congressional approval in order to be implemented directly into U.S. law.

The most controversial scenario for sole Executive Agreements is when they are made pursuant to the President's own, exclusive powers under Article II of the Constitution. These include the

---

17. See *Made in the USA Foundation v. United States*, 56 F. Supp.2d 1226 (N.D. Ala. 1999).

18. See the Case Act, 1 U.S.C. § 112(b).

Recognition Clause (which gives the President the power to receive and appoint ambassadors, and thus (implicitly) to recognize foreign governments) and the Chief Executive's function as Commander-in-Chief of the armed forces. In pursuance of these powers, the President can conclude sole Executive Agreements which will become part of the "Law of the Land" under the Supremacy Clause.

In a series of important cases,[19] the U.S. Supreme Court ruled on the constitutionality of sole Executive Agreements entered into with the purpose of resolving outstanding private claims between nationals of the United States and the government of another country. This type of agreement was usually a prelude to normalization of relations, and thus the Court held that these agreements were pursuant to the President's recognition powers. In these cases, the Supreme Court concluded that the sole Executive Agreement was binding in domestic law, preempted any contrary state laws, and could even affect vested property rights. For example, the *Dames & Moore v. Regan* case[20] was a constitutional challenge to the Algiers Accords which secured the release of the American diplomats held hostage in Iran. The Court ruled that private parties that had claims against Iran (secured by liens against property in the U.S. or pending court actions) had not suffered an uncompensable taking of property, even though those liens and actions were dismissed under the terms of the settlement. Because the parties had the right to litigate their claims against Iran before a newly-created Claims Tribunal in The Hague, due process was satisfied and the exercise of a foreign relations power did not violate a constitutional freedom.

One nettlesome problem remains concerning the status of sole Executive Agreements as the "Law of the Land": can they trump earlier statutes under a "last-in-time" rule? Incredibly, in the entire history of the Republic, this issue has been presented to a court only once. In that case, *Guy W. Capps, Inc. v. United States*,[21] the issue was the status of a sole Executive Agreement entered into by the President with Canada concerning seed potato imports. The agreement manifestly contradicted an earlier statute, and the Fourth Circuit Court of Appeals observed that an agreement concerning foreign commerce did not fall within the zone of the President's exclusive powers under the Constitution. The court thus voided the domestic effect of the agreement.

As executive agreements (whether made as a statute with Congress or under the President's sole powers) continue to flourish as the primary vehicle for the United States' entry into internation-

---

19. See *United States v. Belmont*, 301 U.S. 324 (1937); *United States v. Pink*, 315 U.S. 203 (1942).

20. 453 U.S. 654 (1981).

21. 204 F.2d 655 (4th Cir. 1953).

al commitments, these questions about their permissible scope and preemptive effect will continue to be litigated. Like treaties, executive agreements are often subject to bruising court battles about their proper interpretation and enforcement. Judges should properly defer to the positions of the Executive Branch in many of these disputes. On the other hand, courts are understandably reluctant to countenance a Presidential construction of a treaty which is manifestly wrong, contradicts earlier positions taken by the government, or which violates the vested rights of individuals. Even though international agreements and the treaty power of the political branches are often central to U.S. foreign relations, courts are right to regard matters of treaty construction and enforcement as within their judicial authority.

Chapter 16

Jurisdiction

Jurisdictional controversies often arise between nations, and the vast majority of such disputes are settled in the domestic courts of one of the States involved, not in an international tribunal. Whether it is the prosecution of a foreign defendant, or application of a nation's law to events overseas, or the respect to be given to a foreign tribunal's decisions, jurisdiction can often implicate critical questions of the incorporation of international law into domestic legal systems. That is not to say, though, that international law dictates a code of rules for dealing with jurisdictional disputes. Rather, it provides certain crucial background principles that tend to mark the outer limits of a State's appropriate exercise of various kinds of jurisdiction, and then leaves substantial discretion to nations to work out jurisdictional disputes in a constructive way.

This Chapter will explore this subject by (A) distinguishing various types of jurisdictional questions as they relate to problems of comity and limits on exercises of State jurisdiction, (B) discussing in depth the traditional grounds, or "bases", that States use to assert jurisdiction in assorted legal contexts, and (C) considering some practical problems in the mutual legal assistance that nations extend to each other, especially in criminal law enforcement. Once again, the focus here will primarily be the United States' practice in such matters, although it is vital that the views of other nations be appreciated because the U.S. position in many jurisdictional conflicts is regarded as aggressive and aberrational. Questions involving immunities from jurisdiction under international law—which only arise when it is clear that a State would otherwise have jurisdiction in a particular matter—will be reserved for the next Chapter.

A. Analyzing a Jurisdictional Problem

At the outset of this discussion, it is vital to realize that not all jurisdictional disputes between nations arise in the same way, involve the same national interests, or are to be resolved in the same fashion. When someone speaks of a nation's "jurisdiction," they could be referring to three very different kinds of assertions of competence.

The first is the power of a nation to legislate, to make rules binding on persons, transactions, and relationships that have some connection with that State. This is called, in international law parlance, the jurisdiction to *prescribe*. When Congress passes a law, or an administrative agency issues a regulation, that should be in pursuance of a valid basis of a jurisdiction to prescribe. American lawyers tend to assume that if such a law or regulation is constitutional, or within the proper scope of delegation, then that suffices. The question here is whether the United States has the power and authority to prescribe rules that impact the conduct and behavior of individuals outside the United States.

The second type of jurisdiction is the one that lawyers typically think of in relation to this subject. That is the power of a tribunal to decide a particular dispute or to hear a certain case. This is jurisdiction to *adjudicate*. Traditionally separated into "subject-matter" and "personal" jurisdiction inquiries, lawyers are trained to understand that this is a central problem in civil procedure and constitutional law. Likewise, many of the most spectacular jurisdictional disputes that arise in international law occur when the courts of one nation purport to claim the power to adjudicate a matter involving a foreign national or events that transpired beyond that country's borders.

The third, and last, type of jurisdiction is an important corollary of a nation's jurisdiction to prescribe and adjudicate. That is its power to enforce both its rules and its judgments, and is usually called jurisdiction to *enforce*. Students of this subject tend to forget this last category or to lump it into the previous two, but that would be a grievous mistake. Just as every seasoned litigator knows that it is one thing to win a judgment against a defendant, it can be quite another to actually collect damages or otherwise enforce the court's decree. Likewise, international law may, in certain exceptional cases, allow a State the power to prescribe a particular rule of conduct against the interests of foreign States or nationals, but then sharply limit its ability to enforce that rule directly.

It is vital to keep these three kinds of jurisdiction—prescriptive, adjudication and enforcement—analytically separate. The rules and presumptions that apply to a State's assertion of one of these types of jurisdiction consistent with international law may not apply to another kind. Likewise, the traditional bases or justifications of jurisdiction that States usually invoke may be stronger or weaker depending on the class of jurisdiction that is claimed.

There is a central dilemma lurking here in matters involving conflicting jurisdictional claims made by States. It arises from the Permanent Court of International Justice's 1927 decision in The *LOTUS* Case.[1] That controversy, already discussed here in the context of the formation of customary international law (see Chap-

1. 1927 P.C.I.J. (Ser. A) No. 10 (Fr. v. Tur.).

ter 2(B)), featured a challenge by France of Turkey's assertion of criminal jurisdiction over a French national who committed negligent homicide on a French ship on the high seas that had the effect of injuring or killing a number of Turkish nationals. You might recall that the World Court ruled in that case that France bore the burden of showing that Turkey's exercise of jurisdiction violated international law. This burden allocation was decisive in that case; France could not show a prevailing customary international law that opposed Turkey's exercise of criminal jurisdiction on those facts.

What has come to be called the *"LOTUS* Presumption" has exerted a strong influence on the international law of jurisdiction. Under this rule, States are free to assert their jurisdictional competences to the absolute limit that international law allows. When in doubt, this presumption counsels, States are able to insist on their jurisdiction over a particular individual, matter, or transaction. In short, international law is a permissive system when it comes to State jurisdiction: everything is permitted, save that which is expressly—and unambiguously—rejected.

It does not take much imagination, however, to realize that the *LOTUS* Presumption, and its underlying assumptions about international law and relations, can cause very real mischief. If States are atomistic entities entitled to assert their jurisdiction to the notional limit that international law allows, then conflict will be rife. What is worse, under such a system, States will be *obliged* to make aggressive and contentious assertions of jurisdiction, for fear that failing to do so will constitute some sort of acquiescence or acceptance of another nation's claim of jurisdiction. It is for these reasons that international law (in general) and the United States' law (in particular) have sought to soften the effects of the *LOTUS* Presumption in a variety of ways.

The first of these approaches—and the one with the oldest doctrinal pedigree—is the concept of *comity*. Comity was mentioned in a slightly different context in the earlier discussion about the formation of customary international law (in Chapter 2(B)). In that setting, comity was the idea that States may engage in a particular course of conduct, but *not* out of a sense of legal obligation. Rather, nations may engage in a practice out of courtesy or respect for their neighbors or partners in the international community. In the circumstances of conflicting claims of State jurisdiction and power, comity means more than "mere courtesy and good will." As the U.S. Supreme Court observed in the 1895 decision of *Hilton v. Guyot*, "it is the recognition which one nation allows within its territory of the legislative, executive, or judicial acts of another nation, having due regard both to international duty and convenience, and to the rights of its own citizens or of other persons who are under the protection of its laws."[2]

Comity has been construed by the Supreme Court to mean a number of different things. One aspect is that U.S. courts should not lightly assume that Congress intends to apply legislation extra-territorially to individuals and events occurring outside the United States[3] or to matters clearly subject to international regulation (such as maritime law).[4] Comity is also invoked when an American court decides that, even though it has jurisdiction over a particular matter, it should instead be heard by a foreign tribunal. Whether this is done as a consequence of a choice-of-forum clause between the parties or under the doctrine of forum *non conveniens*, it is still a manifestation of respect for foreign judicial institutions.[5] This praise for the notion of comity has been by no means unanimous. In a recent case, the U.S. Supreme Court explicitly rejected its use, although over the objections of a strong dissent.[6]

The second broad approach that domestic courts have employed to blunt assertive claims of jurisdiction is a kind of interest-balancing. This is the central feature of current doctrine in choice-of-law or conflict of laws (also known as "private international law" in the United Kingdom and Europe). When a tribunal in one jurisdiction has the choice to apply its own law to a transaction or relationship, or the law of another jurisdiction, it usually balances different considerations. A court in New York will be reluctant to grant a divorce for a couple married in France, unless they have become domiciled here. Two contracting parties may have agreed to apply the law of Georgia, even though they are litigating before the courts of California. A tribunal in England may be averse to applying German law to an accident occurring in Berlin if English law would not regard the tort as actionable. Such conflict situations (assuming they are real conflicts), may be resolved by mechanical rules, but, more likely, the forum will balance various interests.

Also, a court considering whether a particular exercise of jurisdiction exceeds international law standards may apply some mechanical rules, but will (more likely) balance the relevant interests. What this can mean is that the *LOTUS* Presumption—which allows a State to assert jurisdiction to the maximum limits allowed—will be substantially softened. Perhaps the best enunciation of this alternative rule is contained in the 1987 *Restatement (Third) of the Foreign Relations Law of the United States*, a publication of

---

2.　159 U.S. 113, 163–64 (1895).

3.　See *Foley Bros., Inc. v. Filardo,* 336 U.S. 281 (1949); *Smith v. United States,* 507 U.S. 197 (1993).

4.　See, e.g., *Lauritzen v. Larsen,* 345 U.S. 571 (1953).

5.　See *The BREMEN v. Zapata Offshore Co.,* 407 U.S. 1 (1972); *Piper Aircraft Co. v. Reyno,* 454 U.S. 235 (1981).

6.　See *Hartford Fire Ins. Co. v. California,* 509 U.S. 764 (1993).

the American Law Institute prepared by eminent academic international lawyers. Although I have previously expressed some concern about the indiscriminate use of this source by U.S. litigators and courts, the *Restatement*'s treatment, in section 403, of limitations on jurisdiction is very significant.

For starters, section 403 concerns only limits on jurisdiction to prescribe. It may have rather less force for situations involving jurisdiction to adjudicate or enforce. The *Restatement* provides that even when a State has a legitimate ground for asserting the effect of its domestic laws on foreign individuals and events, "a state may not exercise jurisdiction to prescribe law with respect to a person or activity having connection with another state when the exercise of such jurisdiction is unreasonable." In short, *Restatement* section 403 challenges the *LOTUS* Presumption, and replaces a muscular system of aggressive assertions of jurisdiction with an approach that requires that any claim of prescriptive jurisdiction satisfy a test of reasonability.[7]

Section 403 goes on to articulate a series of balancing criterion, including

(a) the link of the activity to the territory of the regulating state, i.e., the extent to which the activity takes place within the territory, or has substantial, direct, and foreseeable effect upon or in the territory;

(b) the connections, such as nationality, residence, or economic activity, between the regulating state and the person principally responsible for the activity to be regulated, or between that state and those whom the regulation is designed to protect;

(c) the character of the activity to be regulated, the importance of regulation to the regulating state, the extent to which other states regulate such activities, and the degree to which the desirability of such regulation is generally accepted.

(d) the existence of justified expectations that might be protected or hurt by the regulation;

(e) the importance of the regulation to the international political, legal, or economic system;

(f) the extent to which the regulation is consistent with the traditions of the international system;

(g) the extent to which another state may have an interest in regulating the activity; and

(h) the likelihood of conflict with regulation by another state.

7. See also *Timberlane Lumber Co. v.*   1976).
Bank of America, 549 F.2d 597 (9th Cir.

Section 403 concludes by noting that "When it would not be unreasonable for each of two states to exercise jurisdiction over a person or activity, but the prescriptions by the two states are in conflict, each state has an obligation to evaluate its own as well as the other state's interest in exercising jurisdiction, in light of all the relevant factors [and] a state should defer to the other state if that state's interest is clearly greater."

The rule of reason articulated in section 403 presents a credible and welcome alternative to the "Wild West" world assumed by the *LOTUS* Presumption. Nevertheless, section 403 has been vigorously criticized. The replacement of clear rules for resolving jurisdictional conflicts between States with amorphous interest-balancing standards has been particularly excoriated. U.S. courts have often noted that such jurisdictional conflicts are usually irreconcilable, and that it is rare for one national court or government to backdown in the face of a conflict.[8] For these reasons, the balancing standards of section 403 have been regarded as too elastic, often sanctioning an "unreasonable" assertion of prescriptive jurisdiction, rather than restraining it.

B. Bases of Jurisdiction

If comity, reasonableness, and interest-balancing fail, that leaves the traditional international law rules that mark the outer limits of a State's ability to prescribe, adjudicate and enforce. These justifications—or bases—for jurisdiction have enjoyed a remarkable recognition and observance as customary international law for over two centuries, but they have recently undergone some significant changes. It would be wise to review these bases, starting with those regarded as the strongest.

1. *Territoriality and the Effects Principle.* One of the fundamental tenets of State sovereignty is the idea that a nation may exercise jurisdiction over persons, transactions and events occurring within its territory. As Chief Justice John Marshall noted in 1812, "The jurisdiction of a nation within its own territory is necessarily exclusive and absolute. It is susceptible of no limitation not imposed by itself."[9] Under this reasoning, only the territorial sovereign can decide to exercise jurisdiction over a matter arising within its borders. Consistent with international law, virtually every nation exercises nearly complete jurisdictional competence on the basis of territoriality.

---

8. Compare *Laker Airways v. Sabena, Belgian World Airlines*, 731 F.2d 909 (D.C. Cir. 1984) with *British Airways Bd. v. Laker Airways Ltd.*, [1984] 3 All E.R. 39 (H.L.) (U.K.), reprinted in 23 Int'l Legal Materials 727 (1984).

9. *The SCHOONER EXCHANGE v. McFaddon*, 11 U.S. (7 Cranch) 116, 136 (1812).

The only exceptions to territorial jurisdiction recognized by international law virtually prove the rule. States may *consent* through treaties to certain self-derogations of territorial sovereignty. In past centuries, for example, western colonial powers imposed "capitulary" or "extraterritorial" regimes on such Asian countries as India, China and Japan. Under such capitulations or extrality, a Briton living in Japan would be subject only to the jurisdiction of a British consular court in that nation. (Under a similar regime, a U.S. federal court operated in Shanghai, China from 1906 to 1943.) Today, the only equivalent of these unequal capitulations are "Status of Forces Agreements" (SOFAs) concluded by nations that have military contingents stationed in other countries. SOFAs might govern issues like the criminal prosecution of service-members and their dependents, and such a SOFA was the agreement at issue in *Reid v. Covert* (discussed in the last Chapter in the context of constitutional limitations on treaties).

The controversial aspect of the jurisdictional basis of territoriality does not arise with respect to persons and things within the forum's territory. Rather, the problem occurs when a State wishes to exercise jurisdiction over a person or thing, located *outside* that nation's territory, but that person or thing causes effects *inside* that State's borders. This is known as the "objective territorial principle" or, more descriptively, the "effects principle."

Objective territoriality is simply illustrated by the scenario of a gunman, located just a few feet inside Canadian territory, who fires a weapon into the United States and injures someone on this side of the border. If this sounds fanciful, consider a German decision of 1889 in which a French national, standing on a hillside in France, shouted "Vive la France!" and was later prosecuted for sedition in Germany because his declaration was heard across the frontier.[10] It is no surprise, therefore, that some of the most contentious cases of disputed jurisdiction have arisen when one State purports to exercise jurisdiction on the basis of the effects principle.

Let us take just one example of the many possible areas of controversy: the United States' extraterritorial enforcement of its antitrust laws. The U.S. was among the first countries to legislate strict rules to control monopolistic behavior by business combinations. One would think that in order to make antitrust enforcement effective, such legislation would have to be applied equally to both U.S. and foreign businesses. Otherwise, U.S. businesses would be operating at a substantial disadvantage, while foreign competitors could seek to subvert the U.S. market by making anti-competitive

10. *The Case of B.*, 20 Entscheidungen des Reichgerichts in Strafsachen 148   (1889), 17 Journal du droit international privé (Clunet) 498 (1890).

agreements. But under what theory could the U.S. prosecute or enjoin the monopolistic activities of foreign businesses?

The answer was provided by a panel of the U.S. Court of Appeals for the Second Circuit in *United States v. Aluminum Co. of America* (Alcoa).[11] The complaint charged that Aluminum Ltd., a Canadian entity, had formed in 1931 a cartel (rather brazenly called "the Alliance") with German, Swiss and British companies, in order to corner and control world markets in aluminum. Each member of the Alliance was given a production and sales quota, and at least initially, the U.S. market was not included in the quota. In 1936, the Alliance scheme was changed somewhat and imports into the U.S. were tacitly included in the combination. The United States later charged that the Alliance constituted a violation of section 1 of the Sherman Act that "every contract, combination . . . or conspiracy, in restraint of trade or commerce among the several States, or with foreign nations, is declared to be illegal."[12]

Because four Justices of the Supreme Court were recused in the matter, it was referred to the Second Circuit, and Judge Learned Hand wrote the decision. (His cousin, Augustus Hand, was also on the panel.) The Circuit ruled that the Sherman Act had to be construed consistent with "the limitations customarily observed by nations upon the exercise of their powers." Nevertheless, the Court held that the Sherman Act would only penalize that anti-competitive conduct which had actual effects in the United States. In finding that the 1936 version of the "Alliance" was intended to operate as a cartel in the United States, Judge Hand placed the burden on the defendants to prove that it had no actual impact.

Thus was born the effects doctrine in the extraterritorial application of U.S. antitrust laws. The *Alcoa* precedent has since been recognized by the U.S. Supreme Court,[13] and used in a variety of particular antitrust contexts. Needless to say, our major trading partners—Canada, Europe, and Japan—have vigorously opposed what they regarded as an untoward and illegal extension of United States' prescriptive jurisdiction over competition matters. In the late 1980's, however, the Europeans at least shifted their thinking and began to give qualified support for the use of the effects doctrine.[14] This time it was in vindication of the European Community's own competition policies and directives. The effects doctrine is thus becoming a more widely-recognized aspect of the jurisdictional basis of territoriality.

11. 148 F.2d 416 (2d Cir. 1945).

12. 15 U.S.C. § 1.

13. See *Continental Ore Co. v. Union Carbide & Carbon Corp.*, 370 U.S. 690 (1962).

14. See *Re Wood Pulp Cartel: A. Ahlstrom Osakeyhtio v. E.C. Commission,* [1988] 4 C.M.L.R. 901; *Re The LdPE Cartel: The Community v. Atochem SA,* [1990] 4 C.M.L.R. 382.

2. *Nationality.* Equally significant as a basis of a nation's jurisdiction to prescribe, adjudicate and enforce is nationality. That means a State is in large measure free to require compliance by its nationals, even when they are living abroad. It has been virtually unquestioned that the United States may impose substantial requirements on its nationals resident overseas. For example, the U.S. Supreme Court ruled that the refusal of a U.S. citizen, living in Paris, to obey issued subpoenas and to return to the United States to give testimony in a pending case was properly within the jurisdiction of the offended court.[15] Nor does there seem to be doubt that Congress has the power to legislate penalties for treason, the imposition of income taxes, registration for the draft, and other penalties for U.S. citizens abroad. Indeed, some enactments are particularly focused on the conduct of Americans living abroad. The Foreign Corrupt Practices Act (FCPA) makes it civilly-actionable for an individual or company to engage in bribery of foreign government officials in pursuance of business contracts overseas.

The nationality basis of jurisdiction has the potential, however, to cause substantial conflicts with other countries. This can occasionally occur for individuals. For example, the U.S. Supreme Court has ruled that the United States has jurisdiction to try and punish one of its nationals for an offense committed abroad, even though they might also be a national of the State in which the offense was committed.[16] It is precisely this dilemma that was earlier indicated (in Chapter 7(A)) as being a particular issue for dual nationals.

Corporations tend to be the parties that are most often affected by States' assertions of jurisdiction based on nationality. The most contentious issue in this regard has been the reach of United States' law to the subsidiaries of U.S. companies located overseas. This has arisen particularly in the context of enforcement of U.S. economic sanctions against foreign nations. For example, when Iranian revolutionaries stormed the U.S. embassy in Tehran in 1979 and took U.S. diplomats hostage, the United States "froze" Iranian assets located in U.S. banks. As an additional measure, the order extended to the foreign branches of U.S. banks. Some nations objected to this extraterritorial enforcement of U.S. law within their respective territories, but under the unique circumstances they did not attempt to foil U.S. sanctions. Just a few years later, in 1982, the United States sought to block the construction of a Soviet natural gas pipeline into Western Europe. To this end, the U.S. ordered that U.S. subsidiaries not provide supplies or equipment for the project. European nations howled with protest, and some (including Britain) passed special legislation purporting to block the application of the U.S. sanctions law in their territory and to

---

15. See *Blackmer v. United States,* 284 U.S. 421 (1932).

16. See *Tomoya Kawakita v. United States,* 343 U.S. 717 (1952).

punish any U.S.-owned or U.S.-controlled business that complied with the sanctions.

We have in this scenario a classic "whip-saw." A subsidiary of a U.S. corporation is forced to decide whether to comply with United States' law (asserted under the nationality principle of prescriptive jurisdiction) or to obey the contrary law of the State where it is based (legislated under a territoriality principle). It quite literally is impaled on the horns of a dilemma, made all the more difficult if one (or more) of the competing States imposes criminal sanctions for violation of its law. (This is not an extravagant scenario: an officer of a U.S. bank with a branch in Switzerland was recently forced to disobey an American subpoena to produce bank records or risk being imprisoned for violation of Swiss bank secrecy laws!)

Congress tries to be careful in not imposing regulatory requirements on U.S. businesses operating overseas, especially when such would make them less competitive. The U.S. Supreme Court will interpret an ambiguous Act of Congress as *not* applying extraterritorially in these situations.[17] Aside from inchoate principles of comity, there are no international law principles that would be used to resolve this conflict between nationality and territoriality bases of jurisdiction. A handful of United States cases recognize a doctrine of "foreign sovereign compulsion," in which a U.S. national will be relieved of the obligation to respect U.S. law when to do so would place it in irreconcilable conflict with a foreign nation's law. While some U.S. court decisions have granted this defense, upon showing of a good faith effort to comply with the U.S. law requirements, other judgments have rejected the argument.

3. *Universality.* The remaining bases of jurisdiction have rather more limited scope and applicability than territoriality and nationality. Among these last three, the universal principle of jurisdiction is probably the most significant. Already introduced in the context of the duties of individuals under international law (see Chapter 7(B)), universal jurisdiction means that any nation may prosecute or otherwise assert jurisdiction over persons suspected of having engaged in certain crimes or offenses. Some of these enumerated infractions were established by customary international law and then codified into treaty (such as piracy or slave-trading), others were more recently progressively developed (such as genocide, State-sponsored torture, and the most serious war-crimes). By granting *any* nation the right to assert jurisdiction over universal offenses, the set of possible prosecuting nations is extended beyond that of the perpetrator's State of nationality or the nation where the offense took place.

---

17. See *EEOC v. Arabian American Oil Co.*, 499 U.S. 244 (1991).

The concept of universal jurisdiction is by no means free from controversy. It really does depend on a virtual universal consensus that certain kinds of conduct are so heinous as to grant the right to any nation to prosecute them, even if the State of nationality of the defendant or the nation in which territory the crime took place is not so disposed. Conflicts between a State claiming universal jurisdiction and a nation asserting competence based on territoriality are rife. For example, a recent litigation involved former Chilean President Augusto Pinochet who was held in Britain for extradition to Spain to stand charges for tortures committed in Chile. The Chilean government argued (unsuccessfully) that only Chile, as the territorial sovereign in question, had a right to try Pinochet for those offenses. Likewise, a United States court ruled that a person charged with crimes committed in Nazi concentration camps in Eastern Europe could be extradited to Israel to stand trial there.[18]

The United States has been reluctant to exercise criminal jurisdiction over foreign nationals committing crimes in foreign nations on a theory of universality. The U.S. implementation of the Genocide and Torture Conventions has, to date, not been interpreted to extend so far. A number of European nations have begun to initiate prosecutions for such offenses within the past decade, and, ironically enough, United States courts will often exercise civil jurisdiction based on the Alien Tort Claims Act, previously discussed in Chapter 9(B). The Alien Tort Statute provides that U.S. courts have "jurisdiction of any civil action by an alien for a tort only, committed in violation of the law of nations or a treaty of the United States."[19] This has been construed as extending, at a minimum, to those offenses committed by individuals—with or without color of State authority—that are within universal jurisdiction. For example, a U.S. court held that the Bosnian–Serb leader, Radovan Karadžić, was amenable to a civil suit under the ATS for alleged violations of the law of nations involving genocide, war crimes, and breaches of humanitarian law.[20]

4. *Protective Principle.* In exceptional situations, a State may exercise jurisdiction over conduct that occurs beyond its borders by non-nationals, but which nevertheless is prejudicial to the State's security. The examples most often cited as justifying this exercise of jurisdiction are punishing foreign plots to overthrow a nation's government or to forge its currency. Nevertheless, protective jurisdiction is potentially expansive, based on how a nation defines its national security. For example, one of the asserted bases for Israel to prosecute Adolf Eichmann, one of Hitler's henchmen in carrying out the genocide of Jews in Europe, was a protective theory. This

---

18. See *Matter of Demjanjuk*, 776 F.2d 571 (6th Cir. 1985).

19. 28 U.S.C. § 1350.

20. See *Kadic v. Karadzic*, 70 F.3d 232 (2d Cir.1995).

was probably a substantial stretch, since the State of Israel had obviously not even been founded at the time of the Holocaust, and, even if it had, it might be doubted how Israel's national security interests were substantially affected.

The protective principle has been rarely invoked in U.S. law. There are a handful of statutes that might be seen to punish conduct, engaged in by foreigners outside the United States, which are regarded as impacting U.S. security, and which would not otherwise be covered by some application of the effects doctrine. In a handful of cases, courts have prosecuted foreigners who perjured themselves before U.S. diplomatic or consular officials abroad, and regarded their crimes as having been completed at the time they made their false statements (without the need for further action).[21] Despite its availability and recognition, States seem very cautious in invoking the protective principle as the only, or even a substantial, basis for invoking jurisdiction in a particular matter.

5. *Passive Personality.* The idea that a State could exercise jurisdiction over a crime based on the nationality of a victim has been regarded as the weakest basis for jurisdiction under international law. One might recall that this theory was half-heartedly argued by Turkey in *The LOTUS* Case as grounds for justifying their prosecution of a French officer charged with the negligent homicide of Turkish nationals on the high seas.[22] The Permanent Court of International Justice did not seriously entertain this argument, preferring to side with Turkey's position on other grounds.

Indeed, the United States historically has been critical of the passive personality theory. In an 1887 incident,[23] Mexico attempted to prosecute a U.S. journalist for the publication of a libel against a Mexican national in an American paper. Mexico relied on a passive personality theory for the action, and the United States protested. The criminal complaint was later modified by Mexico to include an allegation that the defamatory publication was actually distributed in Mexico—clearly satisfying an "objective personality" or effects test. The U.S. agreed that this was a permissible basis for Mexico's jurisdiction; the prosecution proceeded, but the defendant was ultimately released.

The United States' opposition to passive personality jurisdiction has decreased recently. In response to threats of international terrorism or organized crime directed at U.S. nationals residing or traveling abroad, Congress has legislated a number of crimes that

---

21. See, e.g., *United States v. Pizzarusso*, 388 F.2d 8 (2d Cir. 1968).

22. See 1927 P.C.I.J. (Ser. A) No. 10 (Fr. v. Tur.).

23. *Cutting* Case, [1887] U.S. Foreign Rel. 757.

can be prosecuted against non-nationals. In one case, *United States v. Yunis*,[24] these laws were challenged on the theory that the passive personality basis of jurisdiction violated customary international law. The defendant had been charged with participation in a hijacking incident in Lebanon in which Americans had been injured and killed. The U.S. Court of Appeals for the D.C. Circuit simply declined to rule on the merits of the defendant's jurisdictional challenge. Once the court confirmed that Congress was express in its intent to extend passive personality jurisdiction to particular crimes, and once it was clear that the normal presumptions against extraterritorial application of U.S. laws had been overcome, the D.C. Circuit refused to "conform the law of the land to the norms of customary international law."

This last holding is suggestive of two things. First, U.S. courts may well find the passive personality principle an appropriate basis for jurisdiction in both criminal and civil cases.[25] (Imagine a civil case arising from a securities fraud perpetrated on U.S. investors abroad.) More importantly, the ruling in *Yunis* indicates that U.S. courts might not be prepared to impose customary international law limits on the exercise of prescriptive and adjudicatory jurisdiction, at least as authorized by Congress. Yet, at the same time, courts have ruled that *compliance* with international law standards of jurisdiction satisfies any due process constitutional concerns for such prosecutions.

C. Extradition and Mutual Assistance

The last mechanism by which States avoid jurisdictional conflicts is through formalized, mutual assistance. These are typically procedures recognized and employed by countries to request aid from other States' executive or judicial authorities in the pursuance of criminal or civil procedures. For example, there are a series of conventions (drafted by the Hague Conference on Private International Law) that establish cross-boundary rules for service of process, taking of evidence, authentication of documents, and other litigation-related events. The United States is a party to many of these treaties, and they often play a significant role in U.S. litigation involving foreign parties. (The Hague Service Convention is so important that it is reprinted as an annex to Rule 4 of the Federal Rules of Civil Procedure.) Lastly, courts in one nation may apply for assistance from the tribunals of another State by dispatching a "letter rogatory" (sometimes also called a "letter of request"). These will often be respected and complied with, at least to the

---

24. 924 F.2d 1086 (D.C. Cir. 1991).   **25.** See *United States v. Benitez*, 741 F.2d 1312 (11th Cir. 1984).

extent that local law does not affirmatively bar the request for cooperation.

Mutual assistance does have its limits, however. Countries will often agree to cooperation in criminal investigations, especially now that some criminal enterprises are organized and often transnational. Such mutual assistance treaties often contain a clause exempting cooperation if the matter involves "sovereignty, security or similar essential interests" of one of the parties. Moreover, it has long been the view of the United States—as expressed by Chief Justice John Marshall in *The ANTELOPE*—that "the Courts of no country execute the penal laws of another."[26] All of this can be a big factor when a foreign litigant seeks to have a foreign judgment enforced or otherwise collected in the United States. U.S. courts will routinely refuse to enforce foreign judgments that they believe would violate American public policy. European courts do the same. (In a number of recent decisions, German courts have refused to enforce U.S. court judgments including punitive damages awards.)

The ultimate form of mutual assistance is *extradition*, the surrender by one State of an individual accused or convicted of a crime in another nation. Originally, extradition (or its less formal equivalent, *rendition*), was at the surrendering government's sole discretion. But at least in the nineteenth century, U.S. courts began to require that an extradition treaty be in force before an individual (whether or not a U.S. citizen) was handed-over to another country.[27] Today, under almost all of the extradition treaties to which the United States is a party, a foreign State desiring surrender of an individual will make an extradition request to the Executive Branch of the government. The only judicial involvement is a cursory examination of whether the person to be surrendered is, in fact, the individual sought, and whether the allegations satisfy a standard of probable cause. No independent review of the merits of the charges is made, what is called the "rule of non-inquiry." Once a court finds a person as extraditable, it remains in the sole discretion of the Secretary of State to have the person surrendered.

The only other task for judges in these situations is to ensure that the requirements of the relevant extradition treaty are fulfilled. Most extradition treaties feature a few possible elements that might affect the proceedings. The first is the rule of *double-criminality*. This means that the defendant's alleged crime must be punishable (usually as a felony) in *both* the requesting and sending States.[28] It may also mean that the charged offense was, in fact, a

---

26. 23 U.S. (10 Wheat.) 66, 123 (1825).

27. See *Valentine v. United States ex rel. Neidecker*, 299 U.S. 5 (1936).

28. See *Factor v. Laubenheimer*, 290 U.S. 276 (1933).

crime at the time it was committed. Many extradition treaties also contain lists of extraditable crimes, and the charged offense must fall within that list. Some extradition controversies have involved questions of how to define a particular offense. (For example, U.S. courts have declined to extradite individuals charged with violating Swiss bank secrecy laws—such a breach of confidence is not usually regarded as a crime under federal or state law.) Periodically, concerns have arisen where the statute of limitations has run (and not been tolled) in one of the relevant countries.

Related to double-criminality is the doctrine of *specialty*, which means that a defendant may only be tried or punished in the requesting State for those crimes for which he was extradited.[29] A requesting State may not seek extradition for bank fraud, and then "bait and switch" and later try the individual for homicide. Likewise, some extradition treaties to which the United States is a party bar the application of the death penalty if the defendant is convicted. In such circumstances—as with the *Soering* Case (discussed in Chapter 9(A))—the relevant U.S. jurisdiction would have to give the necessary assurances that the death penalty would not be imposed in the event of conviction after extradition. Some States go so far as to reserve in their extradition treaties the right not to hand-over their own nationals. The United States makes no such reservation, and will routinely extradite U.S. citizens.[30] This sometimes raises profound due process concerns. With the rule of judicial non-inquiry, it is entirely possible to imagine that an unscrupulous government might collude with a foreign nation to make a spurious extradition request thus resulting in that individual's forced exile from the United States.

The last, and most controversial, feature of most (but not all) extradition treaties is the *political offense exception*. This is a clause that indicates that the sending State is not obliged to extradite a suspect charged with political offenses. This was originally conceived in the 19th century as a way for liberal democracies to avoid surrendering dissidents to authoritarian regimes. But once a political offense exception was recognized, efforts were made to limit it. For example, *attentat* clauses were included in some extradition treaties, which provided that the murder of a head-of-State or head-of-government, or a member of such person's family, was not to be regarded as a political offense.[31]

Some extradition treaties specifically exclude anarchists or those who "envisage the overthrow of the bases of all political

29. See *United States v. Rauscher,* 119 U.S. 407 (1886).

30. See *Charlton v. Kelly,* 229 U.S. 447 (1913).

31. See *In re Pavelic,* [1933–34] Annual Digest of Int'l L. No. 158 (Turin Ct. App. 1934) (Italy).

organizations." Other conventions declined to extend the political offense exception to a "common crime," even if it had a political motivation or purpose. U.S. courts have attempted to distinguish between different sorts of offenses. For example, in a number of matters involving suspected Irish Republican Army (IRA) operatives, the charged assassinations of British soldiers or police were regarded as political offenses, while gratuitous murders of civilians were not. In any event, the 1985 Supplemental Extradition Treaty between the U.K. and U.S. largely eliminated the political offense exception.

Aside from the formal processes of extradition and rendition, there is one other mechanism for apprehending suspects in another country: self-help through forced abduction. Not surprisingly, though, this is frowned-upon in international law. In one recent example, United States agents, working in concert with private Mexican parties, kidnaped a Mexican doctor suspected of being complicit in the torture-murder of a Drug Enforcement Agency agent in Mexico. Upon his forced removal to the United States, the doctor challenged the jurisdiction of the court based on the U.S.-Mexico 1978 Extradition Treaty. Lower courts agreed with the defendant that because the Extradition Treaty had been violated, he should be released. The U.S. Supreme Court ruled, however, that because the treaty was actually silent on the subject of forced abductions as an alternative to formal extradition, there had been no violation, and jurisdiction was proper.[32]

Aside from the interpretive contortions that the Supreme Court had to engage in to reach this result, the decision seems doctrinally misguided. Resorting to forcible abductions to gain custody of a suspect should not be encouraged, especially when there is an extradition treaty in place. In any event, the case proved to be tragically unnecessary and embarrassing: the U.S. government later conceded that it had apprehended the wrong person! These extradition disputes illustrate the ultimate form of jurisdictional conflict in international relations. They will continue to be contentious, and implicate the most basic problems of the application of international rules in domestic law.

32. See *United States v. Alvarez–Machain*, 504 U.S. 655 (1992).

Chapter 17

Jurisdictional Immunities

The international law issue that is most-litigated in U.S. courts is the question of jurisdictional immunities that are to be extended in certain cases featuring foreign parties or raising delicate issues of foreign relations. I refer to these generically as "jurisdictional immunities," but in actuality they include situations not only where U.S. courts decide they lack subject-matter jurisdiction over certain disputes or parties, but also where they prudentially decline to address the merits of certain kinds of claims. Moreover, some of these jurisdictional immunities are actually required under international law and are the subject of substantial customary international law practice and treaty codification. In other situations, the jurisdictional immunities or prudential exemptions that U.S. courts extend actually *exceed* those required under international law.

This Chapter will explore this subject by examining three broad categories of immunities and exemptions: (A) foreign sovereign immunities, (B) the act of state doctrine, and (C) diplomatic, consular, and international organization immunities. In each instance, U.S. practice, statutory provisions, and case law are unique and may well reflect significant differences with those of other nations.

A. Foreign Sovereign Immunities

1. *From Absolute to Relative Immunity*. The immunity that a State enjoys in the domestic courts of other nations has always been a concern of customary international law. Views about foreign sovereign immunity, as reflected in the practice of States, have evolved as conceptions of the role of the State institutions and governments in international relations have also changed, especially over the past two centuries. Also, attitudes about the immunities of States in foreign courts have been altered as domestic legal systems have modified the immunities given to their own sovereigns and governments in their own tribunals.

Originally, conceptions of State immunity were rather weak. In the 17th and 18th centuries it would have been extravagant to suggest that monarchs and governments enjoyed blanket immunity from suit in their own nation's courts, or in the tribunals of foreign nations. But in the early 19th century, a significant sovereign immunity "revolution" occurred, and countries throughout the world began to extend wide immunities from suit to various forms of government institutions. An important case in this transition was the U.S. Supreme Court's 1812 decision in *The Schooner EXCHANGE v. McFaddon*.[1]

That case involved a ship originally owned by Americans. During the Napoleonic wars, France had seized the vessel on the high seas, condemned it as "prize" in its own courts, and rechristened it as a warship (called The BALAOU). Owing to a storm, the EXCHANGE had to put into Philadelphia for repairs. The original owners, shocked (and undoubtedly delighted) to see it at the dock, instituted an action to recover their property, claiming that the French confiscation had violated the law of nations. In 1812, France and the United States were at peace, and the U.S. government entered the proceeding to assert that the vessel was immune from arrest.

The Supreme Court, Chief Justice John Marshall writing, ruled that France enjoyed absolute immunity in the matter, and the case should be dismissed. Key to the Court's decision was the characterization of The BALAOU as a French "public armed ship," part of the "military force which supports the sovereign power, and maintains the dignity and the independence of a nation." Marshall made some citations to earlier publicists writing on this subject, but the real basis of his decision was judicial caution: "the general inability of [courts] to enforce its decisions in cases of this description, [and] that the sovereign power of the nation is alone competent to avenge wrongs committed by a sovereign, [and] that the questions to which such wrongs give birth are rather questions of policy than of law, [and] are for diplomatic, rather than legal discussion."

Despite these pronouncements, the absolute foreign sovereign immunity that *The Schooner EXCHANGE* has often been cited as supporting, may not have been so "absolute" after all. In dictum, Marshall observed that had the issue in the case concerned "the private property of the person who happens to be a prince," domestic courts might have jurisdiction. If the case had concerned a consignment of Virginia hams bound for the Emperor Napoleon's private dining table, the outcome might have been different. Thus was born the distinction of State activities *ius imperii* (on behalf of the government itself) and *ius gestionis* (on the private or commercial account of the sovereign or government official).

From this distinction evolved significant limitations on absolute foreign sovereign immunity. In response to many nations' having government-owned shipping operations engaging in commercial operations, the first multilateral treaty on foreign sovereign

---

1.   11 U.S. (7 Cranch) 116 (1812).

immunity—the 1926 Brussels Convention—was adopted. This instrument withdrew foreign sovereign immunity for State-owned commercial vessels. The problem was not confined to the shipping sector. It has been common practice for many States to have widespread and lucrative commercial operations. Government-owned mines, transport and communications, State trading and marketing arms, and national banks and insurance companies are but a few examples of this trend. (The United States is among a handful of nations that historically has shied-away from government-owned commercial enterprises.) Obviously, a doctrine of absolute foreign sovereign immunity that protected such government-owned commercial entities from lawsuits for breach of contract or other remedies was profoundly distortive in the competitive marketplace.

Beginning after the Second World War—at a time when the role and conception of the State was changing in any event—absolute sovereign immunity came under intense attack. Some European courts began to adopt a "restrictive" form of foreign sovereign immunity, one which did not immunize the commercial activities of foreign governments.[2] The United States began to move towards this position with the 1952 issuance of a State Department opinion on this subject, known as the "Tate Letter."[3] The letter pragmatically concluded that "the Department feels that the widespread and increasing practice of governments of engaging in commercial activities makes necessary a practice which will enable persons doing business with them to have their rights determined in the courts."

Within a few decades, State practice—as largely reflected in the views of Foreign Ministries and domestic tribunals around the world—had shifted to a theory of restrictive immunity for foreign sovereigns, one which carved-out extensive exceptions to claims of immunization from proceedings in other nations' courts. The socialist and Eastern European nations were the last holdouts for absolute foreign sovereign immunity, not surprising in view of their centrally-planned economies structured around State-run enterprises. With the dismantling of such structures in the 1980's and 1990's, these countries also embraced restrictive theories of foreign sovereign immunity.

2. *The U.S. Foreign Sovereign Immunities Act of 1976.* To a surprising degree, questions of foreign sovereign immunity remain a problem for customary international law and domestic case law. Attempts to fully codify this subject in multilateral treaties have

---

2. See, e.g., *Dralle v. Republic of Czechoslovakia*, 1950 Int'l L. Rep. 155 (Austrian S.Ct. 1950).

3. 26 Dep't of State Bulletin 984 (1952).

failed notably. A 1972 European Convention on State Immunity received little attention, and a project by the U.N. International Law Commission (ILC) to draft a comprehensive treaty on this subject has languished in the United Nations. A handful of countries—particularly those from common law traditions—have set-forth the contours of foreign sovereign immunities in statutory form.

The United States adopted such a law in 1976, the Foreign Sovereign Immunities Act (FSIA). The FSIA is an immensely significant statute in many respects. It purports to codify international law on an important subject. It also seeks to convert questions of granting foreign sovereign immunity—which had previously been regarded as matters for political and diplomatic expediency—into judicial and legal questions. The FSIA thus "overrules" Chief Justice Marshall's observation in *The Schooner EXCHANGE*, that the grant (or denial) of foreign sovereign immunity is a purely political matter. Indeed, prior to 1976, the only way that a litigant could initiate a suit against a foreign sovereign in a U.S. court was by first procuring the permission of the State Department. This resulted in threshold proceedings in which State Department lawyers would review potential claims, check for potential diplomatic fall-out, and only then grant a "pass" to file suit. The explicit intent of Congress in legislating the FSIA was to largely remove the role of the Executive Branch from these foreign sovereign immunity determinations.

The last point to be considered about the FSIA is that it is a subtle and complex piece of legislation.[4] It has often been criticized by lawyers, judges, and commentators as difficult to understand and apply, and, even after a quarter-century of experience, many problematic issues continue to arise under the Act. If one reads the FSIA and keeps a few basic points in mind, it should become more comprehensible.

The FSIA is the mechanism for gaining jurisdiction over a foreign sovereign, its officials and agents, its political subdivisions and government offices, and its agencies and instrumentalities.[5] Perhaps the most difficult issue raised under the FSIA is whether a particular entity being sued in a U.S. court is even notionally covered under the Act. This is obvious if a plaintiff's complaint lists the "Republic of France" as a defendant, but it becomes more problematic if the entity being sued is a company in which France owns a 51 percent stake (or, even more tenuously, a company owned by a company owned by the French government). Courts

---

4. The FSIA is codified at 28 U.S.C. §§ 1330, 1332, 1441, 1602–1611.

5. See 28 U.S.C. §§ 1603(a) & (b).

have ruled that individuals working within the scope of their employment or official authority with a foreign State may also be covered in some situations.

It is vital to realize that the FSIA is the *exclusive* avenue for gaining jurisdiction over a foreign sovereign entity in a United States court (whether federal or state). It previously had been suggested that the Alien Tort Claims Act, which gives district courts' jurisdiction over torts in violation of international law, would also extend to foreign sovereigns included as defendants in such suits. In 1989, the U.S. Supreme Court squelched such arguments in a case where an American company complained that Argentina had illegally destroyed its ship during the Falklands War.[6] The Court ruled that a suit against a foreign sovereign may only be brought under the restrictive rules of the FSIA. This decision has, in large measure, blunted the thrust of much human rights litigation in U.S. courts (discussed in Chapter 9(B)), because such suits can only be initiated against private parties, and not the abusing States themselves.

Once it is clear that a particular defendant is covered by the FSIA (and the foreign sovereign entity bears the burden of proof in this regard), the critical provision is 28 U.S.C. § 1604 which indicates that such an entity is presumptively *immune* from the adjudicatory jurisdiction of U.S. courts, *unless* one of the exceptions to immunity (set forth in section 1605) is satisfied. This effectively means that it is the plaintiff in foreign sovereign immunity cases that carries the burden of showing that a U.S. court has jurisdiction over the matter. If this showing cannot be made, the case is dismissed.

The heart of the FSIA is thus the enumerated exceptions to presumptive foreign sovereign immunity. In rough order of importance they are: the commercial activity exception (section 1605(a)(2)), waivers of immunity (section 1605(a)(1)), tortious acts (section 1605(a)(5)), and the newly-legislated terrorist States exception (section 1605(a)(7)). These will be discussed in turn. (Other exceptions covering admiralty claims, expropriated property, real property situated in the U.S., and arbitration agreements have less impact and will be discussed only tangentially in the following discussion.)

The commercial activity exception is the most-litigated exclusion of foreign sovereign immunity under the Act, and also one of the most confusingly drafted. In many respects, the key phrase—"commercial activity"—is inadequately defined by the FSIA to

---

6. See *Argentine Republic v. Amera-*   (1989).
da Hess Shipping Corp., 488 U.S. 428

mean "either a regular course of commercial conduct or a particular commercial transaction or act. The commercial character of an activity shall be determined by reference to the nature of the course of conduct or particular transaction or act, rather than by reference to its purpose."[7] If this sounds simple, it is not. Just because a particular course of conduct can be engaged-in by a private business party, does not make that same act a "commercial activity" if performed by a foreign sovereign. Courts have thus held that a libel action against a State-owned news agency is not a "commercial activity," and that an international cartel's fixing of oil prices was inherently a "sovereign" activity and thus non-commercial.[8] These results were criticized because they seemed to impose peculiarly American standards as to the appropriate role of government in business matters, and the Supreme Court responded in a 1992 decision holding that when a foreign sovereign engages in debt restructuring and finance, that constitutes a commercial activity, and there is thus no immunity.[9]

It is not enough, however, to show that a foreign sovereign or instrumentality has engaged in a commercial activity. A plaintiff must also show some connection between that activity and the United States. Section 1605(a)(2) allows for a withdrawal of immunity where an

> [i] action is based upon a commercial activity carried on in the United States by the foreign state; [ii] or upon an act performed in the United States in connection with a commercial activity of the foreign state elsewhere; [iii] or upon an act outside the territory of the United States in connection with a commercial activity of the foreign state elsewhere and that act causes a direct effect in the United States.[10]

The three "prongs" of the commercial activity exception can be used by plaintiffs singularly or in combination to persuade a court that a foreign sovereign entity had engaged in commercial conduct meriting an exclusion of immunity.

This nexus requirement spelled the doom of a plaintiff's claim in a recent case. Scott Nelson was recruited in the United States to serve as a hospital safety consultant in Saudi Arabia. He arrived at his posting, began to observe some safety irregularities, reported these to his supervisors, whereupon he and his wife were arrested and tortured by Saudi police authorities. (The Saudi government later contended that Nelson had engaged in employment irregulari-

---

7. 28 U.S.C. § 1603(d).

8. See *Yessenin-Volpin v. Novosti Press Agency*, 443 F. Supp. 849 (S.D.N.Y. 1978); *International Ass'n of Machinists & Aerospace Workers v.*

OPEC, 477 F. Supp. 553 (C.D. Cal. 1979).

9. See *Republic of Argentina v. Weltover, Inc.*, 504 U.S. 607 (1992).

10. 28 U.S.C. § 1605(a)(2).

ties, and the Nelsons were only released after a high-level intervention by the U.S. government.) Upon his return to the U.S., Nelson instituted a suit against the Saudi government under the FSIA.

In a 1993 decision, the Supreme Court ruled that Saudi Arabia had immunity in the case.[11] The majority held that to the extent Nelson's complaint arose from his torture, there was no causal link or nexus between his recruitment in the U.S. (which would satisfy prongs i & ii of 1605(a)(2)), his job performance, and his retaliatory torture. (The Court appeared to assume that if the case had been for amounts owing on Nelson's contract, Saudi Arabia would not have enjoyed immunity.) The Court concluded—over a strong dissent—that the police-sponsored torture was a sovereign act that would never be imputed as a commercial activity. Putting aside the naïvete of the assumption that torture and coercion are never used in foreign business practices, the holding in the *Nelson* case demands a high level of showing that a foreign sovereign's commercial conduct caused an effect in the United States.

A number of FSIA exceptions give scope to the idea that a foreign sovereign can consent by *waiver* to jurisdiction in U.S. courts. Sometimes this kind of waiver can be manifested in Friendship, Commerce and Navigation (FCN) Treaties concluded between the U.S. and other nations, and are encompassed in section 1604's reference to pre-existing international agreements to which the United States is a party. More typically, foreign sovereigns or instrumentalities may consent to the jurisdiction of U.S. courts in forum selection clauses found in contracts or arbitration agreements (contemplated in section 1605(a)(1)). Implied waivers are also possible, but only in very narrow circumstances. If a foreign sovereign enters an appearance in a U.S. proceeding, without invoking its immunity, that will be taken as a waiver. Furthermore, if that foreign sovereign files a counterclaim in a pending suit (within the meaning of section 1607), that is also a waiver.

U.S. courts have been virtually unanimous in rejecting arguments for another form of implied waiver. Human rights litigators have contended that if a nation engages in abuses that amount to *ius cogens* violations such as genocide and torture, then it cannot claim foreign sovereign immunity. This idea of universal jurisdiction "canceling out" foreign sovereign immunities has a superficial appeal, until one realizes that the threshold for an implied waiver must necessarily be a high one. That does not mean, though, that in appropriate cases a U.S. court will not creatively find an implied submission to U.S. jurisdiction in litigating a human rights abuse. For example, the Ninth Circuit U.S. Court of Appeals ruled that Argentina had impliedly submitted to U.S. court jurisdiction by

11. *Saudi Arabia v. Nelson*, 507 U.S. 349 (1993).

filing a letter rogatory and pursuing a pretextual investigation of one of its nationals here.[12] Because of that, the plaintiff could litigate damages arising from his torture (but not expropriation of property) at the hands of the Argentine government.

The last major FSIA exception is for "non-commercial torts." This covers situations where

> money damages are sought against a foreign state for personal injury or death, or damage to or loss of property, occurring in the United States and caused by the tortious act or omission of that foreign state or of any official or employee of that foreign state while acting within the scope of his office or employment; except this paragraph shall not apply to—
>
> (A) any claim based upon the exercise or performance or the failure to exercise or perform a discretionary function regardless of whether the discretion be abused, or
>
> (B) any claim arising out of malicious prosecution, abuse of process, libel, slander, misrepresentation, deceit, or interference with contract rights.[13]

As one can tell from reading, this exception is so riddled with conditions as to be almost unavailing for FSIA plaintiffs. The crucial condition of the tort exception is that the incident must occur in the United States. The paradigmatic case contemplated under this exclusion was to allow suit when a foreign government employee injures someone in a vehicular accident in the United States.

Another aspect of the tort exception, the discretionary function carve-out (in section 1605(a)(5)(A)), is particularly problematic. This can conceivably allow a foreign sovereign to claim that it was permitted to commit a tort in the United States because it was in pursuance of some official policy or sanction. Fortunately, this argument for immunity has been rejected where a foreign sovereign has engaged in assassinations or political murders in the United States—no State has the "discretion" to commit that kind of crime. At the opposite end of the spectrum, the suggestion that Nigerian consular officers had the "discretion" to trash a leased office in San Francisco was derisively rejected.[14] In a much-criticized decision, a court held that Norwegian consular officials had the discretion to defy the custody and injunctive orders of a California state court and issue travel documents to a mother and her children, knowing that the mother would later return the kids to Norway. Norway

---

12. See *Siderman de Blake v. Republic of Argentina*, 965 F.2d 699 (9th Cir. 1992).

13. 28 U.S.C. § 1605(a)(5).

14. See *Joseph v. Office of the Consulate General of Nigeria*, 830 F.2d 1018 (9th Cir. 1987).

was thus immunized from a suit by the father for loss of his parental rights.[15]

Recognizing that the FSIA's tort exception often did not allow suit for some of the most egregious incidents, Congress legislated in 1996 a new exclusion. Section 1605(a)(7) permits U.S. nationals to bring suits against foreign sovereigns for personal injury or death arising from "torture, extra judicial killing, air sabotage [and] hostage taking." There is no requirement that the tort occur in the United States, but there is a provision that the defendant State must be one that is designated by the State Department as a State-sponsor of terrorism. (That list now includes Cuba, Iraq, Iran, Libya, North Korea, Sudan and Syria.) A lengthy (10 year) statute of limitation is imposed, as is a requisite that the claimant give the offending foreign State the opportunity to arbitrate. This new FSIA exception has been much-employed since it was enacted, with suits brought for hostage-takings and bombings by Iranian-backed terrorists, and for the destruction of a PanAm flight over Lockerbie, Scotland.

3. *Remaining Issues.* The FSIA was intended to resolve all extant problems and disputes concerning foreign sovereign immunities in U.S. law. Alas, that has not been the case, and many notable issues remain. Many arise from ambiguities in the Act itself, which has been criticized by judges as both confusing in structure and problematic in its technical details. It is worth briefly pointing out some of these additional matters.

One thing to note is that the FSIA combines both subject-matter and personal jurisdiction into one inquiry. The FSIA establishes its own service of process requirements (section 1608), but (assuming those are satisfied) if a court finds that a foreign state is not entitled to immunity under the Act, then that court has jurisdiction. This jurisdiction can extend even to suits brought by foreign plaintiffs against foreign defendants. As long as one of the exceptions of section 1605 is triggered, the suit may proceed even if it has only a tenuous connection with the United States. Although some commentators have criticized this result as an unconstitutional increase of judicial power, the U.S. Supreme Court has ruled that if Congress wishes to open U.S. courts to such suits, it may under its Commerce Clause powers.[16] It is also important to note that, under the FSIA, proceedings are subject to a special removal procedure and that, in any event, no right to a jury trial exists.

Although the role of the State Department as a "gate-keeper" for claims against foreign sovereigns has been substantially reduced under the FSIA, it has not been eliminated altogether. The Execu-

---

15. See *Risk v. Halvorsen*, 936 F.2d 393 (9th Cir. 1991).

16. See *Verlinden, B.V. v. Central Bank of Nigeria*, 461 U.S. 480 (1983).

tive Branch often appears as an *amicus curiae* in cases involving foreign sovereigns, and its views are often respected by the courts. In one type of case, though, the State Department's views may still be dispositive. The FSIA makes no mention of the immunities of heads-of-State or leaders of governments. The Executive Branch has argued that head-of-state immunity remains subject to common law (and customary international law) rules, and that its determination of whether an individual is a head-of-State should be controlling for purposes of any grant (or denial) of immunity by the courts.

The last remaining issue involves execution of judgments against foreign sovereigns and their instrumentalities. In actuality, the FSIA (at sections 1609–1611) sets forth very restrictive rules for enforcement of judgments. If it is difficult enough to satisfy one of the exceptions to immunity (under section 1605) to gain jurisdiction to adjudicate over a foreign sovereign, it is even harder to prevail on an exception to actually enforce a judgment. As currently drafted, the FSIA requires that (1) only commercial property of the foreign sovereign or actual foreign instrumentality that is the defendant in the suit be attached or executed against, and (2) that there must be some link between the property to be attached or executed against and the underlying claim. The diplomatic assets, central bank accounts, and military property of the foreign State are virtually immune from execution.

This has caused substantial miscarriages of justice. In one case, Chilean secret agents entered the United States in 1976 and murdered a Chilean dissident and his American companion in a car-bombing in Washington, D.C. The families brought suit under the FSIA and prevailed under the tort exception to immunity, despite Chilean arguments that they had the "discretion" to assassinate opponents in the U.S. But when it came time to enforce the $5 million judgment, problems arose. The only Chilean assets the plaintiffs could find in the U.S. were the property of the Chilean national airline (LAN). A court later ruled that, under the narrow drafting of the FSIA, LAN was a separate entity from the Chilean government and that, in any event, it was by no means clear that the property to be executed against was related to the underlying political murder.[17] The Second Circuit Court of Appeals acknowledged that this left the plaintiffs with a "right without a remedy." Ultimately, the award was paid by Chile (although without interest) a decade later, after the diplomatic intervention of the United States.

Execution cases thus implicate the "absolute immunity" legacy of foreign sovereign prerogatives. They also involve tricky questions

---

17. See *Letelier v. Republic of Chile,* 748 F.2d 790 (2d Cir. 1984).

of corporate forms, especially when plaintiffs are suing not a foreign sovereign itself, but an instrumentality of the State (usually a trading entity or State-owned corporation). In these instances, international law rules for corporate forms and the principle of not typically "piercing corporate veils" will be respected.[18]

Foreign sovereign immunities will likely remain the single-most litigated bundle of international law issues in U.S. courts. The presence of a definitive (if albeit, complex) statutory regime is one reason why. The increasing globalization of trade and commerce, and the continuing role of State institutions in that process, are other factors. Restrictive immunities of foreign States may also give scope to suits that would have been inconceivable even a few years ago. Insofar as foreign sovereign immunities often involve incredibly delicate issues of foreign relations, they will continue to be contentious and difficult.

B.   The Act of State Doctrine

The act of state doctrine is closely linked with foreign sovereign immunities; so much so that one commentator has called it the "evil twin" of the FSIA. The act of state doctrine is not, however, a jurisdictional defense to a suit, like foreign sovereign immunity is. If a court dismisses a complaint under the FSIA, it does not reach the merits of the case. The act of state doctrine is best thought of as a prudential rule of judicial self-restraint or choice-of-law rule, which results in certain claims being dismissed on their merits. Another thing to realize is that while foreign sovereign immunity is typically raised by a foreign State *defendant* in a case filed in the U.S., the act of state doctrine can be invoked by *any* party in a litigation in order to defeat a particular claim or counter-claim.

The act of state doctrine is solely the creature of Anglo–American common law. It has its roots in early English decisions and is still applied in England today.[19] The tribunals of most other nations in the world reject the doctrine. Unlike foreign sovereign immunities, no argument can be made that an act of state exclusion for matters litigated in domestic courts is affirmatively required by international law.

The first, and most succinct, expression of the act of state doctrine in U.S. case law was in *Underhill v. Hernandez*, where the Supreme Court held: "the courts of one country will not sit in judgment on the acts of the government of another, done within its

---

18. See *First National City Bank v. Banco Para el Commercio Exterior de Cuba*, 462 U.S. 611 (1983).

19. See *Blad v. Bamfield*, 3 Swan. 604, 36 Eng Rep. 992 (Ch. 1674); *Duke of Brunswick v. King of Hanover*, 2 H.L. Cas. 1, 9 Eng. Rep. 993 (1848); *Buttes Gas & Oil Co. v. Hammer*, [1981] 3 All E.R. 616 (H.L. 1981) (U.K.).

own territory."[20] Even in the initial articulation of the doctrine, it was limited to the acts of a government taken with its own territory. On its own terms, the doctrine does not apply to bar adjudication of disputes involving acts of foreign governments taken outside of its own territory, or (perhaps more problematically) to acts with effects outside of its own territory.

Despite this qualification, U.S. courts recognized early-on that the act of state doctrine had the potential to cause profound injustice. In one notorious example, *Bernstein v. Van Heyghen Freres Société Anonyme*,[21] the Second Circuit ruled that the Nazis' confiscations of Jewish property in Germany qualified as an act of state and thus dismissed plaintiff's suit to recover such items. In response to this decision, the Executive Branch began a policy of issuing what came to be known as "Bernstein letters," in which the U.S. government indicated that it had no objection to a U.S. court adjudicating a dispute involving the actions of a foreign government. The use of Bernstein letters indicated that courts regarded the act of state doctrine as a kind of "escape valve," an implicit request by the political branches of the government to the courts not to consider a dispute because of potential embarrassment to U.S. foreign policy. When the President indicated that judicial review of foreign acts would not be a problem (as, obviously, would be the case of actions taken by Nazi Germany, which the U.S. defeated in World War Two), then the case could proceed.

In a 1964 decision, the U.S. Supreme Court put the act of state doctrine on a potentially broader footing. In *Banco Nacional de Cuba v. Sabbatino*,[22] the issue was the propriety of Castro Cuba's expropriation decrees of American sugar plantations. Banco Nacional had sued Sabbatino, the receiver of a U.S. company expropriated by Cuba, for funds in his possession. Sabbatino raised, as a defense to Banco Nacional's claim, that the expropriations were illegal under customary international law (see Chapter 8(C)). Banco Nacional asserted that, to the extent that Sabbatino's claim depended on placing in issue Cuba's act of state carried out in its own territory, it was barred. The *Sabbatino* case thus featured the offensive use of the act of state doctrine by a plaintiff.

In the event, the Supreme Court agreed that the act of state doctrine applied to bar the counterclaim. The Court confirmed that the doctrine was not required by sovereignty or by international law. Rather, the Court's rationale for the doctrine was a constitutional separation of powers problems that would arise when the judiciary attempted to resolve issues dependent on characterizations of acts of foreign governments. The Court was concerned that

20. *Underhill v. Hernandez*, 168 U.S. 250, 252 (1897).

21. 163 F.2d 246 (2d Cir. 1947).

22. 376 U.S. 398 (1964).

customary international law was too vague to give U.S. judges a definitive basis to make those decisions. Moreover, judicial efficiency was not served by having U.S. courts resolve disputes (like mass Cuban expropriations) by piecemeal litigation. Lastly, the Court indicated that the act of state doctrine was a *mandatory* rule of judicial rectitude; courts would have to abstain in such cases, even if the Executive Branch had issued a Bernstein letter.

The *Sabbatino* case reflected the high-water mark for the act of state doctrine. Under that ruling, any case which involved an action by a recognized foreign government (even an expropriation contrary to customary international law), within its own territory, would be barred from adjudication by U.S. courts, unless there was a controlling treaty provision between the U.S. and that foreign country. The "treaty exception" to the act of state doctrine has been consistently recognized by the courts. If there is a treaty "on-point," U.S. courts generally feel they are competent to rule on the merits of a foreign nation's allegedly illegal acts.[23]

Since 1964, the *Sabbatino* version of the act of state doctrine has been substantially eroded. This has partially been achieved by legislative action. Within months of the *Sabbatino* decision, Congress enacted an antidote: the Second Hickenlooper Amendment.[24] That Amendment provided that a taking in violation of international law could still be adjudicated in U.S. courts, notwithstanding the act of state doctrine, provided that the asserted claim was for a property right, and that the President had not specifically filed a notice barring the suit. Courts have also carved out exceptions to the act of state doctrine for cases involving human rights abuses committed by governments. This result was confirmed by Congress when it legislated the Torture Victim Protection Act (TVPA) in 1992,[25] the functional equivalent of the Alien Tort Claims Act for U.S. plaintiffs. Attempts, however, to create a commercial-activity exception for the doctrine, like the one for foreign sovereign immunities, have been less successful.[26] That means that a case against a foreign sovereign involving a commercial matter will be jurisdictionally allowed under the FSIA, but might be rejected on act of state grounds.

The latest occasion for the Supreme Court to rule on the act of state doctrine was in *W.S. Kirkpatrick & Co., Inc. v. Environmental Tectonics Corp., Int'l*, handed down in 1990.[27] This case involved a charge by one U.S. contractor that another had used bribery in

23. See, e.g., *Kalamazoo Spice Extraction Co. v. Provisional Military Government of Socialist Ethiopia*, 729 F.2d 422 (6th Cir. 1984).

24. See 22 U.S.C. § 2370(e)(2).

25. See 28 U.S.C. § 1350 note.

26. But see *Alfred Dunhill of London, Inc. v. Republic of Cuba*, 425 U.S. 682 (1976).

27. 493 U.S. 400 (1990).

order to win a lucrative contract from the Nigerian government. The defendant argued that this matter implicated an act of state and was thus not justiciable. The Supreme Court rejected this contention, distinguishing situations where a party sought to "declare invalid the official act of a foreign sovereign performed within its own territory" (covered by the doctrine), from cases where a court merely imputes "unlawful motivation" to foreign officials (which is not covered). As Justice Scalia concluded:

> The short of the matter is this: Courts in the United States have the power, and ordinarily the obligation, to decide cases and controversies properly presented to them. The act of state doctrine does not establish an exception for cases and controversies that may embarrass foreign governments, but merely requires that, in the process of deciding, the acts of foreign sovereigns taken within their own jurisdictions shall be deemed valid. That doctrine has no application to the present case because the validity of no foreign sovereign act is at issue.[28]

The *Kirkpatrick* case may well have narrowed the act of state doctrine to the vanishing point. Although broadly stated in both *Underhill* and *Sabbatino*, the treaty, human rights, and (perhaps) commercial exceptions have limited its preclusive effect. *Kirkpatrick*'s emphasis on the doctrine as a choice-of-law rule having to do only with respect afforded to foreign acts means that only in the most exceptional cases will disputes be barred from adjudication in U.S. courts. Despite these caveats, the act of state doctrine remains a significant aspect of litigation involving international law rights and duties in U.S. courts.

C. Diplomatic, Consular and Organizational Immunity

Diplomatic immunity counts as one of the oldest of international law doctrines. It traces its doctrinal roots to ancient times and is obviously an essential component of international relations. Diplomacy would be impossible if there were a substantial risk that envoys would be harmed by receiving States, or if they were not adequately protected as they carried out their duties. Diplomatic immunity has thus evolved from a form of extraterritoriality, known as *droit du quartier*, with the diplomat and embassy being considered to be under the sovereign jurisdiction of the sending State. Embassies—despite what the popular press reports–are no longer considered to be the territory of the foreign State that occupies them. And even though a nation's ambassador is considered to be the personification and representative of the sending

---

28. Id. at 409.

State, that is no longer considered the basis for diplomatic immunities and privileges.

Today, the scope of diplomatic immunities is premised on the functional duties of diplomatic personnel. The type and intensity of diplomatic immunities and privileges granted under international law thus depend on the nature of particular diplomatic officials and establishments. At this juncture, it is necessary to distinguish two broad types of foreign representative personnel stationed in a receiving nation. *Diplomats* typically represent the sending State in all political and military relations with the host government. *Consuls* are a distinct category of officials. Also an ancient institution (from Greece), consuls are charged with protecting the interests of their nationals resident in a host country. Consuls also issue visas and passports to travelers, as well as handle commercial and business relations between the sending and receiving States. A consul is usually, but not always, a national of the sending State. (A consul who is a national of the host State is called an "honorary consul" and is only afforded the most rudimentary immunities.)

For centuries, the privileges and immunities of diplomats and consuls were an issue for customary international law, and there was an elaborate ceremony and protocol for such matters. Finally, these rules were codified in the 1961 Vienna Convention on Diplomatic Relations (VCDR) and the 1963 Vienna Convention on Consular Relations (VCCR). The chief premise of these conventions is that diplomatic and consular personnel should be afforded those protections to allow them to exercise their functions and duties. Diplomats are usually granted complete immunity from the host State's criminal jurisdiction and also from most civil proceedings (except when they act in a personal, commercial capacity). Consuls, on the other hand, have only a limited immunity for conduct carried out in pursuance of their functions. Diplomatic and consular properties and communications are generally privileged from interference by the host State, and visiting diplomats and consuls get relief from the host State's taxes and personal obligations. It should be borne in mind that diplomatic immunities are not personal and absolute—they can be waived be the envoy's home government for whatever reason.

Abuses of diplomatic immunities and privileges are rare, but when they occur they are notorious. Some manifestations of these affronts are simply aggravating, such as foreign envoys in Washington, D.C. who illegally park their vehicles and then defiantly refuse to pay the tickets. Others are much more serious. Diplomatic shipments to and from embassies—what is known as the "diplomatic pouch" (even though they can be the size of railroad containers)—have been used to smuggle weapons and narcotics into a host State. Under the VCDR, such pouches are supposed to be inviolable, immune from inspection or scanning, although this rule has been violated in exceptional cases (such as the release of a Nigerian dissident, found drugged and bound in a diplomatic container awaiting shipment at London's Heathrow Airport). Consular pouches may be scanned and challenged, and the sending nation has the choice of either opening the package or having it returned.

Even more contentious is the immunity granted to diplomatic premises. On occasion, host States have entered embassies or consulates in order to extinguish fires or rescue kidnaped individuals. These incidents have been sharply protested, as was the Iranian militants' take-over of the U.S. embassy in Tehran in 1979. Another wrinkle to the "inviolability" of leased diplomatic premises is that if a country is a "deadbeat" tenant and has not paid its rent, it may not be lawfully evicted.[29] Needless to say, this rule has suppressed the willingness of commercial property owners to lease space to diplomatic establishments.

By far and away the most politically explosive issue surrounding diplomatic immunity is when envoys (or their families) quite literally get away with murder. (This is not an issue for consuls since they have only a limited form of immunity.) Since diplomats have absolute immunity from the receiving State's criminal jurisdiction, when an envoy commits a serious crime, the receiving State can only demand either that the sending State waive his immunity or that he immediately leave (this is called being declared *persona non grata*, or, in diplomatic argot, "being PNG'ed"). As grossly unfair as this seems, it is important to keep in mind that serious criminal acts by diplomats are exceptionally rare. Moreover, the position of the United States is that such diplomatic immunities are necessary to ensure that members of the U.S. Foreign Service are not harassed (or worse) on pretextual charges.

Added to the mix of diplomatic and consular immunities are those of international organizations, their staff, and accredited representatives. Known generically as "international organization immunities," this is actually three distinct subjects. The official representatives of States to international organizations (such as the foreign missions to the United Nations in New York) are assimilated to foreign embassies. Although U.S. relations with some of the U.N. missions have been testy, the United States has typically respected their privileges and immunities. The U.S. has imposed size limits on the missions and has periodically limited the movements of mission staff. With the sole exceptions of the abortive closing of the Palestine Liberation Organization's U.N. mission in

---

29. See, e.g., *767 Third Ave. Assocs. v. Permanent Mission of Zaire to the* *United Nations,* 988 F.2d 295 (2d Cir. 1993).

1987 and the prosecution of a Cuban mission official for espionage in 1963,[30] the immunities of U.N. missions have been respected.

As for the privileges and immunities of international organizations themselves (for more on which, see Chapter 6), these are typically regulated by the constituent instrument of the institution or by special agreement among the members. The 1946 Convention on the Privileges and Immunities of the United Nations and the 1947 Headquarters Agreement are the key instruments for the U.N. Under these agreements, the institutions enjoy immunity from host State courts for almost all kinds of actions. The most contentious kind of law-suit has been those by employees against their organizations for wrongful termination or employment discrimination. Under U.S. practice, such suits are governed by the International Organization Immunities Act (IOIA),[31] which grants a form of absolute immunity to such institutions, irrespective of whether the underlying claim is really commercial in character.[32] U.S. courts have in a handful of cases found that the international institution has waived its immunity to some sorts of contractual claims.[33]

The last issue with international organization immunity has to do with the protections afforded to the staffs of such institutions. Given the nature of their work, they are often considered at risk, especially for coercion by their own States of nationality. In a series of cases, the International Court of Justice has ruled that U.N. employees are subject to civil service protections (through the U.N. Administrative Tribunal), even though their States of nationality may in some situations dictate their terms of employment through secondment policies. More importantly, the immunities and privileges of U.N. staff, even occasional employees or experts, are applicable as against their State of nationality.[34] The substantive protections include immunities from harassing civil litigation brought in reference to acts carried out in the course of the staff member's employment.[35] Once again, the immunities of international institution staff are functional in character. They are limited to those necessary for the neutral and efficient operation of the organization. (In one famous instance,[36] a New York traffic court

---

30. See *United States ex rel. Casanova v. Fitzpatrick*, 214 F. Supp. 425 (S.D.N.Y. 1963).

31. See 22 U.S.C. § 288 et seq.

32. See *Mendaro v. World Bank*, 717 F.2d 610 (D.C. Cir.1983).

33. See *Lutcher S.A. Celulose e Papel v. Inter–American Development Bank*, 382 F.2d 454 (D.C. Cir. 1967).

34. See *Applicability of Article VI, Section 22, of the Convention on the*

Privileges and Immunities of the United Nations, 1989 I.C.J. 177.

35. See *Difference Relating to Immunity from Legal Process of a Special Rapporteur of the Commission on Human Rights*, 1999 I.C.J. ___ (Opinion of April 29).

36. See *Westchester County v. Ranollo*, 67 N.Y.S.2d 31 (City Ct. New Rochelle 1946).

imposed a fine against the U.N. Secretary–General's chauffeur for speeding, despite a plea of immunity!)

Diplomatic, consular and organizational immunities reflect an important value of international law as applied in domestic legal systems: the necessity of protecting the essential mechanisms of communication and diplomacy between nations. While these privileges and immunities appear anachronistic and formalistic, they retain substantial vitality in both customary international law and treaty codification. When combined with related doctrines of foreign sovereign immunity and acts of state, they can represent a formidable barrier to litigate certain types of foreign relations disputes in U.S. courts. Jurisdictional immunities to what would otherwise be the unquestioned competence of domestic tribunals to hear certain kinds of cases will remain controversial. To the extent U.S. practice differs from international rules (whether by being too gracious or grudging towards outside interests), these controversies will intensify. The complexities and contradictions of this subject are what makes it so challenging for international lawyers.

*

PART FOUR

WAR AND PEACE

Chapter 18

Counter–Measures

The ultimate test of international law is how well it manages conflict between States and other international actors. So far, this volume has demonstrated that international law is fully-formed as a legal system—with clear sources and methods, a diversity of subjects and objects, as well as the ability positively to interact with domestic legal systems. Even so, international law would be a failure if it could not adequately meet the needs of the international community in constructively resolving the problems that arise in international affairs. The only real way to measure the success of the international legal system is by its ability to resolve peacefully those international disputes.

This final Part of the book examines the cluster of issues implicated in international law's management of conflict. This Chapter will review the ways that States practically enforce or demand their rights under international law, chiefly by measures that fall short of the use of military force or war. Chapter 19 considers the ways in which the international community has imposed controls on recourse to armed conflict and the restraints placed on States in initiating hostilities. This topic also includes the role of the United Nations in the maintenance of international peace and security, and as the agent of collective security. The role of international law does not end with a declaration of war between countries. Over centuries, international law has developed a definitive law of war, which today includes substantial protections of civilians, noncombatants, prisoners, and other individuals deserving protection. The laws of war, also known as "international humanitarian law," will be reviewed in Chapter 20. Finally, the many mechanisms available under international law for the peaceful settlement of disputes will be assayed in Chapter 21. These include the institutions of negotiated-settlement and arbitration, as well as the significant role and jurisdiction of the International Court of Justice.

Already in this book I have characterized the process of making international law as a struggle. States and other international actors competitively bid for new rules of customary international law, actively negotiate new treaties, aggressively assert their domestic jurisdictions over international matters, and generally compete to shape a "market-place" of international law values, doctrines, systems and institutions. This struggle for law requires that a State carefully consider its options when its international law rights have been violated or transgressed by another nation. How exactly do international actors enforce international law rights and duties?

This topic is known today as the international law of "counter-measures." Counter-measures, or "self-help," is a necessary part of any legal system that lacks strong "vertical" enforcement like the international community. There is no world policeman to command or coerce obedience to international law rules; instead, States and other actors rely on a combination of mechanisms to win respect and compliance for these duties. Counter-measures have been traditionally divided into two categories: *forcible* (involving recourse to armed conflict) and *non-forcible* (not involving military power).

The use of forcible means to coerce another nation to comply with an international law right or duty is now governed by the background rules of the control of armed conflict and the law of the United Nations Charter (discussed at great length in the next Chapter). It is worth remembering that, until 1945 at least, the use of armed force in response to an unfriendly or illegal act by another State was a common occurrence. In 1914, for example, U.S. forces occupied the Mexican city of Veracruz after Mexican authorities refused to salute the American flag following an incident where rowdy American sailors had been arrested on shore-leave and promptly released with an apology. The United States justified its use of armed force as legitimate reprisal and as "a means of enforcing redress for a specific indignity."[1]

In a similar fashion, an arbitral tribunal ruled in 1928 that States could engage in forcible reprisals in response to illegal acts, but only after a demand for redress had been made to the offending nation, and only in a way that was proportional to the injury.[2] Despite attempts to control the use of armed reprisals in international relations, there was an inevitable tendency for hostilities to escalate in these situations. Moreover, the self-judging conduct of States in taking matters into their own hands caused substantial problems. It was for these reasons that the U.N. Charter specifically abrogated the "right" of States to engage unilaterally in the

---

1. Veracruz Incident, 1914 U.S. Foreign Relations 448–95.

2. See *Naulilaa Incident* Arbitration (Port. v. Ger.), 2 U.N. Rep. Int'l Arb. Awards 1012 (1928).

threat or use of force as a means to command other nations to obey or respect international legal obligations.

As a consequence of the substantial elimination of forcible counter-measures in international law, States were left only with the option to engage in measures short of war to create an environment that was conducive to the development of international law rules and the peaceful settlement of disputes. Non-forcible counter-measures came to be divided into two categories. The first was *reprisals*—an illegal act made in response to another State's illegal conduct. The other type of counter-measure was *retorsions*—an unfriendly, but legal, response made to another nation's illegal act.

Retorsions have been relatively uncontroversial in international law. A retorsion might include the withdrawal of diplomats and embassy staff by an offended nation. Certain forms of voluntary aid or support (either bilateral or through multilateral institutions) might be terminated. Retorsions also include the imposition of economic sanctions against target countries, a perennial favorite tactic in hard-ball international relations. Because no State can usually claim it is *legally* entitled to trade with another nation, these sanctions are typically regarded as being lawful. Nevertheless, there is a growing body of opinion that indicates that severe forms of economic sanctions might run afoul of some international norms, particularly the free-trade disciplines of the World Trade Organization (WTO) or relevant human rights regimes. Moreover, the World Court has ruled that, by entering a Friendship, Commerce and Navigation (FCN) Treaty with another State, a country might foreswear its customary international law right to engage in economic sanctions as a retorsion.[3] Despite this, the U.S. has maintained long-standing economic sanctions against Cuba, North Korea and Iraq, as well as supporting forms of technology bans against many unfriendly nations. The real question with economic sanctions as a type of retorsion may not be their legality, but, rather, their effectiveness in advancing the foreign policy goals of the sanctioning nation.

Most commentators agree that non-forcible reprisals remain necessary to promote respect for international obligations. Without some kind of threat to take action (even if it is illegal action) in the face of unlawful conduct, then many nations will flout international law. Under this vision of a "muscular" international law, we need a bit of punch and counter-punch in order to persuade recalcitrant nations to respect their duties under custom or treaties. But at what point does a system of counter-measures become *too* energetic

3. See *Military and Paramilitary Activities in and against Nicaragua* (Nicar. v. U.S.), 1986 I.C.J. 14 (Merits Phase).

and in fact contribute to instability and conflict in international relations? In addition, if counter-measures are chiefly used by the rich and powerful nations of the world, does that mean that weaker States are reduced to a position of meekly acquiescing to the demands of their more powerful neighbors or simply foregoing their remedies when their rights are violated?

Perhaps the best illustration of this dynamic of counter-measures can be seen in the *Air Services Agreement* Arbitration of 1978 between the United States and France.[4] The underlying dispute arose in connection with a 1946 bilateral Air Services Agreement between France and the United States. As might be recalled from Chapter 10(A), these treaties regulate every aspect of scheduled commercial aviation between two nations. Under the 1946 agreement, the American airline, Pan Am, was given the right to operate a scheduled route between Paris and London. Because of aggressive subsidies being provided by the French government to Air France, Pan Am desired to substitute a 747 aircraft on the route with a smaller craft, what is called a "change in gauge." The 1946 treaty was arguably silent or ambiguous as to whether an air carrier could substitute a smaller for a larger aircraft. The French government steadfastly refused, and the basis for the refusal ranged from assertions of national honor (for Pan Am to fly anything smaller than a 747 into Paris would be an affront) to the more pragmatic reason that Air France rather enjoyed the prospect of forcing its competitor to run a grossly unprofitable route. Finally, the French dropped all pretenses and simply compelled Pan Am to cease its flights to Paris.

At this juncture, the U.S. government proposed arbitration as a way to resolve the dispute. For nearly two years, the French refused this invitation to resolve the dispute in this manner. Finally, the United States made a reprisal in the form of suspending Air France's Paris–Los Angeles route, long established under the 1946 agreement. This got the French government's attention, and France finally agreed to arbitration. The two questions submitted to the panel were (1) whether Pan Am could change gauge, and (2) could the United States unilaterally suspend Air France's route to Los Angeles? The first matter was quickly resolved in favor of Pan Am, but the second question implicated the international law of counter-measures.

The arbitral tribunal first had to respond to France's suggestion that because the 1946 agreement provided for arbitration, then it was impermissible for the U.S. to engage in unilateral self-help measures. The tribunal ruled, however, that it had been *France* which had stone-walled the arbitration process, and it was only the

4. 18 U.N. Rep. Int'l Arb. Awards 417 (1978).

United States's retaliatory move terminating the L.A. route that brought France to the negotiating-table. In short, the tribunal ruled that counter-measures were a necessary part of the "punch" and "counter-punch" that was often needed in international relations in order for States to decide to submit their disputes to arbitration or some other method of binding settlement.

The tribunal did indicate, however, that there was a risk of escalation in any use of counter-measures. France could have, conceivably, cut-off Pan Am's New York–Paris run, and then the United States could have retaliated by economic sanctions outside of the air sector, and so on. Nevertheless, the tribunal ruled that the U.S. response in terminating Air France's Los Angeles run— although a violation of the 1946 agreement—was a permissible, and proportional, response to France's earlier refusal to allow Pan Am to change gauge. Despite its endorsement of non-forcible reprisals as a means of enforcing international law rights, the tribunal did observe that once an effective dispute-settlement mechanism was triggered, then all counter-measures should cease. In this case, once the arbitral tribunal had jurisdiction over the matter, neither France nor the U.S. could take unilateral measures without the panel's permission. A similar ruling was made by the International Court of Justice in 1980, validating the U.S. freezing of Iranian assets in response to the take-over of the U.S. embassy in Tehran.[5]

The holding of the *Air Services Agreement* Arbitration permits a wide ambit of discretion to States which believe themselves to be victims of an international law violation. They may proportionally seek to punish the offender by engaging in their own retaliatory response—a response that would itself be illegal, but for the earlier unlawful act of the other side. This rule precisely matches the principle under the Vienna Convention on the Law of Treaties (VCLT) that only where there has been a material breach of an agreement can another party terminate or suspend performance (see Chapter 3(E)). This means that States must be cautious in taking the first step of what may later be characterized as an anticipatory breach. Both of these rules (of counter-measures in *Air Services* and material breach in VCLT) are intended to give States the option to respond to the perceived illegal acts of other nations, but only within a limited scope. Such retaliations also carry with them the risk that a later arbitration might rule that there had been no initial violation or material breach, and that, therefore, it was the *responder's* actions that were the first to cross the threshold of illegality.

5. See *United States Diplomatic and Consular Staff in Tehran* Case (U.S. v. Iran), 1980 I.C.J. 3.

Substantial concerns have been raised about the use of counter-measures. The U.N. International Law Commission (ILC) has currently under consideration Draft Articles on State Responsibility which might vastly limit their use in any situation where there is available a dispute-settlement mechanism. Many nations oppose such a limit, though, because it means that the advantage will go to the State that makes the first move in a confrontation. (Any later response would be characterized as a counter-measure and thus be limited under this scheme.) Whether the background international law rules of counter-measures are even susceptible to some sort of regulation by codification remains to be seen.

A more difficult issue is raised when a State takes a reprisal against the nationals of the offending nation, resident within its own boundaries. For example, the United States seized Cuban nationals' assets located in the U.S. after Castro's rise to power and also required the registration of Iranian nationals living here after the Hostage Crisis. Such retaliations may be consistent with rules of State Responsibility towards aliens, but still might run afoul of human rights norms. (The United States has recently offered restitution to Japanese nationals who were resident in Latin American countries in 1941 (at the outbreak of World War Two), and were forcibly removed to the United States for internment.)

Before leaving the subject of counter-measures, it is worth discussing the remedies available for international law violations. Oftentimes when nations are engaging in a struggle for law, their primary objective is to clarify what the relevant international law is. So instead of actually seeking any form of monetary redress from an offending nation, the goal may be simply a form of *satisfaction*—that the malefactor nation admits its wrong-doing and undertakes to conform its future conduct to international law norms. Many international tribunals will routinely order satisfaction as the sole or primary remedy for many forms of international law violations. In this sense, seeking satisfaction for a violation of a customary international law norm or the breach of a treaty is a kind of declaratory judgment action, a clarification of the content of an international law right or duty.

Whether international tribunals can order *restitution*—affirmatively order a nation to engage in certain remedial conduct—is more controversial. As just one example of this confusion, two different arbitrations were obliged to consider the legal remedies available for Libya's expropriation of foreign oil concessions in the 1970's. One tribunal rejected the availability of a remedy of specific performance (requiring that Libya restitute the expropriated properties), while the other said such relief was possible.[6] Earlier

---

6. Compare *BP Exploration Co. (Libya) v. Libyan Arab Republic,* 53 Int'l Law Reports 297 (1979) (Arb. 1973 & 1974) with *Texas Overseas* Petroleum

decisions of the World Court are certainly suggestive that restitutionary remedies are available in certain narrow, well-defined circumstances.[7]

Lastly, cash awards are a typical form of remedy for international law violations. Sometimes these are made as a form of settlement. A government might make amends without admitting any international fault or liability, what is known as an *"ex gratia* payment."* (For example, the U.S. made such a settlement to China after it accidentally bombed and destroyed the Chinese embassy in Belgrade in May 1999 during the Kosovo intervention.) Entire classes of claims between nations are often resolved through the device of lump sum agreements. Under this plan, a State will pay a certain amount to another nation to settle a large number of claims of its nationals. The recipient State will then distribute such funds to its national claimants through a domestic claims institution. (In the United States, that is the Foreign Claims Settlement Commission, a part of the U.S. Department of Justice.)

International tribunals will often award indemnities for violations of international law obligations. These tend to be in the form of compensatory damages only, although more and more frequently, interest payments will also be awarded in recognition of the fact that judgments are often paid decades after the injurious conduct occurs. Alas, attorneys' fees or other litigation-related sanctions are almost never awarded by international dispute settlement institutions. Likewise, the award of exemplary or punitive damages—intended to punish a malefactor State, instead of merely compensating the injured nation—are virtually unheard of.[8]

The international law of counter-measures governs the practical way that States enforce their rights in a decentralized international legal system. It is no surprise that how and when States have resort to measures short of war in these circumstances can themselves give rise to substantial disputes. Nevertheless, non-forcible counter-measures (whether reprisals or retorsions) will remain a significant aspect of international legal practice. Nor should it be assumed that such matters are the concern only of States and foreign ministries. Private parties are often caught in the middle of such disputes (think of the role of Pan Am in the *Air Services* Arbitration). So it is vitally important for all international lawyers to understand the ways that international law responds to, and offers remedies for, violations of its rights and duties.

Company v. Libyan Arab Republic, 53 id. 389 (Arb. 1975 & 1977).

7. See *Case Concerning the Factory at Chorzow* (Ger. v. Pol.), 1928 P.C.I.J. (ser. A) No. 17.

8. But see *The I'M ALONE* Arbitration (Canada v. U.S.), 3 U.N. Rep. Int'l Arb. Awards 1609 (1933).

Chapter 19

Control of Armed Conflict

This Chapter explores the ways that international law prevents and manages the outbreak of hostilities between nations, as well as promotes international peace and security. This topic is known as the *ius ad bellum* and considers the prohibition on the use of force in international relations. (How international law controls the actual conduct of hostilities, the *ius in bello*, will be narrated in the next Chapter.) The best way to proceed in examining this subject— perhaps the most controversial subject in all of international law and relations—is, first, to consider the position of international law on uses of force prior to the adoption of the United Nations Charter in 1945. Next, the law of the Charter and its very detailed regime for regulating recourse to the use or threat of armed force will be reviewed. Lastly, the actual operation of the Charter's system of collective security and peacekeeping, as actuated through the decisions of the U.N. Security Council and General Assembly, will be assessed.

A. Limiting War Before the U.N. Charter

Control of international conflict is a problem as old as humankind itself. Ancient peoples embraced a distinction between just and unjust wars—conflicts that were initiated for rightful reasons, and those that were not. Just war theory has always had a strong connection with natural law principles, whether espoused by St. Augustine, St. Thomas Aquinas, Grotius or Pufendorf. The difficulty with distinctions to control conflict based on the justness of the reasons given to initiate conflict is that such justifications are infinitely elastic and malleable. By the time of the Middle Ages, it was acknowledged that each State in a conflict could legitimately regard itself as being engaged in a just war. Such a concession manifestly undermined the persuasiveness and reliability of just war theory as the basis for making legal distinctions in the *ius ad bellum*.

Modern efforts to impose legal restrictions on international conflict began in 1907. The Hague Convention II of that year outlawed "recourse to armed force for the recovery of contract debts claimed from the Government of one country by the Government of another country as being due its nationals." Despite this welcome development, that treaty exempted situations where the debtor State refused arbitration or, having accepted it, declined to pay the award. Despite this caveat, the Hague Convention II was part of a larger pattern of bilateral conventions which imposed a duty on States to attempt to resolve their differences through arbitration, rather than immediately declaring war.

It was the Covenant of the League of Nations, adopted in 1919 as part of the Treaty of Versailles that ended World War One, which ushered in the first global system for collective security and protection of international peace and security. The primary feature of the Covenant system was a compulsory dispute settlement mechanism (operated by the Council of the League), to which States had to submit as a condition preparatory to initiating hostilities. If a nation "jumped the gun" and began a war before the League institutions had the chance to adjust the dispute, then that Party would have violated Covenant Article XVI, and the League Council could recommend action against the aggressor. The critical weakness of the League Covenant was the requirement of unanimity in the Council to trigger collective security, and, even when that was achieved, member States still had the option whether or not to use force against the aggressor.

The League had some initial success in controlling conflict, particularly in the Balkans (with the Greco–Bulgarian crisis of 1925) and Latin America (with the Chaco War between Paraguay and Bolivia in 1932–35). Starting with Japan's 1931 invasion of Chinese Manchuria (which led to the creation of the puppet State of Manchukuo, discussed in Chapter 5(A)), the League found itself powerless to restrain its members. Nazi Germany forcibly occupied and remilitarized the Rhineland in 1936, in deliberate violation of its commitments under the Versailles Treaty. The worst failure of the League was in its lack of political will to stop Mussolini's Italy from invading Ethiopia in 1935 and 1936. It is generally believed that Italy could have been restrained by stronger economic sanctions or threats of military retaliation, but neither France or Britain desired to do so. And the fact that both the United States and Soviet Union were not members of the League further weakened its position. It was thus just a matter of time that the League system of collective security collapsed after Germany occupied the Czechoslovak Sudetenland in 1938 and then invaded Poland in September 1939.

One of the ironies of the League's failure was that it was occurring at a time when there was a growing international consensus to limit war. The Kellogg–Briand Pact of 1928 (formally known as the General Treaty for the Renunciation of War), grandiloquently "outlawed" war by declaring that it "condemn[s] recourse to war for the solution of international controversies, and renounce[s] it an instrument of national policy.... " The Pact is still notionally in force and has been regarded at a minimum as a declaration by countries not to be the first to resort to armed conflict. Indeed, the Pact was cited by the Nuremberg International Military Tribunal as the basis for its ruling that customary international had, prior to 1939, recognized the planning or waging of aggressive war as "the supreme international crime."

One last point should be made about the pre-Charter position of international law as to the conditions for using armed force. Self-defense had always been recognized in custom as a permissible basis for initiating armed hostilities. The question was whether a State could, in its sole judgement, decide that it was justified in initiating armed force. The German Nazi leadership at Nuremberg had, in fact, attempted to argue that its 1939 invasion of Poland was justified based on anticipatory self-defense (that Poland was just about to attack Germany).

Customary international law had already developed rules for limiting the use of force in these situations. In the famous CARO-LINE incident, the United States conceded that Great Britain had been entitled to use force and invade part of New York in 1837 in order to disrupt a group of rebels who were planning on attacking Canada. Secretary of State Daniel Webster observed that an antici-patory reaction is permissible in those situations where the "neces-sity of that self-defense is instant, overwhelming, and leaving no choice of means and no moment for deliberation."[1] In this diplo-matic correspondence, the British government agreed that it was also incumbent upon itself to show that its armed response was proportional to the threat it perceived and the necessity of the situation. These conditions of imminence and proportionality re-main important background rules for use of force in self-defense under the U.N. Charter system.

B. The Law of the U.N. Charter

1. *Force and Aggression.* The heart of the U.N. Charter's system to control conflict is Article 2, paragraph 4: "All Members shall refrain in their international relations from the threat or use of force against the territorial integrity or political independence of any state, or in any other manner inconsistent with the Purposes of the United Nations." This can be regarded as the "prime directive" of modern international law, at least when it comes to the funda-mental question of the place of conflict in the relations of States.

---

1. The CAROLINE Incident, 2 John   Law 412 (1906).
Bassett Moore, DIGEST OF International

But despite the clear command of Article 2(4), there remain substantial doubts about its scope and meaning.

Essential to understanding the sweep of Article 2(4) is the meaning of two terms and concepts: "force" and "aggression." The word "force" is used in the very language of Article 2(4). It has come to be understood as referring only to armed or military force. Despite the suggestion of some countries that severe forms of economic coercion (like trade sanctions) should rise to the level of "force," and thus be prohibited by Charter Article 2(4), this has been rejected in practice. Obviously some forms of action that bear on trade—such as a naval blockade of a nation's coastline—have a military element and are regarded as force within the meaning of Article 2(4)'s prohibition.

Likewise, Article 2(4)'s mention of "territorial integrity" and "political independence" of States is broadly understood to cover any kind of military action that interferes with a nation's political autonomy or practical sovereignty. A temporary occupation of part of a nation's territory is barred by Article 2(4), just as a quick raid to topple the government of a neighboring nation. Lastly, Article 2(4) prohibits not only "use[s]" of force, but also the "threat" of using force. Although this aspect of Article 2(4) is not so well-understood in practice, it might indicate that States are under an obligation not to engage in certain kinds of intimidation that would lead to the use of armed force.

The ultimate purpose of the United Nations' system to control conflict is to prevent aggressive war. The Charter undertakes to rework the theoretical basis for States to initiate hostilities. The Charter is indifferent as to whether a nation may feel it has been wronged in such a way as to merit a response with force. In this sense, the Charter reflects a rejection of a just war rationale for armed conflict. Instead, the Charter substitutes a legalist vision for controlling conflict: no State has the right to engage in aggressive war for any reason. Although the word "aggression" does not appear in Article 2(4), it is included in Charter Article 1 (denominated the "Purposes of the United Nations") and in Article 39.

Aggression is a notoriously difficult concept to pin-down. A United States delegate to the United Nations in 1950 observed that it may be impossible legally to define it. Nevertheless, the U.N. General Assembly attempted to do just that in a 1974 Resolution.[2] In large measure, this Resolution acknowledged what many nations regarded as the practical reality of this inquiry: aggression was whatever the international community and political organs of the U.N. (and particularly the Security Council) said it was in any

2. See Resolution on the Definition of Aggression, G.A. Res. 3314 (XXIX), GAOR 29th Sess., Supp. 31, at 42 (1974).

specific confrontation. The Resolution was careful to observe that the State that is the first to use force in a particular situation would be deemed the aggressor, absent some showing of a legitimate claim of self-defense. Article III of the Resolution provided a handy check-list of situations in which aggression would be assumed, including military occupations (however temporary), bombardments or blockades, and direct attacks. This provision also went on to note that some forms of low-intensity conflict—such as sending "armed bands" or "groups" against another State with sufficiently grave effects—could rise to the level of aggression, and thus also be banned under the Charter.

2. *Justifications for Use of Force.* All of this begs the question of whether there are any permissible excuses for the use of force that would otherwise be prohibited under Charter Article 2(4). Some commentators and States have forcefully asserted that Article 2(4)'s proscription on the use of force cannot admit to *any* exceptions. If it did, these authorities claim, the exceptions would quickly swallow the rule and provide pretextual grounds for countries to engage in aggression or intervention in the affairs of other nations. Despite these assertions, State practice and the views of the relevant U.N. organs are strongly suggestive that certain justifications to aggression are permissible under the U.N. Charter and international law. Clearly, the Charter provides that enforcement action by the U.N. Security Council is not considered aggression within the meaning of Article 2(4). This will be discussed further at the conclusion of the Chapter.

Other putative exceptions to Article 2(4) are either more dubious or more problematic. For example, it has been suggested that a State may waive the prohibition on the use of force and actually invite foreign military intervention. A handful of mutual security treaties allow for a group of nations to carry-out a military intervention in the territory of one of the parties. (The convention creating the Republic of Cyprus in 1960 has such a clause, which was relied upon by Turkey for its 1974 invasion.) Likewise, invitation was among the many ostensible justifications used by the United States in its 1983 invasion of the Caribbean island nation of Grenada. It was asserted that an invitation was either triggered by Grenada's involvement in the Organization of Eastern Caribbean States or was specifically made by the Governor–General of the island.

The really divisive use of invitation as a justification for armed intervention arises in the context of civil wars. In such situations, each rival government can claim the right to invite an allied State to intervene and help it win the war. The traditional international law rule for such insurgencies was that aid and support could only be offered to the "legitimate" government that had been properly recognized under international law (see Chapter 5(B)). The problem with this position was devastatingly revealed in the course of the Spanish Civil War (1936–39), when Republican forces were recognized and supported by France and the Soviet Union, whereas Nationalist insurgents were supported by Nazi Germany and Fascist Italy. Each side claimed it was the legitimate government of Spain, and their respective allies justified their interventions based on invitation. The same confluence of factors arose in the Vietnam War, with U.S. forces supporting the South and the Soviets allied with the North.

Attempts to resolve this riddle by distinguishing between external, or international, wars (on the one hand) and truly internal conflicts (on the other) have been unavailing. While only international conflicts would notionally be covered by Charter Article 2(4)'s prohibition on intervention, the truth is that even truly internal conflicts have the grave potential to upset international peace and security. It was inevitable, therefore, that the traditional rule of giving aid to the "legitimate" government in a civil war was degraded over time. Efforts to substitute it with a rule of providing no aid to *either* side in an internal conflict have also been criticized, since such a policy tends to support the better-established government forces. (In the recent troubles in Yugoslavia, the new government of Bosnia–Herzegovina complained that an arms embargo equally applied to Bosnian and Serbian sides unfairly disadvantaged them.) Issues of involvement in civil wars have, in some measure, been resolved by domestic law. The United States, for example, has the Neutrality Act of 1794, which prohibits U.S. citizens from participating in rebellions against recognized governments with which the U.S. is "at peace."[3]

A second potential justification for a use of armed force that would otherwise be a violation of Article 2(4) is humanitarian intervention. Mentioned already in Chapter 9(B), this is the practice of a nation or nations unilaterally using force or intervening in a State charged with perpetrating grave human rights abuses against its own nationals. A number of publicists have suggested that if the human rights crisis is truly serious, and the intervening State is limited in its objectives in removing the abusing government from power, then humanitarian intervention might be legitimate under international law. Other commentators, and quite a few States, have asserted, however, that humanitarian intervention could become a pretext for continued meddling in the affairs of nations, particularly those in the developing world.

Historic examples of true humanitarian interventions are exceedingly rare. They must certainly be distinguished from situa-

---

3.   18 U.S.C. § 960.

tions where a State is intervening into another nation in order to protect its *own* nationals from abuse by the host government. This might be regarded as a form of self-defense (discussed below), and examples would include Belgium's 1964 intervention in the Congo, Israel's 1976 Entebbe raid into Uganda, and U.S. invasions of Grenada in 1983 and Panama in 1989. Likewise, many humanitarian interventions may have really been a cover for other foreign policy objectives. India's invasion of East Pakistan (Bangladesh) in 1971 may have been as much to support a war of national liberation, than it was to end human rights abuses. Tanzania's overthrow of Uganda's Idi Amin was more about the exercise of a right to self-defense. Vietnam's invasion of Cambodia and overthrow of the genocidal Khmer Rouge government in 1979 was surely a fine example of humanitarian intervention, and yet the members of the United Nations nearly unanimously denounced it.

The international community has thus been very reluctant to recognize humanitarian interventions that are invoked unilaterally. France's intervention in the Central African Empire in the 1980's might be legitimately regarded as a humanitarian intervention, and it received only muted criticism in the United Nations. Other humanitarian interventions have actually been ordered by the U.N. Security Council, pursuant to its collective security powers under Chapter VII of the Charter (discussed below). These have been regarded as consistent with the Charter as a matter of international law, although of questionable practical impact. After the Gulf War, northern Iraq was actually occupied by Coalition forces in order to prevent Saddam Hussein's government from retaliating against the Kurdish population there. The U.N. had directed an intervention into Haiti, but that was averted by a last-minute settlement. Also, the U.N. ordered a humanitarian intervention into the "failed State" of Somalia in 1992, in order to ensure distribution of food relief supplies. The mission gradually expanded to restoring law and order, and was severely hampered by opposition generated by local armed factions. In 1999, the U.N. permitted an intervention into what had been Indonesian-occupied East Timor. The dangers of a humanitarian intervention mission "creeping" into more political or strategic objectives are manifest, and that is another reason it has been distrusted as an international law doctrine.

One must at least comment about the 1998–99 NATO intervention in Kosovo, a province of Serbia where that government in the late 1990's was escalating human rights abuses against the predominately Muslim population. The reason why this intervention was undertaken as a unilateral regional enforcement action by the North Atlantic Treaty Organization was that there was a substantial likelihood that the U.N. Security Council would not have agreed to sponsor it (both the Russians and the Chinese had threatened a veto on that measure). Although virtually none of the NATO members justified the intervention on humanitarian grounds, a number of commentators have. This still raises concerns about the level of imminence (how severe are the human rights abuses in the country) and proportionality (how much force can be used in the intervention) as elements of the humanitarian intervention doctrine. These issues will certainly have to be resolved before unilateral forms of humanitarian intervention will be permitted as a justification for a use of force otherwise in violation of Charter Article 2(4).

That leaves one last potential justification for a use of force, covered under Article 2(4). That is self-defense. At the outset, it should be noted that U.N. Charter Article 51 explicitly recognizes self-defense as an "inherent right ... if an armed attack occurs." The idea of self-defense as an inherent right of States is a clear indication that it was recognized in customary international law, and, moreover, that the Charter system of collective security was never intended to strip nations of their ability to respond effectively to an armed attack. Indeed, it has generally been acknowledged that States are free to respond to an armed attack in any manner they choose, consistent only with the general strictures of proportionality and while also observing the laws of war (discussed in the next Chapter).

The more difficult question presented by self-defense arises in situations of a collective response to an armed attack. Charter Article 51 refers both to "individual or collective self-defence." This has been understood to mean that a State which has been the victim of an armed attack is free to summon help from its neighbors and allies. This makes entirely good sense, for if the collective security mechanism of the Security Council fails (and it consistently has), the only way that a small or weak nation can respond to an attack is by receiving help. Nevertheless, questions have been raised about the limits of collective self-defense under Article 51 and (even more generally) the conditions that give rise to an "armed attack" within the meaning of that exception to Article 2(4)'s ban on the use of force.

These issues were addressed by the International Court of Justice in one of the most contentious and controversial cases it has ever decided: *Military and Paramilitary Activities in and against Nicaragua.* The case arose out of the United States' efforts to destabilize and topple the left-leaning Sandinista government in Nicaragua in the early 1980's. The Sandinistas had come to power by overthrowing the U.S.-backed, authoritarian Somoza regime. This was a period of profound political instability in Central America, with many right-wing governments under pressure from leftist insurgents, especially in El Salvador, Guatemala and Honduras. Although the Reagan Administration made a tepid effort to negotiate with the Sandinistas, relations quickly turned frosty, and the U.S. began to fund, supply, arm and train a group of guerrillas— known as the *contras*—which began to launch raids into Nicaragua from neighboring nations. In addition, the United States imposed a general trade embargo on Nicaragua and went so far as to mine Nicaraguan harbors covertly.

In response to these events, Nicaragua initiated a case against the U.S. at the World Court. In the first stage of the case, the ICJ considered whether it had jurisdiction over the United States. In its 1984 decision,[4] to be discussed further in Chapter 21, the World Court ruled that it did have jurisdiction and that the case was otherwise admissible. In a sharp reaction, the Reagan Administration withdrew from the Court and declared that it would have no further involvement with the merits of the *Nicaragua* Case. That meant that U.S. essentially defaulted on Nicaragua's claims, and the Court was left to decide their veracity without the participation of U.S. counsel. The Court had also earlier rejected an intervention request by El Salvador. These procedural events proved to be most unfortunate, since the Court assumed facts that, as it later turned out, were inaccurate.

The heart of the dispute decided by the ICJ was the U.S. assertion that it was permitted to use force against Nicaragua (whether in the form of support for the *contras* or direct action) because it was engaging in collective self-defense on behalf of El Salvador. El Salvador, the U.S. argued, was the victim of an armed attack by Nicaraguan-backed rebels. The ICJ rejected this defense, based on its reading of Charter Article 51 and the background rules of customary international law for *ius ad bellum*.[5] The Court found, as a matter of fact, that El Salvador had made no formal request to the United States to engage in collective self-defense against Nicaragua. Without such an appeal, the Court reasoned, collective self-defense could not be invoked. In short, international law does not give States the right to foist assistance on an unwilling partner. This makes sense, but on the facts of the *Nicaragua* Case, it was manifest that El Salvador had been on record as believing that insurgent forces were being supported by the Nicaragua Sandinistas, and had requested aid from the United States to repel that intervention.

The ICJ went on to make, however, the crucial ruling of the case. It held that, in any event, Nicaragua's aid to the El Salvador rebels had not risen to the level of an "armed attack" under

4. 1984 I.C.J. 392 (Jurisdictional   **5.** 1986 I.C.J. 14 (Merits Phase).
Phase).

Charter Article 51. The Court found that it was the United States that was the first to cross the "trip-wire" of an "armed-attack," and, therefore, it was found to be the aggressor under Article 2(4). This rule—similar in structure to the VCLT's provision on material breach and the *Air Service* Arbitration's principle of counter-measures—requires that a State be cautious in reacting to a potential international law violation by another nation. For if a country does not fully appreciate the situation, it might later be found to be the aggressor.

Another key element to be appreciated about the *Nicaragua* Case was that it was chiefly decided on the basis of customary international law. Owing to a jurisdictional wrinkle in the case (to be discussed further in Chapter 21), the ICJ was obliged to read Article 51 and the custom of self-defense together. Although Article 51 provides some procedural safeguards to the exercise of self-defense under the Charter—such as notifying the U.N. Security Council in such situations—the Court was able to derive most of its holding from background rules of international law.

This is significant because certain scenarios, such as the exercise of anticipatory self-defense (before an actual armed attack occurs), may still be permissible under the rule of *The CAROLINE* incident. For example, the U.S. quarantine of Cuba during the 1963 Missile Crisis and the 1981 Israeli bombing of the Iraqi nuclear facility were each justified on the grounds of anticipatory self-defense. Since in neither instance had their been an actual use of armed force by either Cuba or Iraq, this was the only possible justification for intervention. And although criticized at the time as exceeding the ambit of Charter Article 51, many commentators and States have accepted the notion that there might be a very limited exception for anticipatory reaction.

C. Collective Security, Peacekeeping and Enforcement

If Article 2(4)'s proscription of use of force is the "prime directive" of modern international law, it is only natural that States will struggle to establish the outer limits of that obligation and any potential exceptions. While the U.N. Charter's legal approach for controlling conflict has been intensely criticized, it does reflect a notable improvement on the League of Nations' model. The United Nations' legal controls on its Members' resort to armed conflict can only be as successful as the underlying collective security regime that the U.N. manages. States will only refrain from aggression if they have the certain knowledge that breaches of the peace will be the subject of immediate economic sanctions and, much more importantly, decisive military response by the wider international community.

The key to the United Nation's collective security regime is the Security Council, the 15–member body consisting of 5 permanent members (Britain, China, France, Russia and the United States) and 10 non-permanent members that each serve a rotating 2–year term. Any permanent member can wield a veto of any substantive action. To order any response to a breach of the peace or an act of aggression requires 9 votes, including the concurrences of the permanent members. (An abstention by a permanent member does not stand as a veto, but it does not count for the needed 9 votes.) Thus to order any credible response to aggression requires a high level of political will by the members of the Security Council, and either the support or silent acquiescence of each of the permanent members.

The original intent of the Charter system was to prevent or suppress dangerous regional powers from militarizing and challenging the authority of the Great Powers. The system of collective security under the Charter was never intended to address Great Power conflict or rivalries acted out between the proxies of the Security Council's permanent members. The Charter's plan was that the Security Council would, in the face of an act of aggression, declare a violation of the Charter under Article 39 and then order all Member States of the U.N. to impose economic sanctions or other penalties. If such sanctions are ineffectual in reversing the unlawful conduct, then the Council can, under Article 42, order the mobilization of air, sea or land forces. U.N. Members are obliged not to give any support to the outlaw nation. Under Charter Article 43, States were supposed to have negotiated agreements with the U.N. to provide military contingents for the U.N.'s use under the command of the Security Council and its Military Staff Committee. No such agreements have ever been concluded, and thus on those few occasions where the U.N. has ordered an enforcement action under Chapter VII of the Charter, ad hoc coalitions of forces have been assembled for the task.

It is fair to say that the entire collective security mechanism of the U.N. Charter was nullified during the Cold War. The Security Council literally could not act against aggressor nations because, almost inevitably, each one was a proxy of either the United States or Soviet Union, and thus the Americans (and their allies) or the Soviets could be counted-upon to veto any responsive resolution. The only exception to this Security Council gridlock was the serendipitous action taken by the U.N. at the beginning of the Korean War. The Soviets had been boycotting the Council and thus were not there to cast the necessary veto of the enforcement action.

(Since that occurrence, no permanent member representative has ever failed to attend a meeting of the Council!)

The grid-lock on Security Council action profoundly disappointed the international community in the 1950's and 1960's. In response, the U.N. General Assembly began to assert its authority to be able to order certain kinds of actions without Security Council approval. Thus was born the use of U.N. peacekeeping forces, authorized under Chapter VI of the Charter. Developed by the dynamic U.N. Secretary General, Dag Hammarskjöld of Sweden, the first uses of peacekeepers occurred in the aftermath of the Middle East Suez Crisis in 1956 and the 1960–63 Katanga Rebellion in Congo. Essential to the creation of the U.N. Emergency Force for the Sinai (UNEF) and the U.N. Force for the Congo (ONUC)—U.N. peacekeeping forces are inevitably given unwieldy acronyms—was permission for their deployment by the host States. Unlike enforcement actions against malefactor countries, which can only be ordered by the Security Council acting under Chapter VII, peacekeeping forces are consensual (with the permission of the host State) and can thus be established and funded by the General Assembly under Chapter VI of the Charter. In a significant decision,[6] the World Court upheld the right of the General Assembly to create such forces and also to require that all Member States pay their share of the expenses.

Peacekeeping has become a central mission of the United Nations. Oftentimes, however, the ultimate goals of such operations have been frustrated. In many situations, the U.N. peacekeeping force was inserted as a buffer between warring States. Regrettably, the presence of the U.N. peacekeepers often does not promote the negotiation of a final political settlement. U.N. peacekeepers have been stationed on the Indian–Pakistan border since 1947, in Cyprus since 1975, and in southern Lebanon since the early 1980's. More recently, U.N. peacekeepers have been used for a task very different from merely separating bickering nations. U.N. forces have been successfully used for election monitoring in El Salvador and Namibia, although to little or no effect in Angola and Western Sahara. In a wider sense, U.N. peacekeepers might be enlisted for "democracy and nation building" in parts of the world ravaged by conflict. U.N. forces in the Balkans and in Cambodia have certainly played that role.

Iraq's invasion of Kuwait in August 1990 revived Chapter VII's collective security regime which had been moribund for over 40 years. The combination of factors that led to the United Nations' response was extraordinary. The Cold War was over, and both Russia and China were anxious to let the U.N. operate to its full

6. See *Certain Expenses* Opinion,
1962 I.C.J. 151.

potential. Iraq was a dangerous, mid-sized power, precisely the regional bully that the Security Council was intended to discipline. Iraq had no allies on the Council. Lastly, and no less important, Iraq's invasion of small, helpless Kuwait was so audacious and unlawful that even the most jaded and callous of diplomats or leaders could not help being appalled.

Within hours of the invasion, the U.N. Security Council met and began to adopt a series of resolutions imposing various diplomatic, economic, trade and transport sanctions against Iraq. From the very beginning, the Council signaled its intent to invoke Chapter VII and follow it to its logical, and necessary, conclusion. Finally, after waiting nearly 4 months for the Iraqis to withdraw from Kuwait, the Council adopted Resolution 678 which "authorized Member States co-operating with the Government of Kuwait ... to use all necessary means" to eject Iraq from Kuwait, unless Iraq withdrew by January 15, 1991. When the deadline passed, the Gulf War began. Within a few months it was over, and Iraq was compelled to accept a peace imposed by the Council in its Resolution 687, including mandatory disarmament (something that nearly a decade later Iraq has refused fully to do) and payment of reparations to Kuwait and other countries injured by Iraq's aggression (managed through a body known as the U.N. Compensation Commission (UNCC)).

The Gulf War was hailed as, at long last, the ultimate vindication of the United Nation's collective security mandate. But such enthusiasm was unwarranted. Since 1991, there has been little political will to respond to violations of international peace and security. U.N. action in the Balkans was ineffectual, and in Rwanda may have actually contributed to a genocide claiming nearly a million lives. The U.N. has also tended to defer to regional security organizations in undertaking enforcement action, as occurred in Liberia and Sierra Leone in West Africa. Lastly, NATO's usurpation of the Security Council's role in fashioning a response to Serbian outrages in Kosovo may have also been indicative of a "new" Cold War mentality.

Ironically, it has even been suggested that the U.N. Security Council has become too powerful and needs to be legally restrained. It has been seriously suggested that the World Court should exercise a form of "judicial review" over Council determinations that certain acts constitute a "threat to the peace, breach of the peace, or act of aggression" within the meaning of Charter Article 39, which is the "trigger" for Chapter VII enforcement actions.

For example, in the bombing of a Pan Am flight over Lockerbie, Scotland, Libyan terrorists were implicated. The U.S. and Britain requested the extradition of these suspects from Libya.

Under the authority of the 1971 Montreal Convention for the Suppression of Unlawful Acts against the Safety of Civil Aviation, Libya refused, arguing that under that treaty it had the right to prosecute the suspects themselves under the *"ex dedere aux judicare"* principle (for more on which, see Chapter 7(B)). The U.N. Security Council, acting under Chapter VI, requested that Libya hand-over the suspects. Libya still declined and initiated an action before the World Court. During the pendency of the case, the Security Council passed another resolution, but this time under the authority of Chapter *VII* of the Charter, *ordering* the extradition. In preliminary rulings the Court flirted with, but ultimately declined to exercise some form of review of Council decisions under Chapter VII.[7] Because Libya in 1999 turned over the suspects for trial before a Scottish court in The Netherlands, it is not entirely clear whether the ICJ will issue a definitive ruling on whether there are any legal limits to the exercise of the Council's powers under the Charter.

International law controls on armed conflict will thus continue to reflect a mix of customary international law principles, interpretations of the U.N. Charter's clarion commands of Articles 2(4) and 51, the "constitutional" law of the U.N. as the chief guarantor of international peace and security, and the political reality of States pursuing different national objectives. Make no mistake, the question of when it is appropriate for a nation to resort to war, as well as the mechanisms for collective security, are today more and more regulated by legal considerations.

7. See *Lockerbie* Case (Libya v. U.S./ U.K.), 1992 I.C.J. 3, 114 (Provisional Measures).

Chapter 20

Laws of War

The rule of law in international affairs does not end with the outbreak of war between States. From the most ancient times, the law of nations has always included rules by which States attempt to moderate the effects of conflict and govern the conduct of hostilities. The law of nations was traditionally divided into two branches—those rules governing nations in their peaceful relations and those norms used in warfare. Grotius' famous tract, *De jure belli ac pacis*, first published in 1625, was organized in this fashion, as were many of the writings of contemporary publicists. The laws of war, the *ius in bello*, were a significant aspect of medieval and early-modern State relations. Chivalry and restraint gradually gave way to the horrors of "modern" conflict, featuring total warfare, the involvement of large civilian populations, and the emergence of new, and ever deadlier, means of killing.

This Chapter considers the contemporary relevance of the laws of war by first examining that body of rules concerning the conduct of hostilities on both land and sea, including the regulation and limitation of certain kinds of weapons and armaments. Next, it is important to chart the transformation of the "laws of war" into "international humanitarian law," with its emphasis on the protection of civilians and other persons not directly involved as combatants. Lastly, it is worth considering some aspects of emerging issues in the law of international armed conflict, including belligerent occupations and protection of the environment and cultural heritage.

Beginning in the 18th and 19th centuries, international law developed an elaborate set of rules regarding naval warfare, and, particularly, the conditions under which the vessels of enemy or neutral nations could be subject to capture, or what was known as "prize." The law of naval captures was administered by the prize courts of maritime Powers (such as Britain, France and Holland) and was extraordinarily uniform and consistent in application. These prize courts applied virtually the same rules in determining the enemy character of ships and cargoes found at sea during hostilities, the status of certain kinds of products as contraband (and thus subject to seizure), and the circumstances in which a blockade could be effectively enforced against an enemy coastline. The body of prize law jurisprudence was staggeringly large, and

226

exceedingly well-documented in the admiralty decisions of all maritime Powers (including that of the fledgling United States). It was because of this well-established customary international law that the U.S. Supreme Court could confidently decide, in *The PAQUETE HABANA* (discussed in Chapter 2(B)), that small coastal fishing boats were exempt from capture. In addition to customary law sources, the norms of naval captures of neutral ships and cargoes were the subject of the first modern treaty on the laws of war, the 1856 Paris Declaration.

In contrast to naval warfare, little effort had been made to systematize or codify rules of combat on land. The first such effort was the 1863 Code of Francis Lieber, an advisor to the Union Armies during the Civil War. That document galvanized subsequent international negotiations to develop a treaty for the laws of war on land, first at Brussels in 1874 and then at the First Hague Peace Conference, held in 1899. The Hague Peace Conference was the first major multilateral meeting devoted to a broad range of international issues. Convened by Tsar Nicholas II in order to advance his agenda of global disarmament and demilitarization (especially for Russia's rivals, Germany and Japan), the Conference also deliberated the creation of new dispute-settlement institutions (discussed in the next Chapter) and codification of the laws of war.

The result of the 1899 Hague Peace Conference was a package of no less than six instruments on the *ius in bello*. Some of these treaties were dedicated to abolishing the use of certain forms of dangerous weapons (such as expanding bullets or poison gases), or certain means of warfare (such as dropping bombs from balloons). In addition, the delegates were able to conclude a general codification of the Laws and Customs of War on Land. The 1899 meeting was so successful that the delegates enthusiastically endorsed a follow-up session in 1907, the Second Hague Peace Conference. Many more delegates, representing most of the nations in the world at that time, attended. This meeting adopted even more agreements, some of which reiterated in form and substance the 1899 Conference's achievements. In addition, some arms control conventions were concluded (on the use of automatic submarine contact mines and naval bombardments) and also full codifications on land and naval warfare (as well as specific treaties on neutrality and the formalities for the opening of hostilities).

The combined work-product of the 1899 and 1907 Hague Peace Conferences on the laws of war is known simply as the "Hague Law." The primary thrust of this body of conventional law was to regularize expectations by belligerent States as to how their enemies would conduct hostilities, treat prisoners of war and hospital facilities, and also to build confidence that certain kinds of weapons or tactics would not be employed in wartime. The critical underlying principles of the Hague Law were that unnecessary suffering and indiscriminate killing would be avoided in military conflicts (achieved through the abolition of certain kinds of munitions and delivery-systems), and, moreover, that military necessity was the benchmark for determining the proper restraints on hostilities. Lastly, and most importantly, the delegates at the Hague Peace Conferences recognized that the laws of war were just at the beginning of a process of codification and clarification, and that customary international law norms remained significant. Included in each of the Hague treaties was the Martens Clause (named after the Russian international lawyer who proposed it), incorporating customary norms into the treaty regimes.

The treaties negotiated at the Hague Peace Conferences were widely ratified, but as for whether they were successful in controlling the worst excesses of war, one simple, ironic fact can be noted. The Third Hague Peace Conference had been scheduled for the year 1915, but had to be canceled owing to the outbreak of the First World War. In many respects, World War One was the bloodiest conflict in human history (military casualties exceeded those even in World War Two). The war featured wholesale slaughters on the battlefield, indiscriminate sinkings of ships by submarines, and even the use of chemical weapons. Based on this evidence, the treaties concluded at the Hague Peace Conferences cannot be regarded as a success. Nevertheless, the Hague Law has spurred no less than three initiatives in the laws of war.

The first has been a consistent use of international law in an attempt to control and reduce dangerous or indiscriminate armaments and modes of warfare, and particularly abolishing weapons of mass destruction. Some military tactics, such as use of submarines to attack enemy shipping, proved so popular that there never formed a universal consensus to abolish the practice. Likewise, although many nations abhorred the use of poison gas in World War One, few nations were initially willing to take the chance of unilaterally denouncing their use and destroying all of their stockpiles. In this sense, the best deterrent against the use of chemical weapons was that each side in a conflict had them and was prepared to retaliate if the other side used them first. (That was why Nazi Germany declined to employ chemical weapons in World War Two.)

It was only in the 1990's that a comprehensive and verifiable ban on chemical weapons, including their production and stockpiling, managed through an elaborate regime with international inspectors based in Vienna, was finally adopted. A similar ban on biological weapons was signed in 1972. Nevertheless, there have been notable violations of these accords, and it has been proven that Iraq used weapons of mass destruction against Iran in the

1980's and against its own Kurdish population in the 1990's. Efforts to ban anti-personnel land-mines—millions of which have been laid and left, resulting in thousands of deaths and injuries each year—finally culminated in the 1997 Ottawa Convention, although the United States has (so far) declined to ratify it.

The most contentious question in disarmament has, of course, been nuclear weapons. Quite a number of arms control conventions have attempted to address the proliferation, testing and use of nuclear weapons. The 1968 Non–Proliferation Treaty established a multilateral regime to control the spread of nuclear weapons-making technology, while, at the same time, encouraging the peaceful use of nuclear energy through the inspections and assistance of the International Atomic Energy Agency (IAEA). Additionally, nuclear Powers have agreed to forego most forms of nuclear testing and deployment, including on the seabed, in outer space and the atmosphere. (France's unilateral decision to terminate its atmospheric nuclear testing in the Pacific was mentioned in Chapter 3(A)). A new Comprehensive Nuclear Test Ban Treaty is now pending, although its advice and consent was refused by the United States Senate in 1999. Finally, numerous bilateral treaties, chiefly between the United States and the Soviet Union (now Russia), have attempted to decrease the actual numbers of nuclear warheads deployed by each side, as well as severely limit certain kinds of destabilizing nuclear weapons systems (including anti-ballistic missiles (ABMs) using "Star Wars" technology).

Despite these developments, many nations clamored for an authoritative ruling on the lawfulness of the use of nuclear weapons under the modern laws of war. In 1961, the U.N. General Assembly (which is charged, under the Charter, with making recommendations on disarmament) adopted a resolution declaring the use of nuclear weapons unlawful.[1] Because General Assembly resolutions lack binding effect (see Chapter 4(B)), this was not even regarded as a credible evidence of State practice and customary international law. After some false starts, the General Assembly requested the International Court of Justice to render an advisory opinion on this subject.

In 1996, the Court issued its opinion.[2] The ICJ concluded that threats or employments of nuclear weapons were governed by the same background rules for control of international conflict (discussed in the last Chapter) as any other use of force. But, when asked to opine as to whether nuclear weapons could be used under *any* circumstances (even in legitimate self-defense under Charter

---

1. G.A. Res. 1653 (XVI), GAOR 13th Sess., Supp. (1961).

2. *Legality of the Threat or Use of Nuclear Weapons* Opinion, 1996 I.C.J. 226.

Article 51), the Court deadlocked. In a split decision (the Court's President casting the deciding vote), the ICJ ruled that while:

> the threat or use of nuclear weapons would generally be contrary to the rules of international armed conflict, ... in view of the current state of international law ... the Court cannot conclude definitely whether the threat or use of nuclear weapons would be lawful or unlawful in an extreme circumstance of self-defence, in which the very survival of a State would be at stake.

Thus, in one of the most controversial opinions ever asked of it, the Court essentially declared a *non-liquet*, a deliberate gap in the substance of international law.

The second legacy of the Hague Law was a very different emphasis in the laws of war for protection of civilians, prisoners of war, and other individuals who are non-combatants (*hors de combat*). After the total conflict of World War Two–where civilian populations were targeted for destruction (if not annihilation) by belligerent forces and were particularly vulnerable to air bombardment, occupation, and enslavement–efforts began to negotiate a new thrust for the laws of war. Led by the International Committee of the Red Cross (ICRC), a Swiss non-governmental organization that had been earlier recognized as the principal agency for the protection of non-combatants in wartime, the 1949 Geneva Conventions for the Protection of War Victims were negotiated. The four agreements included instruments on wounded and sick soldiers in the field, wounded, sick and shipwrecked sailors at sea, prisoners of war, and civilians. The four conventions contained a series of common articles (including a form of Martens Clause on custom), as well as very detailed rules and protections for the different classes of non-combatants.

Together the Geneva Conventions are known as the "Geneva Law," or, more descriptively, *international humanitarian law*. Although the Geneva Conventions have been widely ratified (and the U.S. is a party to all four), serious concerns have arisen as to their application in certain kinds of situations. For example, it has remained unclear whether the protections of the Geneva Conventions applied only to individuals involved in international conflicts, as opposed to civil wars. In reality, civilians tend to be brutalized more in internal conflicts. Common Article 3 of the Geneva Conventions attempted to extend the reach of the treaties to civil wars, and this was later acknowledged by the ICJ in the *Nicaragua* Case.[3] In a further development in 1977, two Additional Protocols were negotiated for the Geneva Conventions, and they apply its protections to most internal conflicts and wars of national liberation

---

3.   See 1986 I.C.J. 14, 113–14.

(although not to situations of "internal disturbances and tensions, such as riots, isolated and sporadic acts of violence").

This principle was recognized by the International Criminal Tribunal for the Former Yugoslavia (ICTFY), established by the U.N. Security Council in 1993 to "try those persons responsible for serious breaches of international humanitarian law committed on the territory of the Former Yugoslavia." As part of the broad pattern of international law holding individuals responsible for their own acts (see Chapter 7(B)), especially in the wake of Nuremberg and the Nazi atrocities, the ICTFY has had the opportunity to clarify and apply many aspects of international humanitarian law. (A U.N.-established Tribunal for Rwanda–which shares the ICTFY's prosecutorial staff and appeals judges–has also made important contributions in this regard.) In one decision,[4] the ICTFY's Appeals Chamber rejected a defendant's claim that the Tribunal lacked jurisdiction over him because his alleged crimes occurred in the course of an internal conflict, and thus were not covered under either the Geneva Conventions, Protocols, or customary international law.

The last bequest of the Hague Law was the clarification of issues of treatment of enemy nationals and their property in time of war. Although outright confiscations of private property have always been a common feature of military operations, international law has attempted to ameliorate the harsh effects of such measures. Even so, in the United States at least, the President still has exceptionally broad powers to register and control the property of enemy aliens, under the authority of the Trading with the Enemy Act.[5] Such measures can even extend, unfortunately, to the supervision, or even the internment, of such individuals. The 1949 Geneva Convention Relative to the Protection of Civilian Persons in Time of War does, to some degree, restrain this kind of reprisal.

A more nettlesome problem is raised by belligerent occupation, when one warring State physically controls the territory of another, prior to any disposition by treaty or peace accord. The Hague Conventions provided detailed rules for such occupations, stating (among other things) that the occupant is entitled to maintain order and to utilize the resources of the country for its own military needs. Nevertheless, the occupying Power is obliged to respect the local law then-prevailing and to consider the population and economic assets of the territory as a *usufruct*, or trust. The rules of belligerent occupation become difficult to enforce in situations where the subjugation has persisted for a long time. For example, Israel's occupation of the West Bank and Gaza Strip since 1967 was

---

4. *Prosecutor v. Tadić*, 35 Int'l Legal Materials 32 (1996) (ICTFY App. 1995).

5. 50 U.S.C. §§ 21–24.

criticized as not being in strict accordance with the Hague and Geneva Conventions.

In the last few decades, the laws of war have taken a particular interest in protecting the environment during times of conflict. The 1977 Additional Geneva Protocol I prohibits States from "employ[ing] methods or means of warfare which are intended, or may be expected, to cause widespread, long-term and severe damage to the natural environment." Another treaty signed the same year requires nations not to make hostile use of environmental modification techniques (the ENMOD Convention). This progressive development of international law was necessitated by certain new forms of warfare (particularly in Vietnam, where mass defoliation efforts took place). The question of whether these rules had entered customary international law was raised in 1991, when Saddam Hussein's occupying forces wantonly opened Kuwaiti oil wells and set them on fire, as well as deliberately caused a massive oil spill in the Persian Gulf.

Finally, international law has stepped-up efforts to protect cultural heritage and property during wartime. Although it had always been respected that literary and artistic works were immune from capture under the law of naval prize,[6] protection of art works and historic sites was rarely respected on land. The destruction of significant historic monuments in Europe during the World Wars, as well as the wholesale looting of valuable artworks by the Nazis, led to the negotiation of the 1954 Hague Convention and Protocol for the Protection of Cultural Property in the Event of Armed Conflict. This instrument, which was amended in 1998, has received broad support, although well-publicized breaches during the Balkans conflict (including the virtual destruction of the historic city of Dubrovnic) suggest that much remains to be done in this regard.

That may as well be one's general conclusion as to the efficacy of the laws of war. Despite the extraordinary leaps forward in the development of the *ius in bello* and international humanitarian law, the 20th century saw some of the bloodiest conflicts since the vicious religious wars of Grotius' time in the early 1600's. Nevertheless, the creation of an International Criminal Court (discussed in Chapter 7(B)), as an avenue for prosecutions of war criminals, may accelerate further the strengthening of the laws of war. The continued commitment of major military Powers to prosecute their own officers and service-members for infractions of international humanitarian law may offer the most promising means of actually enforcing that body of law.

6. See *The MARQUIS DE SOM-MERUELES*, Stew. Adm. 482 (Vice   Adm. Ct. Halifax 1815) (U.K.).

Chapter 21

Peaceful Settlement of Disputes

Now that we come to the concluding pages of this volume, it remains to be seen how international institutions actually resolve legal disputes between States and other international actors. This topic is known as the peaceful settlement of international disputes, and it is a matter that obviously has occupied much attention in this study. The very structure of the sources and methods of international law contributes to a sense of confidence that there are neutral and objective rules for resolving controversies between countries. International law doctrines have sufficient specificity in order to give concrete guidance to such resolutions, and the availability of domestic legal remedies and procedures may actually reinforce the binding nature of international legal obligation. The entire framework of international law thus leads nations, organizations, individuals, and businesses to the expectation that disputes between international legal persons will be settled peaceably, efficiently, and fairly under an international rule of law.

It makes sense to end this book by closely examining the precise institutional machinery that is available to achieve this critical objective for international legal order. Consequently, this Chapter will first explore some generic issues on this topic—the obligation of States to settle disputes peacefully and the role of the United Nations in that regard. Next, the significant role of international arbitration will be discussed. The history, jurisdiction, and operating procedures of the World Court will then be fully canvassed. A consideration of future trends in international adjudication will conclude the book.

A. Negotiation, Conciliation and Arbitration

An affirmative obligation upon States to resolve peacefully disputes is a relatively new development in international law. The first multilateral effort in this regard was the League of Nations' 1928 General Act for the Pacific Settlement of International Disputes. This instrument created a duty for States to submit legal disputes first to conciliation (discussed below), and, if that failed, to more binding arbitration or adjudication. The 1928 General Act has today only a handful of signatories (the U.S. is not one), and its current relevance in international dispute resolution has been doubted. Nevertheless, it spawned a large number of bilateral treaties, of which the United States is party to many, that impose a similar requirement of peacefully resolving disputes and which grant jurisdiction to particular institutions to carry out those procedures. Such provisions in treaties are known as *compromissory clauses*. Some of these are quite simple, while others (including that in the 1982 Law of the Sea Treaty—see Chapter 11) are quite complex and offer a bewildering array of different options.

Before proceeding, it should be noted that the very phrase "dispute" is a term-of-art in international law. A dispute conveys the sense of an authentic disagreement between nations that has risen to a level that requires peaceful adjustment. Somewhat analogous to the U.S. Constitution's "Case or Controversy" requirement for exercise of the judicial power of the federal courts, an international dispute must be appropriately concrete, specific and contested in order to trigger an obligation of peaceful settlement under the 1928 General Act, the U.N. Charter, or various other treaties. Coupled with this narrowing construction of a "dispute" in international relations are also a variety of prudential doctrines that international tribunals employ to avoid resolving certain kinds of issues. (These will be considered below in the context of the ICJ's admissibility rulings.)

Once the threshold of an authentic dispute is reached, the way that the vast majority of such matters are resolved is simply through bilateral negotiation and adjustment. No outsiders are summoned in such instances, and the proceedings are confidential and (usually) never revealed. Negotiation reflects the real "push-and-pull" of international diplomacy; the ultimate resolution of the dispute remains in the hands of the parties, giving them the right to compromise and settle without outside scrutiny or accountability. It is no wonder that, even when negotiation is accompanied by the mediation efforts of other countries or organizations (think of the U.S. role in Middle East peace talks), negotiation is the preferred mode of international discourse.

A slightly more formal mechanism for dispute settlement is conciliation. First initiated with the so-called Bryan Treaties of 1914–21 (named after then-Secretary of State William Jennings Bryan), conciliation commissions were envisioned as a non-binding method for nations to resolve disputes. Commissioners are drawn from uninvolved States, and they make recommendations to the parties to settle the matter. This is intended to be more formal than mere mediation but is certainly not third-party arbitration or adjudication (discussed below). Interestingly, a Protocol to the Vienna Convention on the Law of Treaties (VCLT) makes conciliation the preferred means of settlement for disputes that arise under that treaty.

Related to the practice of conciliation are commissions of inquiry. These can be thought of as fact-finding bodies, charged with objectively collecting information about particular incidents, and then advising the disputants as to what actually happened. No legal conclusions are reached by such commissions; rather, the goal is that, by submitting the facts to the parties, the States involved will be in a better position to resolve the dispute themselves. This has proven crucial in a variety of circumstances.

In one notorious incident it quite likely averted a war. In 1904, Russia's European fleet was sailing to the Pacific in order to join a campaign against Japan. While off the British coast in the North Sea, and in a dense fog, the Russian naval commander suddenly became convinced that he was being attacked by Japanese torpedo boats. (This was quite a stretch, since the nearest Japanese vessel was 10,000 miles and two oceans away!) He ordered his ships to open fire, and after doing so, he learned that he had just sunk a number of English fishing boats, killing many fishermen. The British government was outraged, but in an effort to avoid war, a commission of inquiry was convened (consisting of 5 naval officers from other countries).[1] The commission laid the entire blame for the incident on Russia, although it concluded that, while certainly reckless and bizarre, the Russian admiral's conduct was not intentional. Commissions of inquiry have been used in subsequent naval incidents,[2] as well as to report on election results, World Bank lending practices, and war crimes violations (under the 1977 Geneva Additional Protocol I).

The United Nations Charter can itself be regarded as a dispute settlement mechanism. Article 2(3) provides that "All Members shall settle their international disputes by peaceful means, in such a manner that international peace and security, and justice, are not endangered." It is entirely possible for the U.N. Security Council to regard a legal dispute between States as a potential cause of a breach of the peace. Indeed, the Council has even regarded some forms of domestic policies and legal claims as contributing to international instability. South Africa's former policy of *apartheid* was subject to withering condemnation in the United Nations, notwithstanding Charter Article 2(7)'s provision that certain domestic matters are outside the U.N.'s remit. Likewise, Charter Article 33 allows the Security Council to call upon a variety of dispute settlement options to contesting States, including (under the authority of Article 36(3)) recommending that the parties submit a legal dispute to the International Court of Justice.

---

1. See Dogger Bank Incident (Gr. Brit. v. Russ.), Hague Ct. Rep. (Scott) 403 (Comm'n Inquiry 1905).

2. See RED CRUSADER Incident (U.K. v. Den.), Hague Ct. Rep.2d (Scott) 135 (Comm'n Inquiry 1962).

Unlike the old Council of the League of Nations, the Security Council does not typically involve itself in mediation or conciliation of legal disputes. Instead, it is often the United Nations Secretary–General who is most immediately engaged in mediation of disputes. In fact, the use of the Secretary–General's "good offices" has been a consistent feature of global crisis management. In one recent example, the U.N.'s role in resolving a notorious altercation between States illustrates the many rounds of dispute-settlement that one particular incident can generate.

As has already been narrated (in Chapter 3(A)), France undertook in the 1970's to stop atmospheric nuclear testing on its South Pacific isles. But in the 1980's, France resumed underground nuclear testing on those islands. A number of environmental groups protested this action, and one of them—Greenpeace International—dispatched its flagship, The RAINBOW WARRIOR, to observe the tests just outside France's territorial seas. The publicity generated by Greenpeace vastly aggravated the French government, so it adopted a unique course of action to resolve this problem. In 1985, France dispatched two secret agents (posing as husband and wife) to New Zealand, where the RAINBOW WARRIOR was in port for repairs. The agents proceeded to blow-up the ship, killing a Dutch national who was on board. Obviously having rather low regard for the New Zealand police, the French agents barely bothered to cover their tracks. They were arrested within an hour of their sabotage.

Not surprisingly, the New Zealand government regarded France's action as tantamount to an act of war. The agents were promptly charged with murder and bound-over for trial. The French government reacted initially with denials, but then changed course and expressed outrage at New Zealand's refusal to release the agents. France retaliated by cutting-off lamb and butter imports from New Zealand. (For a country where sheep and cattle outnumber people by a factor of 100–to–1, this was a potent response.) It was at this juncture, that the U.N. Secretary–General, Perez de Cuéllar, offered to mediate the dispute.[3] In return for France's apology, withdrawal of economic sanctions, and an indemnity of $7 million (compensation to the Dutch family and to Greenpeace having already been made), New Zealand agreed to release the two agents to French custody, *provided* they serve a 3–year sentence on the French Polynesian prison island of Hao.

No sooner had the ink dried on this negotiated settlement did France proceed to break it. France withdrew both the agents from Hao (one for "maternity leave" and the other for medical reasons),

---

3. See U.N. Secretary General: Ruling Pertaining to the Differences between France and New Zealand arising from The RAINBOW WARRIOR Affair, 26 Int'l Legal Materials 1346 (1987).

and never returned them. New Zealand vigorously protested, and a new round of dispute-settlement began. Because of a clause in the Secretary–General's agreed settlement, New Zealand initiated binding arbitration proceedings. The arbitral tribunal issued its award in 1990, holding that although France had violated its 1986 undertakings, it could not order specific performance (for more on this see Chapter 18). Despite that, the tribunal ordered France to make a $2 million contribution to a France–New Zealand friendship fund.[4] (A subsequent attempt by New Zealand to have the ICJ rule on the legality of France's resumption of underground nuclear testing also failed.[5]) Thus ended probably one of the most bizarre legal disputes in recent history.

The arbitral tribunal used in *The RAINBOW WARRIOR* Affair was paradigmatic in many ways. For starters, it was *ad hoc*— created to resolve a single dispute. From its beginnings in ancient Greece and revived in the 1794 Jay Treaty between the U.S. and Britain, arbitration was intended as an occasional judicial institution to deal with a particular matter or a set of related claims. When proceedings ended, the arbitral tribunal was disbanded. There was nothing permanent in most arbitrations, although some claims settlement institutions (such as the Iran–U.S. Claims Tribunal) have lasted for decades. The establishment of the Permanent Court of Arbitration (PCA) in 1899, another of the achievements of the First Hague Peace Conference, was a bit of a misnomer. The PCA merely provided facilities for international arbitration (including lists of available arbitrators); it was not, itself, a regular judicial institution.

The organization of *The RAINBOW WARRIOR* Arbitration was also typical. The panel consisted of three arbitrators. One was selected by New Zealand, the other by France. These are known as the "party-appointed" arbitrators. The last arbitrator was picked by agreement of the two governments. (In other situations, the two party-appointed arbitrators mutually pick a president for the tribunal.) The number of arbitrators for a particular tribunal and the manner of their appointment are set by the parties in terms-of-reference called a *compromis*. The *compromis* might also detail the procedures to be followed for the arbitration, the exact issues to be resolved, and any time-limits for the proceedings. If the *compromis* contemplates arbitration of a set of claims, the tribunal's jurisdiction will be carefully circumscribed. (The 1981 Algiers Accord established the Iran Claims Tribunal and imposed about a dozen

---

4. *RAINBOW WARRIOR* Arbitration (N.Z. v. Fr.), 82 Int'l L. Rep. 499 (1990).

5. *Request for an Examination of the Situation in Accordance with Paragraph 3 of the Court's Judgment of 20 December 1974* Case (Austl./N.Z. v. Fr.), 1995 I.C.J. 288.

different jurisdictional requirements for arbitrable claims.) Despite these customary understandings for the operation of arbitral tribunals, problems do arise when one of the parties (usually the respondent State) refuses to appoint their arbitrator, in hopes of thereby stymying the proceedings.[6] Some general arbitration agreements (such as the 1948 Bogotá Pact for Inter–American disputes), as well as some *compromis*, have elaborate provisions to prevent attempts to frustrate the arbitral process.

International arbitration between States has waxed and waned in popularity over the past two centuries. In the 1800's, before the advent of permanent adjudication institutions (to be considered next), *ad hoc* arbitral bodies were exceedingly common. International claims settlement commissions were often invoked, although sometimes in circumstances which suggested a strong element of coercion and economic imperialism (Venezuela and Mexico were required in nearly two dozen instances to submit foreign nationals' claims to such bodies). For these reasons, international arbitration declined in significance, particularly after World War Two and the period of decolonization in the 1960's. Ironically, international *commercial* arbitration (between private parties) came more into vogue during that same period (a development that was mentioned in Chapter 13(1)).

The establishment of the Iran–U.S. Claims Tribunal, under the January 1981 Algiers Accords, reversed the trend away from international public arbitration involving States and State entities. Created in the aftermath of the 1979 Hostage Crisis, the Tribunal illustrated that even for those nations whose relationship could only be charitably described as abysmal could still resolve their outstanding legal disputes. Political tensions did periodically intrude into the Tribunal's work. (In one notorious instance, two Iranian arbitrators attempted to choke one of the neutral arbitrators, in order to create a provocation to suspend operations at the Tribunal.) Despite these isolated occurrences, the Tribunal has over the past 20 years been able to resolve thousands of private claims (mostly by U.S. companies and individuals against Iran, in an amount exceeding $2 billion), as well as conclude some difficult disputes between Iran and the United States. Indeed, for many years the only official point-of-contact between the Iranian and American governments was the Tribunal in The Hague. The Tribunal has also successfully contributed to the international law jurisprudence on State Responsibility and diplomatic protection issues (discussed in Chapter 8).

Taking their cue from the Tribunal's success, more and more arbitral tribunals have been convened in the last decade in order to

6. See *Peace Treaties* Opinion, 1950 I.C.J. 221.

resolve investment matters, territorial disputes and economic controversies. Some general structural issues do remain, and they bear on the institutional success of international arbitration. Some of these implicate the inherent ability of arbitral bodies to protect themselves from fraud and to discipline unscrupulous parties (and their counsel). Although such abuse in uncommon, it does periodically occur.[7]

At the other extreme, a few commentators have expressed concern that some arbitrations have operated beyond the remit provided for in their *compromis*, by deciding issues not before them or by not deciding cases based on the rule of law. In one instance, the *Chazimal* Arbitration,[8] the tribunal defied the explicit instructions of the *compromis* and quite literally "split-the-baby" by dividing the disputed territory. The U.S. refused to accept the award, and it was only until 1963 that the matter was finally resolved. Other challenges of an arbitral tribunal's exceeding its authority (*exces de pouvoir*) have, however, been rejected by the World Court.[9]

Lastly, there remain concerns about the effective enforcement of arbitral awards. The adoption of the 1958 New York Convention (discussed in Chapter 13(1)) has partially addressed this issue, although reservations that some States Parties have attached to the treaty have limited its force. Periodically, a domestic court will refuse to give effect to an arbitral award made by a tribunal in another country, either on grounds of inconsistency with public policy or a due process failing in the arbitral proceedings.[10] Although until recently the idea of "appealing" arbitral awards to a higher body would have been regarded as heresy (the finality of arbitration being one of its singular attractions), this might have to be considered as an aspect of improving the efficacy of both international commercial and public arbitration.

B. The World Court

Proposals for the creation of an international adjudicatory body were first made in earnest at the Hague Peace Conferences of 1899 and 1907. In spite of the relative allure of international arbitration, many States believed that international law could not truly be effectively followed and enforced until there was a permanent

---

7. See *La Abra Silver Mining Co. v. United States*, 175 U.S. 423 (1899); *Federal Reserve Bank of New York v. Gordon Williams*, 708 F. Supp. 48 (S.D.N.Y. 1989).

8. See *International Title to the Chazimal Tract*, [1911] Foreign Relations of the U.S. 573 (Arb. 1911).

9. See *Case Concerning the Arbitral Award of 31 July 1989*, 1990 I.C.J. 64.

10. See *Iran Aircraft Indus. v. Avco Corp.*, 980 F.2d 141 (2d Cir. 1992).

institution for settling inter-State disputes. Plans for the creation of such a court foundered in 1907 when some nations objected to a tribunal with a limited number of judges (these States wanted a judge appointed for every member nation, making for an unwieldy bench), and Germany generally opposed a tribunal with anything but optional jurisdiction. As already noted, the establishment of the Permanent Court of Arbitration (PCA) was a middling consolation prize—it was merely a facilitation center for arbitration, not a permanent judicial body. It was only in 1920, with the end of World War One and the creation of the League of Nations that the Permanent Court of International Justice (PCIJ) was founded at The Peace Palace, in The Hague in The Netherlands. The PCIJ (as noted in Chapter 6) was conceived as a separate institution from the League, with potentially different memberships. A Commission of Jurists drafted the PCIJ Statute in 1920, and the text of that effort is largely reflected in the current Statute of the ICJ. Indeed, for all practical purposes, the ICJ (created as part of the U.N. in 1945) is the successor to the PCIJ, and they are together referred to as the "World Court."

1. *Organization of the World Court.* The structure and operating procedures of the ICJ are fairly straight-forward. The current Court consists of 15 members, each of whom serve 9–year terms. By tradition (and that is all it is), each of the permanent members of the Security Council has a national on the Court. The remaining 10 seats are distributed by region, in order to give the Court as wide a perspective of the world's legal systems as possible. Judges are picked in their individual capacity. They are not political appointees by their respective governments. Actually, the method of nominating and electing ICJ judges can be fairly called byzantine. The national groups of four PCA arbitrators each nominate outstanding international lawyers from government ministries, law faculties, the bench and bar. Judges are elected when they receive a majority vote in each of the U.N. Security Council and the General Assembly.

Despite what has sometimes been suggested by commentators, the judges of the ICJ are rarely politicized. Even at the height of the Cold War, judges from Eastern Europe and the Socialist bloc did not always vote with what were perceived to be Soviet interests in some cases. (Manfred Lachs, a judge from Poland who served over 26 years on the Court, routinely voted in surprising ways.) According to the Court's Statute, however, in any case where one (or more) of the parties are not represented on the bench by a judge of its nationality, then that litigant can appoint a judge *ad hoc*. A holdover of the practice of "party-appointed arbitrators," *ad hoc* judges almost invariably vote in favor of the legal arguments advanced by the State which named them. This has come to be expected, although judges *ad hoc* may exercise some subtle influence on the Court's deliberations, especially in cases where the legal issues may turn on the interpretation of treaties written in an arcane language or on a fuller understanding of particular local laws or customs.

The World Court traditionally hears cases in plenary sessions, with a full bench of 15 judges (or 16 or 17, if there are *ad hoc* judges appointed). A majority vote determines the case. (In case of a tie, the President gets to cast the deciding ballot.) Because the Court hears cases in full benches, the proceedings can be exceedingly slow, and it can take some time for the Court to render a decision. (The fact that proceedings consist of long speeches read laboriously from scripts, and then simultaneously translated into French and English, does not help.) Proposals to utilize *chambers* of the Court, consisting (usually) of 5 hand-picked judges to hear cases, has received mixed reviews. A decision of a Court chamber has the same binding effect as one made by the full bench, and (presumably) the same "precedential" weight (although remember there is no strict doctrine of *stare decisis* in international law). Recent plans to inaugurate a special chamber on international environmental disputes, as well as one for summary procedures, have yet to bear fruit.

The operating procedures of the World Court would hardly matter if its docket consisted of one or two cases a year. Like international arbitration, the Court has gone through periods of dizzying popularity and profound irrelevance. The PCIJ was heavily-employed during the inter-War years, as was the ICJ from 1945 to 1960. But from 1960 to about 1985, the Court went on the skids, the result of a premeditated boycott of developing nations from the Third World who believed that the ICJ did not (and could not) represent or reflect their interests. But, slowly, the Court regained its stature. In a series of wise rulings on border disputes (both land and maritime), the Court acquired the trust of many nations around the world.

In early 2000, the Court's docket consisted of a staggeringly large number of 24 cases. Of these, 4 were boundary cases. But of the remainder, one involved environmental issues, two concerned treatment of aliens, two dealt with aerial incidents, and the rest implicated uses of armed force (in such global hot-spots as the Persian Gulf, Africa, and the Balkans). The Court had never been as busy and as much needed as it was at the beginning of the new Millennium.

2. *The Court's Jurisdiction.* How, then, does the Court get its cases? It is vital to realize that every matter which comes before the ICJ does so because of the consent of the litigants. The only

question is how that consent is manifested. The Court does not—
and cannot—exercise a mandatory form of jurisdiction over States.
And, remember, only States may be parties before the Court.
Article 36(1) of the Statute of the Court thus provides that: "The
jurisdiction of the Court comprises all cases which the parties refer
to it and all matters specially provided for in the Charter of the
United Nations or in treaties and conventions in force."

The most common, and uncontroversial, way for the Court to
receive a case is by the special agreement of the parties to submit it
specially by *compromis*. This is an especially popular vehicle for
seizing the Court in boundary or other territorial disputes. In such
circumstances, the parties have each concluded that the political
costs of losing the case are less than escalating the dispute. Both
sides are prepared to lose, in effect, so submitting it to the adjudication of the Court provides a valuable, "face-saving" device for an
embattled government. When cases are submitted by *compromis*,
the Court proceeds immediately to briefing on the merits since
there is no conceivable jurisdictional concern.

An increasingly accepted way to invoke the ICJ's jurisdiction is
through *compromissory clauses* included in bilateral and multilateral conventions. Such provisions allow, in the event of a dispute
arising under the treaty, that the matter will be submitted to the
Court. Although a compromissory clause need not be formally-
drafted, it must unambiguously indicate that the ICJ has been
selected to resolve any future disputes that might arise under the
treaty. Equivocal undertakings to have the ICJ settle a dispute are
insufficient.[11] At last count, there are approximately 300 conventions with clauses that raise the Court's jurisdiction. Of these, the
United States is party to about a hundred, including the Friendship, Commerce and Navigation (FCN) treaties that the U.S. concludes with many nations. FCN Treaties were the basis of the U.S.
suit against Iran in the Hostage Crisis,[12] and Nicaragua's suit
against the U.S. arising from the *Contra* Affair.[13] In the event that
a respondent State objects to the jurisdiction of the Court, it is up
to the ICJ (under Article 36(6) of its Statute) to decide the jurisdictional matter. In cases involving compromissory clauses, the inquiry is usually limited to the question of whether the dispute before
the Courts falls within the relevant treaty containing the clause.

Aside from special agreements and compromissory clauses, the
ICJ can also acquire, in exceptional cases, matters on appeal from
other bodies. While it would be incorrect to regard the Court as

---

11. See *Aegean Sea Continental Shelf Case* (Gr. v. Tur.), 1978 I.C.J. 3.

12. *Case Concerning United States Diplomatic and Consular Staff in Teh-ran* (U.S. v. Iran), 1980 I.C.J. 3.

13. *Case Concerning Military and Paramilitary Activities in and against Nicaragua* (Nicar. v. U.S.), 1984 I.C.J. 392.

having appellate jurisdiction in any real sense, a handful of treaties or agreements give the Court the power to review decisions by other bodies. Until recently, the ICJ was the court of final recourse for decisions from the U.N. Administrative Tribunal (UNAT), a staff grievance body. The World Court periodically reviews decisions from the International Civil Aviation Organization (ICAO), often in relation to aerial incidents. The possibility that the U.N. Security Council could mandatorily refer disputes to the Court for legal determination has never been accepted.[14]

That leaves, as a final basis of the Court's authority, what is rather misleadingly called its "compulsory jurisdiction." This is premised on Statute Article 36, paragraphs 2 and 3:

2.   The states parties to the present Statute may at any time declare that they recognize as compulsory ipso facto and without special agreement, in relation to any other state accepting the same obligation, the jurisdiction of the Court in all legal disputes concerning:

a.   the interpretation of a treaty;

b.   any question of international law;

c.   the existence of any fact which, if established, would constitute a breach of an international obligation;

d.   the nature or extent of the reparation to be made for the breach of an international obligation.

3.   The declarations referred to above may be made unconditionally or on condition of reciprocity on the part of several or certain states, or for a certain time.

Of the nearly 190 nations that are parties to the Court's Statute, only about 62 currently have made "optional clause" declarations under Article 36. Of the five permanent members of the Security Council, only the United Kingdom today accepts the compulsory jurisdiction of the Court. The United States had an optional clause declaration in force from 1946 until 1985, when it was withdrawn in the heat of the *Nicaragua* litigation.

One need not look far for the reason for the relative unpopularity of optional clause jurisdiction. Filing an Article 36 declaration exposes States to suits brought by any other nation that has filed a similar declaration. That would invoke the Court's jurisdiction over disputes that may not even be in the contemplation of a State when it makes its declaration, and, in many cases, countries have been quite queasy about making such broad, advance concessions. Virtually none of the States that have made an Article 36 declaration have accepted the ICJ's jurisdiction unconditionally. Article 36(2)

---

14. See *Corfu Channel* Case (U.K. v. Alb.), 1949 I.C.J. 31.

establishes an incredibly broad ambit for disputes covered by a declaration—virtually anything involving the content of international law obligations (including treaty interpretations) and remedies for the breach of such a duty. Most countries have, therefore, applied substantial reservations to their acceptances. It is worth reviewing the scope of these typical reservations, if for no other reason that to examine the relative failure of the Court's "compulsory" jurisdiction.

Many countries, for example, exclude any matter from the Court's jurisdiction which is being handled by an alternative dispute resolution mechanism. This makes good sense; there is no point to triggering the Court's involvement if another arbitration is handling the case, or if the dispute is in negotiation or mediation. Other declarations specifically exclude certain kinds of disputes. (Canada's, for example, withdraws jurisdiction for any matter involving law of the sea issues, and particularly any matters involving Arctic claims or fisheries enforcement.[15])

Many optional clause reservations also place time limits on the filing of claims. The United Kingdom's 1969 Declaration, for example, provides that the Court will *not* have jurisdiction where

> any other Party to the dispute has accepted the compulsory jurisdiction of the [Court] only in relation to or for the purpose of the dispute; or where the acceptance of the Court's compulsory jurisdiction ... was deposited or ratified less than twelve months prior to the filing of the application bringing the dispute before the Court.

This was intended to avoid what is known as the "hit-and-run" tactic. All the Court requires, under Statute Article 36, is that the two litigating States have in force, *on the same day*, a declaration. But for Britain's reservation, it would have been conceivable for another State, on Day 1, to file an optional clause declaration, to sue Britain before the Court on Day 2, and then to withdraw its declaration (before any other nation could file an Application) on Day 3. Britain's craftily-drafted Declaration requires that a potential applicant State expose itself to litigation for at least a year prior to filing against the U.K.

By far and away, the two most controversial reservations to optional clause jurisdiction were those appended by the United States to its 1946 Declaration. The first, known as the Connally Reservation (for the Senator who proposed it), simply provided that the Court would not have jurisdiction over "disputes with regard to matters which are essentially within the domestic jurisdiction of the United States of America as determined by the United States."

---

15. See *Fisheries Jurisdiction* Case (Sp. v. Can.), 1998 I.C.J. ___ (Dec. 4).

This was essentially seen as an escape valve; the U.S. would accept the Court's compulsory jurisdiction (thereby setting a good example), but it always had the option to take it back if it decided that a case was in its "domestic jurisdiction." Had this reservation simply required that the Court could not rule on domestic matters and still let the Court decide the issue (as Statute Article 36(6) allows), then it would have been unobjectionable. It was the self-judging character of the Connally Reservation that was so corrosive of international expectations.

These provisions were challenged as reservations that were inconsistent with the object and purpose of an optional clause declaration (see Chapter 3(C)). In the *Norwegian Loans* Case, which featured an identical clause in France's Declaration, the Court could have struck it out on that ground. But, instead, the ICJ came-up with a positively fiendish response to the use of these clauses. The Court permitted States to make such a reservation, but also allowed respondent States to invoke the reservation *against* an applicant. Because optional clause declarations must be read reciprocally under Statute Article 36(3), a defendant State before the Court may pick-and-choose among its opponent's reservations and use them. Norway thus invoked France's self-judging reservation and declared that France's case involved a matter within Norway's "domestic jurisdiction," as decided by Norway. That was the end of the case.[16] In fact, it was the end of every case brought by the United States against another State with an optional clause. Every time the U.S. sued, the other nation simply invoked the Connally Reservation. What was intended as the ultimate "shield" to be used by the United States to avoid embarrassing World Court litigation was consistently used as a "sword" by its opponents. Ironically, in the one dispute where the U.S. would have most liked to have invoked the reservation—in the *Nicaragua* Case—it did not.

If the Connally Reservation is proof positive that the most important rule of all in international affairs is the law of unintended consequences, the second reservation made by the 1946 U.S. Declaration was equally equivocal. The multilateral treaty exception (or "Vandenburg Amendment") excluded disputes arising under such treaties "unless (1) all parties to the treaty affected by the decision are also parties to the case before the Court, or (2) the United States specially agrees to jurisdiction." The purpose of this was to prevent the U.S. from getting in the middle of a whip-saw situation. The Court could conceivably make a ruling on treaty interpretation in a case involving one of our treaty partners. But because such a ruling is not necessarily binding in disputes with

16. See *Norwegian Loans* (Fr. v. Nor.), 1957 I.C.J. 9.

other parties to the treaty, there was a risk that the U.S. would be obliged to take contrary positions or perform mutually contradictory actions. While the Vandenburg Amendment was successfully invoked by the United States in the *Nicaragua* Case, its only effect was to force the ICJ into premising its rulings on uses of force (see Chapter 19(B)) on customary law, and not the U.N. Charter.

All in all, the ICJ's compulsory jurisdiction has been regarded as a failure. It is very unlikely that the United States will ever again file an optional clause declaration. With the advent of many treaties containing compromissory clauses, and with the willingness of States to submit disputes by special agreement, optional clause cases may become a rarity. Those countries that traditionally have been the most vociferous supporters of compulsory jurisdiction are now vexed with its application. Those States that have active declarations are regarded as targets of opportunity. (Australia recently has been hit with a number of suits that can only charitably be described as ill-conceived.) Lastly, the Court itself does not seem to like premising its jurisdiction on this basis. Compulsory jurisdiction cases are usually bitterly-contested. After all, if a respondent State had really wanted to be before the Court, it would have consented by other means.

3. *Admissibility, Provisional Measures and Interventions.* Just because the Court has jurisdiction with some basis under the Statute—*compromis*, compromissory clause or optional clause—does not necessarily mean that the ICJ will actually hear the case. Over nearly eighty years, the World Court has developed a number of prudential grounds for finding a case *inadmissible*, and thus declining to decide it. These grounds are analogous to the prudential reasons that U.S. federal courts often refuse to hear cases, even though jurisdiction is otherwise proper. For example, the Court will dismiss a case if its subject-matter has become moot, as when in the *Nuclear Test* Cases France unilaterally declared that it would no longer conduct atmospheric testing.[17] Although the Court was careful to say that it would remain seized of the issue (just in case the French decided to change their minds), the dispute was, for all intents and purposes, concluded. Likewise, the ICJ will not decide a case if the dispute is not sufficiently ripe, or well-developed.[18]

Somewhat more controversially, the Court will dismiss a case because of failure to exhaust local remedies,[19] a rule borrowed from the international law of diplomatic protection (discussed in Chapter 8(B)). Likewise, the ICJ will not hear a case if there are indispens-

---

17. See 1974 I.C.J. 253 (Austl./N.Z. v. Fr.).

18. See *Electricity Company of Sofia and Bulgaria* (Bulg. v. Belg.), 1939 P.C.I.J. (ser. A/B) No. 77.

19. See *Interhandel* Case (Switz. v. U.S.), 1959 I.C.J. 6.

able parties that are missing in the litigation.[20] In what was probably its nadir, the Court refused to adjudicate a dispute involving South Africa's illegal occupation of South West Africa (Namibia) because the applicant countries lacked standing to bring the claim. This was despite the fact that both Ethiopia and Liberia had been members of the League of Nations which had issued the original mandate for South West Africa, that South Africa had allegedly violated. As it turned out, it was only the Court's standing that was damaged by this decision,[21] and, because of it, countries from the developing world avoided the ICJ for nearly two decades. Perhaps as a consequence of this, the Court has flatly rejected other forms of admissibility challenges, most notably arguments that certain forms of "political questions" should be avoided by the Court.[22]

Among other aspects of the World Court's procedures, it is important to note the ICJ's power to indicate provisional measures. These are interim measures of protection, ensuring the equality of the parties while the proceedings are underway. If the issue in the case is a border conflict, the Court might order provisional measures for a cease-fire and no further aggressive action to be taken by the two sides while the case is pending. While the ostensible standard for the Court to indicate provisional measures is irreparable prejudice, the ICJ will often grant measures even when the underlying jurisdiction of the Court looks doubtful.[23] What this means is that many cases are split into three procedural phases before the Court: (1) an order about provisional measures; (2) a ruling about jurisdiction; and (3) a judgment on the merits. Some of the ICJ's orders for provisional measures have been ignored by the parties—such as Iran's refusal to release the U.S. hostages in 1979, and the United States' later refusal to stay executions in cases involving the Vienna Convention on Consular Relations.

Traditionally, the World Court has been parsimonious in granting leave for third-parties to intervene in cases before the Court. The ICJ Statute, in Articles 62 and 63, provides authority for such interventions, and (one would have thought) such would be desirable in order to promote wider settlement of disputes. The Court's refusal to allow El Salvador to intervene in the *Nicaragua* Case was savaged by critics. Although the Court is correct to be concerned about intervention being used as a ruse to introduce new parties and issues into pending cases, and it has therefore established a high level of showing for prejudice, this procedural bar has lately

---

20. See *Monetary Gold Removed from Rome in 1943* (Italy v. Fr. /U.K./U.S.), 1954 I.C.J. 19.

21. See *South West Africa* Cases (Eth./Lib. v. S. Afr.), 1966 I.C.J. 4.

22. See *Nicaragua* Case, 1984 I.C.J. 392 (Jurisdiction).

23. See *Aegean Sea Continental Shelf Case* (Gr. v. Tur.), 1976 I.C.J. 3 (Provisional Measures).

been lowered. In two recent cases, the ICJ has allowed interventions by third-States that would be affected by maritime delimitation findings.

4. *Advisory Jurisdiction.* The foregoing has considered the World Court's contentious jurisdiction—cases involving States as opposing litigants. But as has been considered in substantial detail in this volume, many of the Court's most significant rulings have come in advisory opinions requested by an organ of the United Nations or one of its specialized agencies. Almost all of the critical decisions as to the "constitutional law" of the U.N. have come through the ICJ's advisory rulings (consider the *Reparations for Injuries* Opinion discussed in Chapter 6, or the *Certain Expenses* Opinion in Chapter 19(C)).

Under the Court's Statute, the U.N. General Assembly, Security Council, and Economic and Social Council can each request advisory opinions, as can certain specialized agencies. The Court will not answer a request for an advisory opinion if it is propounded by an inappropriate body. For example, the ICJ refused to answer a request for an advisory opinion by the World Health Organization (WHO) on the legality of the use of nuclear weapons in armed conflict, since such a question had nothing to do with the WHO's central mission of disease prevention and public health.[24] (As was noted in the previous Chapter, the ICJ did reply to a similar request made by the U.N. General Assembly, which is charged with disarmament questions.)

Nor will the Court allow a request for an advisory opinion be used as a way to force it to render a decision in what is really a contentious dispute between nations, where one or more of the States interested are not inclined to accept the Court's jurisdiction in the matter. For example, in the *Eastern Carelia* Opinion, the PCIJ refused to entertain a request for an advisory opinion on the legal status of disputed territory claimed both by Finland and the Soviet Union when it was manifest that the Soviets would not participate.[25] The Court will issue an opinion, even if States have an interest in the matter, so long as their rights and duties under international law are not being directly adjudicated.[26]

C. The Future of International Adjudication

There is no better way to conclude this volume than by briefly reflecting on the outlook for the peaceful settlement of disputes in international relations. As I observed in the very first Chapter,

---

24. See *Legality of the Use by a State of Nuclear Weapons in Armed Conflict* Opinion, 1996 I.C.J. 66 (July 8).

25. See 1923 P.C.I.J. (Ser. B), No. 5.

26. See *Western Sahara* Opinion, 1975 I.C.J. 12.

international law will continue to remain a primitive legal system, largely bereft of the traditional indicia of most domestic legal orders, including a World Parliament and global enforcement arm. Certainly, international law has managed very nicely without these features. Among the extraordinary developments of the 20th century in this area of law—including the emergence of human rights as a central value, the diversification of the subjects and objects of international law, and the deepening doctrinal sophistication of the discipline—has been the growth of well-respected international dispute settlement institutions.

Indeed, we see today a proliferation of such bodies. We have a continued role for inter-State public arbitrations (including claims tribunals), as well as private commercial arbitration. There have been new commissions monitoring and enforcing international human rights and humanitarian law norms. Tribunals for vindicating individual responsibility under international law, including the just-established International Criminal Court, will likely play a significant role. In addition to such global adjudicatory bodies as the World Court, we have specialized bodies (of which the International Tribunal for the Law of the Sea is a good example), as well as institutions created by regional organizations. Lastly, one should not forget that domestic courts are playing an increasing part in recognizing and enforcing international law rights and duties.

Have we become victims of our success? Do we have too many international courts competing with each other for a narrow jurisdiction and a limited docket of cases? This has been suggested, but I cannot really credit this criticism. These institutions have been created by the demands of the international community. Using a market metaphor, those dispute settlement mechanisms that will prove their worth will survive and flourish. Those that have been fashioned in anticipation of a need that has not materialized will wither away and die. If anything, there is as greater demand today for coordinating the decisions of international tribunals with those of domestic courts. (It has been proposed that national courts might want to refer certain kinds of international law questions to the ICJ, but (so far) there have been no takers.)

The creation of new—and better—international dispute resolution mechanisms is part of a larger struggle for law in international relations. The only real test of international law's success is whether it serves the needs of the international community—not just States, but also any individual, organization, church, or business that operates across frontiers and is concerned with relations and transactions on a global scale. Managing conflict and resolving disputes is just one aspect of serving the needs of a global community that craves peace, expects economic prosperity, and demands justice. The challenge of international law today is more than building better institutions of international law-making and law-compliance. Like this volume—which has focused on the frameworks of international legal order—international law is about the anticipation of a better future. It is a prospect that every international lawyer can share.

Select Bibliography

GENERAL WORKS ON INTERNATIONAL LAW

Ian Brownlie, *Principles of Public International Law* (5th ed. 1998)

Encyclopedia of Public International Law (R. Bernhardt ed. 1981–92)

Louis Henkin, *International law: politics and values* (1995)

Rosalyn Higgins, *Problems and Process: International Law and How to Use It* (1994)

L. Oppenheim, *International Law* (9th ed. Robert Jennings & Arthur Watt 1992)

Recueil des Cours (Hague Academy of International Law)

Restatement (Third) of the Foreign Relations Law of the United States (American Law Institute 1987)

Marjorie Whiteman, *Digest of International Law* (1936–73)

http://www.asil.org (American Society of International Law)

1. NATURE AND HISTORY OF INTERNATIONAL LAW

Fontes Historiae Iuris Gentium: Sources Relating to the History of International Law (W.G. Grewe ed. 1985–92)

Thomas M. Franck, *The Power of Legitimacy Among Nations* (1990)

Martti Koskenniemi, *From Apology to Utopia: The Structure of International Legal Argument* (1989)

John Bassett Moore, *A Digest of International Law* (1906)

Myres S. McDougal & W.M. Reisman, *International Law in Contemporary Perspective* (1981)

Arthur Nussbaum, *A Concise History of the Law of Nations* (rev. ed. 1954)

Religion and International Law (Mark Janis ed. 1999)

Oscar Schachter, *International Law in Theory and Practice* (1991)

J.H.W. Verzijl, *International Law in Historical Perspective* (1968–91)

2. GENERAL PRINCIPLES AND CUSTOMARY INTERNATIONAL LAW

Bin Cheng, *General Principles of Law as Applied by International Courts and Tribunals* (rep. 1987)

Anthony D'Amato, *The Concept of Custom in International Law* (1971)

H.W.A. Thirlway, *International customary law and codification* (1972)

http://www.un.org/law/ilc/index.htm (U.N. International Law Commission)

3. TREATIES

Douglas M. Johnston, *Consent and Commitment in the World Community: The Classification and Analysis of International Instruments* (1997)

Jan Klabbers, *The Concept of Treaty in International Law* (1996)

A.D. McNair, *The Law of Treaties* (2d ed. 1961)

Shabtai Rosenne, *Developments in the law of treaties, 1945–1986* (1989).

Ian Sinclair, *The Vienna Convention on the Law of Treaties* (2d ed. 1984)

Mark E. Villiger, *Customary international law and treaties* (1997)

http://untreaty.un.org (U.N. Treaty Index)

4. OTHER SOURCES AND EVIDENCES

Thomas M. Franck, *Fairness in International Law and Institutions* (1995)

Hersch Lauterpacht, *The Development of International Law by the International Court* (rep. 1982)

Mohamed Shahabuddeen, *Precedent in the World Court* (1996)

5. STATES: IDENTITY, RECOGNITION AND SUCCESSION

James Crawford, *The Creation of States in International Law* (1979)

Hersch Lauterpacht, *Recognition in International Law* (1947)

D.P. O'Connell, *State Succession in Municipal Law and International Law* (1967)

Stefan Talmon, *Recognition of Governments in International Law* (1998)

N.L. Wallace–Bruce, *Claims to Statehood in International Law* (1994)

6. INTERNATIONAL ORGANIZATIONS

C.F. Amerasinghe, *The Law of the International Civil Service as Applied by International Administrative Tribunals* (1988)

D.W. Bowett, *The Law of International Institutions* (4th ed. 1982)

Charter of the United Nations: A Commentary (Bruno Simma ed. 1995)

E. Osmanzyk, *Encyclopedia of the United Nations and International Organizations* (2d ed. 1990)

United Nations: Law, Policies and Practice (Rudiger Wolfrum ed. 1995)

http://www.un.org (U.N. main web-site)

7. INDIVIDUALS IN INTERNATIONAL LAW

R. Donner, *The Regulation of Nationality in International Law* (2d ed. 1994)

International Criminal Law (M. Cherif Bassiouni ed. 1998)

C.A. Norgaard, *The Position of the Individual in International Law* (1962)

8. STATE RESPONSIBILITY AND DIPLOMATIC PROTECTION

C.F. Amerasinghe, *State Responsibility for Injuries to Nationals* (1967)

Edwin M. Borchard, *The diplomatic protection of citizens abroad: or the law of international claims* (rep. 1970)

Ian Brownlie, *State Responsibility* (1983)

The Iran–United States Claims Tribunal: its contribution to the law of state responsibility (Richard B. Lillich, Daniel Barstow Magraw & David J. Bederman eds. 1998)

International law of state responsibility for injuries to aliens (Richard B. Lillich ed. 1983)

9. HUMAN RIGHTS

Basic Documents on Human Rights (Ian Brownlie 3d ed. 1992)

M.J. Bossuyt, *Guide to the 'Travaux Préparatoires' of the International Covenant on Civil and Political Rights* (1987)

Antonio Cassese, *Human Rights in a Changing World* (1990)

S. Davidson, *The Inter–American Court of Human Rights* (1992)

Guide to International Human Rights Practice (Hurst Hannum 3d ed. 1999)

David J. Harris, M. O'Boyle & Colin Warbrick, *Law of the European Convention on Human Rights* (1995)

Dominic McGoldrick, *Human Rights Committee: its role in the development of the International Covenant on Civil and Political Rights* (1991)

J.G. Merrills, *The Development of International Law by the European Court of Human Rights* (2d ed. 1993)

Henry J. Steiner and Philip Alston, *International human rights in context* (1996)

Beth Stephens & Michael Ratner, *International human rights litigation in U.S. courts* (1996)

A Systematic Guide to the Case Law of the European Court of Human Rights, 1960–1994 (P. Kempees ed. 1996)

The United Nations and Human Rights: A Critical Appraisal (P. Alston ed. 1992)

http://www1.umn.edu/humanrts (Human Rights Library)

10. STATE TERRITORY AND COMMON AREAS

Y.Z. Blum, *Historic Titles in International Law* (1965)

Q.C. Christol, *Space Law: Past, Present and Future* (1991)

P.S. Dempsey, *Law and Foreign Policy in International Aviation* (1987)

R.Y. Jennings, *The Acquisition of Territory in International Law* (1962)

Christopher C. Joyner, *Antarctica and the Law of the Sea* (1992)

Donald R. Rothwell, *The Polar regions and the development of international law* (1996)

11. Law of the Sea

R.P. Anand, *Origin and Development of the Law of the Sea* (1983)

E.D. Brown, *The International Law of the Sea* (1992)

R.R. Churchill & A.V. Lowe, *The Law of the Sea* (2d ed. 1988)

United Nations Convention on the Law of the Sea, 1982: A Commentary (Myron H. Nordquist ed. 1985–97)

D.P. O'Connell, *The International Law of the Sea* (1982–84)

http://www.un.org/Depts/los/index.htm (U.N. site on Oceans Law)

12. International Environmental Law

Basis Documents on International Environmental Law (H. Hohmann 3d ed. 1992)

P.W. Birnie & A. Boyle, *International Law and the Environment* (1992)

International Environmental Law: Multilateral Treaties (W.E. Burhenne ed. 1996)

Alexandre Kiss & Dinah Shelton, *International Environmental Law* (1991)

Ved Nanda, *International Environmental Law and Policy* (1995)

Philippe Sands, *Principles of International Environmental Law* (1995)

Edith Brown Weiss, *In fairness to future generations ; international law, common patrimony, and intergenerational equity* (1989)

13. International Economic Law

Hazel Fox, *International Economic Law and Developing Countries* (1992)

F.V. Garcia–Amador, *The Emerging International Law of Development* (1990)

Robert Hudec, *The GATT Legal System and World Trade Diplomacy* (2d ed. 1990)

Robert Hudec, *Enforcing International Trade Law: The Evolution of the Modern GATT Legal System* (1993)

John H. Jackson & W.J. Davey, *International Economic Relations* (2d ed. 1989)

David Palmeter & Petros C. Mavroidis, *Dispute settlement in the World Trade Organization: practice and procedure* (1999)

Ignaz Seidl–Hohenveldern, *International Economic Law* (2d ed. 1992)

http://www.wto.org/wto/dispute/dispute.htm (World Trade Organization dispute panels)

14. INTERNATIONAL LAW AND DOMESTIC LAW

B. Conforti, *International Law and the Role of Domestic Legal Systems* (1993)

C. Economides, *The Relationship between International and Domestic Law* (1993)

Louis Henkin, *Foreign Affairs and the United States Constitution* (2d ed. 1996)

International Law and Municipal Law (G.I. Tunkin & R. Wolfrum eds. 1988)

15. INTERNATIONAL AGREEMENTS IN U.S. LAW

National Treaty Law and Practice (Austria, Chile, Colombia, Japan, The Netherlands, United States) (Monroe Leigh, Merritt R. Blakeslee and L. Benjamin Ederington, eds. 1999)

National Treaty Law and Practice (France, Germany, India, Switzerland, Thailand, United Kingdom) (Monroe Leigh & Merritt R. Blakeslee, eds. 1994)

Parliamentary Participation in the Making and Operation of Treaties: A Comparative Study (Frederick M. Abbott & Stefan Riesenfeld eds. 1994).

16. JURISDICTION

J.-G. Castel, *Extraterritoriality in International Trade* (1988)

The extraterritorial application of national laws (Dieter Lange & Gary Born eds. 1987)

17. JURISDICTIONAL IMMUNITIES

Peter H.F. Bekker, *The legal position of intergovernmental organizations* (1994)

Joseph W. Dellapenna, *Suing foreign governments and their corporations* (1988)

E. Denza, *Diplomatic Law: Commentary on the Vienna Convention on Diplomatic Relations* (2d ed. 1998)

R. Jennings, *The Place of the Jurisdictional Immunity of States in International and Municipal Law* (1987)

Satow's Guide to Diplomatic Practice (L. Gore–Booth 6th ed. 1988)

Christophe Schreuer, *State Immunity: Some Recent Developments* (1988)

B. Sen, *A Diplomat's Handbook of International Law and Practice* (3d ed. 1988)

18. COUNTER-MEASURES

O.Y. Elagab, *The Legality of Non–Forcible Countermeasures in International Law* (1988)

Elizabeth Zoller, *Peacetime Unilateral Remedies: An Analysis of Countermeasures* (1984)

19. CONTROL OF ARMED CONFLICT

Ian Brownlie, *International Law and the Use of Force* (1963)

Yoram Dinstein, *War, Aggression and Self–Defence* (2d ed. 1994)

Louis Henkin, *Right v. Might: International Law and the Use of Force* (2d ed. 1991)

Law and Force in the New International Order (Lori Damrosch & David J. Scheffer eds. 1992)

John Norton Moore, *Law and civil war in the modern world* (1974)

Sean D. Murphy, *Humanitarian intervention: the United Nations in an evolving world order* (1996)

Fernando R. Tesón, *Humanitarian Intervention: An Inquiry Into Law and Morality* (2d ed. 1997)

United Nations Legal Order (Oscar Schachter & Christopher C. Joyner eds. 1995)

20. LAWS OF WAR

M. Cherif Bassiouni, *Crimes against humanity in international criminal law* (1999)

E. Benevisti, *The International Law of Occupation* (1993)

Documents on the Laws of War (A. Roberts & R. Guelff 4th ed. 1999)

L.C. Green, *The Contemporary Law of Armed Conflict* (1993)

F. Kalshoven, *Constraints on the Waging of War* (1987)

Virginia Morris & Michael P. Scharf, *An insider's guide to the international criminal tribunal for the former Yugoslavia* (1995)

The Statute of the International Criminal Court: a documentary history (M. Cherif Bassiouni ed. 1998)

Theodor Meron, *Henry's wars and Shakespeare's laws: perspectives on the law of war in the later Middle Ages* (1993)

Theodor Meron, *Human rights in internal strife: their international protection* (1987)

San Remo Manual on International Law Applicable to Armed Conflicts at Sea (L. Doswald–Beck ed. 1995)

http://www.un.org/icty (International Criminal Tribunal for the Former Yugoslavia)

http://www.un.org/law/icc/index.html (International Criminal Court)

21. PEACEFUL SETTLEMENT OF DISPUTES

Charles N. Brower & Jason D. Brueschke, *The Iran–United States Claims Tribunal* (1998)

Fact-Finding Before International Tribunals (R. Lillich ed. 1992)

G.C. Fitzmaurice, *Law and Practice of the International Court of Justice* (1986)

Christine Gray, *Judicial Remedies in International Law* (1990)

International Courts for the Twenty–First Century (Mark Janis ed. 1992)

E.D. McWhinney, *Judicial Settlement of International Disputes* (1991)

J.G. Merrills, *International Dispute Settlement* (3d ed. 1998)

W.M. Reisman, *Systems of control in international adjudication and arbitration: breakdown and repair* (1992)

Shabtai Rosenne, *The law and practice of the International Court, 1920–1996* (1997)

Nagendra Singh, *The Role and Record of the International Court of Justice* (1989)

Stephen M. Schwebel, *International arbitration: three salient problems* (1987)

A.M. Stuyt, *Survey of International Arbitrations, 1794–1989* (1990)

Stephen Toope, *Mixed International Arbitration* (1990)

http://www.icj-cij.org (International Court of Justice)

TABLE OF CASES AND ARBITRATIONS

References are to Pages

TABLE OF TREATIES AND OTHER DOCUMENTS

Other Diplomatic and Legal Documents

*

INDEX

269